IT'S NOT UNUSUAL

IT'S NOT UNUSUAL

A History of Lesbian and Gay Britain in the Twentieth Century

Alkarim Jivani

MICHAEL O'MARA BOOKS LIMITED

By arrangement with the BBC

For Jonathan

First published in 1997 in Great Britain by
Michael O'Mara Books Limited
9 Lion Yard, Tremadoc Road
London sw4 7nq
by arrangement with the BBC

This book accompanies the BBC2 television series,
produced by Wall To Wall Television Limited

A CIP catalogue record for this book is available from the British Library

ISBN 1-85479-205-9

Picture Research by Tom Graves

Designed and typeset by Martin Bristow

Printed and bound in Slovenia
by Printing House Delo – Tiskarna
by arrangement with Korotan Ljubljana

CONTENTS

ACKNOWLEDGMENTS

My deepest gratitude goes to the thirty-six men and women whose testimony makes up the backbone of the book. Without them it would not have been possible. Thanks are also due to Jane Root who suggested that I write the book in the first place, to Ian Leese, Ian MacMillan and all at Wall To Wall TV. I also owe a debt of gratitude to Annie Reid and David Roberts at Michael O'Mara Books for their unfailing expertise and support. My thanks also go to Alice Rawsthorn, Gurinder Chadha and Paul Mayeda Berges for their pep talks, to Peter Chatterton for his technological advice and reassuring words when the computer crashed, to Tom Gowling and Alan Bailey for letting me have the run of their library and, most of all, to Jonathan Merrison for his kindness and patience while I toiled.

PICTURE ACKNOWLEDGMENTS

The photographs of the contributors – except where indicated below – belong to the contributors themselves and have been reproduced here with their kind permission. (Mander & Michenson Theatre Collection – M&M; Hulton Getty – HG; Syndication International – SI; Private Collection – PC)

p16 (Charles Brookfield) M&M; p18 (Noël Coward, *The Vortex*) M&M; p17 (Beverley Nichols) HG; p19 (Noël Coward and the Duke and Duchess of Kent) HG; p20 (Frith Banbury) M&M; p23 (Vesta Tilley) M&M; p24, *top* (Tallulah Bankhead) PC; p24, *below* (Josephine Baker) PC; p25 (Violet Trefusis) Weidenfeld & Nicholson Archive; p26 (Vita Sackville-West) © Evelyn Irons; p27 (Radclyffe Hall) HG; p29 (Radclyffe Hall and Una Troubridge) HG; p39 (Foyles Luncheon) HG; p42 (Marlene Dietrich) PC; p44 (Greta Garbo) PC; p45 (Quentin Crisp) © Wall To Wall TV; p47 (Harold and Vita at Sissinghurst) Weidenfeld & Nicholson Archive; p48 (Vita Sackville-West with her dog) © Evelyn Irons; p51 (Lyons Corner House) HG; p83 (Vera Lynn) HG; p90 (Film still from *Brief Encounter*) SI; p95 (Sharley McLean) Robert Workman; p97 (Guy Burgess, *left*, and Donald Maclean, *right*) HG; p104 (Sir Edward Marsh) HG; p105 (Emlyn Williams, John Gielgud and Noël Coward) HG; p107 (Oscar Wilde plaque unveiled by Sir Compton Mackenzie, accompanied by H Montgomery Hyde) HG; p109 (Lord Montagu) SI; p113 (Lord Montagu, Michael Pitt-Rivers and Peter Wildeblood) HG; p114 (Lord Wolfenden) SI; p123 (Alan Turing) courtesy of the National Portrait Gallery, London; p129 (E M Forster with Benjamin Britten) HG; p132 (Film still from *The Killing of Sister George*) SI; p135 (On the set of *The Killing of Sister George*) SI; p140 (Danny la Rue) SI; p142, *top* (*Round the Horne*) © BBC Worldwide Ltd 1991; p142, *below* (Film still from *The Trials of Oscar Wilde*) SI; p143 (Film still from *Victim*) SI; p145 (On the set of *Victim*) PC; p149 (Cecil Beaton) HG; p156 (Pat Arrowsmith) HG; p160 (Gay Pride 1994) HG/Steve Eason; p167 (Gay March) Robert Workman; p171 (Gay Liberation March 1977) HG; p173 (Bang) Robert Workman; p178 (Sauna raid) Robert Workman; p179 (Derek Ogg) Simon Cox; p182 (Film still from *The Rocky Horror Show*) Flashbacks; p191 (Remembrance Day and the Cenotaph 1995) HG/Steve Eason; p196 (Lesbian and Gay Pride 1994) HG/Steve Eason; p197 (Gay Pride Festival 1996) HG/Steve Eason; p199 (Lesbian and Gay Pride March 1995) HG/Mark Lynch; p200 (Cathy Peace) Simon Cox; p202 (Ann Lewis and Marika Savage) Simon Cox; p205 (Pink-coloured tank) HG/Steve Eason

INTRODUCTION

Recently a veteran of the Women's Liberation Movement was taken slightly aback when her adolescent daughter asked in all seriousness, 'Mummy did you really burn your bra in the Sixties?' Underneath the amusing naiveté of the question is a deeper point: as the generations succeed one another, myths build up about what life was really like for the people who came before us. Historical accounts generally concentrate on the works of the great and the good and deal with significant dates and momentous events. The result is that what gets preserved from the past is as far removed from everyday life as caviar and white bread. This is particularly true for gay men and lesbians whose voices have been silenced either through fear or through a lack of confidence in the relevance of what they have to say. In fact it is the experience of those who are different from the mainstream that is of most consequence if only because it illuminates the rest.

Until recently the gay past has been another country, but lately a few postcards have begun to trickle through so that the early part of this century is not as foreign a territory as it used to be. This book will add to that correspondence with the testimonies of thirty-six men and women who cover the ground from the end of the First World War to the Nineties. They participated in – or were witnesses to – some of the historical milestones of the twentieth century, such as the banning of *The Well of Loneliness*, the liberation of the Nazi concentration camps, the witch-hunts of the Fifties, the setting up of the Homosexual Law Reform Society, the start of the Gay Liberation Front which put the camp into campaigning, the siege at Greenham Common, the advent of AIDS and the battle against Clause 28. What was it like to be there and to be gay? Read the newspaper reports of these events and you won't find it described there. Very little of the gay experience was deemed worthy of record. As far as they were concerned we didn't exist.

However, this isn't just an account of significant events in gay and lesbian history. It tells, also, of what gay men and lesbians wore, the slang they used, the music they listened to, the places where they met and the people that they loved. The interviewees cover the ground from Evelyn Irons who was a friend of both Radclyffe Hall and Vita Sackville-West to Grace Hughes, a young woman who came out at school in the Nineties, at the age of thirteen. In between there are people who fought the fight for nine long years between 1958 and 1967 to get the law reformed and those who carried the battle further through the Gay Liberation Front to make it clear that 'Gay is Good' – a common slogan shouted out during the early Gay Pride marches. Their accounts are illuminating, funny and poignant, but most of all they are important. Important not only as historical records in their own right, but important so that in the future our children or our children's children aren't so ignorant that they have to ask the gay and lesbian equivalent of 'Mummy did you really burn your bra in the Sixties?'

PART ONE   1918-39

omosexuality, to paraphrase Philip Larkin, began in 1918, between the death of Queen Victoria and Marlene's début on screen. It was only then that the word 'homosexual' began to gain any kind of currency. What was important about this new word was that it was descriptive rather than disparaging. Until then, what gay men and lesbians did was either expressed in euphemisms – such as the constant references to Oscar Wilde's 'unspeakable crime' – or else in pejorative terms, most notably 'invert'. Although the word 'homosexual' had been coined in 1869 by a Hungarian physician, Karoly Maria Benkert, it lay dormant until late in the nineteenth century when it began to be used by academics and sexologists. By the end of the First World War it had passed from the rarefied world of scientists into the discourse of the intelligentsia and a few years after that it had inveigled its way into the vocabulary of the upmarket press when, in October 1926, the *New York Times* used it in a book review.

Nomenclature has an unparalleled power – we name those things that are important to us, hence the notion that the Inuit people of Alaska have fifty different words to describe snow. By the same token the minting of a new term to describe gay and lesbian sexual relations, marked the beginning of a new attitude towards the people who practised them. The difference was that rather than being regarded as a vice, a weakness of character – as it had been in Oscar Wilde's day – it was now regarded as a disease. The work of Richard von Krafft-Ebing, Havelock Ellis and Sigmund Freud was beginning to have an influence in defining the 'homosexual' as distinct from the 'invert' which could refer to any number of sexual practices which were considered abnormal by the mores of the day.

'Bona to vada your jolly old eek again!'
Gay slang meaning: 'Nice to see your face once more!'

Of course the majority of gay men and lesbians did not use any of these abstruse terms to describe themselves, and the words 'invert' or 'homosexual' featured as frequently in their vocabulary as 'antidisestablishmentarianism'. Among the upper and middle classes – the Bloomsbury set for example – the terms most commonly used between the wars were 'queer' for gay men and 'Sapphist' for lesbians, but further down the social scale there was a rich argot, studded with a camp sensibility. Several decades before, a synonym for gay was 'earnest' which must have caused much chuckling among those in the know when *The Importance of Being Earnest* was premièred. Oscar Wilde's play was packed with in-jokes and coded references which were given a further twist when, at the opening night, Wilde and a number of his friends turned up wearing green carnations in their lapels. When the curtain rose, the leading man was also sporting a green carnation thus reinforcing the notion that the actors, the writer and his friends were bound together in a secret confraternity. Between the wars, the most common phrase to inquire whether someone was gay or not was to ask: 'Is she so?' but almost as popular a way of phrasing the same question was: 'Is he musical?' The acronym to describe someone who was sexually available was TBH – 'to be had'. So one might say of a friend, 'He doesn't think he's musical but he's probably TBH.'

The purpose behind slang of any kind is to keep eavesdropping outsiders from catching the drift of what you are saying and in this respect gay men used a secret language called Polari which would have baffled all. Although the origins of the language are obscure, it appears to have originated with show people and gypsies in the nineteenth century. It contains elements of pig Latin and prison slang as well as back-slang where certain words are simply reversed. The Latin influences can be seen in the use of the word 'bona' to mean good and 'vada' to mean look and other words are just reversals of the conventional English word like 'riah' for hair. Unsurprisingly there was an uncommonly large number of words to describe parts of the body so 'ecafe' was back-slang for face which was abbreviated to 'eek' by the late Fifties and early Sixties, hence Kenneth Williams's regular greeting in the radio comedy, *Round the Horne*, 'Bona to vada your jolly old eek again!' 'Lallies' were legs, 'thews' were thighs, 'lappers' were hands, 'ocals' were eyes, men were 'omes', women were 'palones', gay men were 'ome-palones' and policemen were 'Brenda' (short for Brenda Bracelets). So should one Polari speaker want to tell his companion in a crowded bar that the handsome man with the strapping legs standing next to the woman was a police informer, he would simply say 'Vada the bona ome with the huge thews next to the palone – he is a friend of Brenda's' and nobody would be any the wiser.

By the first few decades of this century, Polari had become common usage in theatrical circles and that's where Terry Gardener picked it up. Terry's father had been the stage manager of a drag revue in the First World War and Terry himself started dressing up between the wars and learnt Polari from two drag queens who went busking around the East End with a barrel organ. 'Of course being ladies they couldn't pull a barrel organ around so they paid an ome – which is another word for a man – to pull the barrel organ and because they didn't want him to know what they were talking about they talked in Polari.' The routine was to busk the streets and then repair to a café where they would sit with their cup of tea and slice of bread and dripping amongst all the working men – 'reigning supreme', as Terry aptly describes them – divvying up the money and gossiping about the waitresses. Both these topics of conversation required keeping everybody else in the dark. 'They didn't want him to know how much money they were doing because they'd perhaps only pay him duay biancsay a day. And in case you don't know what duay biancsay is, that was half a crown. And the "palone vadas ome palone very cod" meant you were getting some very funny looks from her serving the tea. They would hold whole conversations like that and count any amount of money.'

Polari was particularly prevalent in the theatre which is probably where Kenneth Williams picked it up. It wasn't till the Sixties with *Round the Horne*, however, that it reached a general public. Barry Took (who came from West End musical theatre) and Marty Feldman (who had worked in fairgrounds) developed two camp characters for Williams and Hugh Paddick – Julian and his friend Sandy – who spoke a patois composed of two parts English to one part Polari. Julian and Sandy were out-of-work actors who set up a new venture every week including Bona Pets and the Bona Nature Clinic. They were a huge success and managed to get away with some extremely filthy jokes because nobody was sure precisely what they were talking about.

As a result of the success of *Round the Horne* many Polari words like 'naff', 'drag', 'slap' and 'rough trade' have been absorbed into the language, and Kenneth Williams's work on the programme has given him an enduring appeal – the BBC still does a roaring trade in audio-cassettes of the Julian and Sandy excerpts. However, he remained thoroughly dissatisfied with his achievements because he had always wanted to be accepted as a straight actor. Even as late as the Fifties, Williams's sexuality meant very few serious parts came his way and he ended up in comedy and revue by default. If you didn't want to be pigeon-holed you kept your trap shut. This was certainly the experience of Frith Banbury, who had to be cautious who knew about his sexuality. Frith, who was at Oxford in the late Twenties and went to RADA after that, says that the spectre of Oscar Wilde still hung over actors even though decades had passed since Wilde's death in 1900. 'For quite a long time after the Wilde case, the leaders of the [theatrical] profession were fairly homophobic . . . There were people like Alan Aynsworth who played in *The Importance of Being Earnest* – I think he was the original Algy . . . and an actor called Charles Brookfield and the bitterness was quite horrifying . . . Wilde had been an enormous show-off and there's nothing people like more than to see somebody taken down a few pegs . . . What one wanted was to be cast in a lot of parts which one would not

necessarily have been cast in if one had been, in one's behaviour and attitudes, too obviously homosexual.'

Charles Brookfield – whom Frith mentions – had been one of the chief informers against Wilde. The Marquess of Queensberry had hired private detectives to collect dirt on Wilde's private life with little success till Brookfield volunteered himself. According to a book published by Frank Harris, one of Wilde's friends, in New York in 1916, Brookfield had 'constituted himself private prosecutor in this case and raked Piccadilly to find witnesses against Oscar Wilde'. The curious thing about it was that, at the time, Brookfield was appearing at the Haymarket Theatre in Wilde's *An Ideal Husband*, albeit in a very small part – Lord Goring's valet. After Wilde's successful conviction, Brookfield and his friends entertained Queensberry to dinner to mark the event. Brookfield was later appointed Censor of Plays in the Lord Chamberlain's office – the government department which kept a close eye on all theatrical presentations – possibly for his enthusiastic work in the Wilde case.

An indication of how the stigma surrounding the Wilde case lingered on for decades after his death is given by the writer Beverley Nichols. As an adolescent, he was caught by his father reading one of Wilde's books and the reaction was extreme. Nichols's father struck him, spat on the book and tore up the pages. He only calmed down when a baffled Nichols asked why Wilde was considered so abhorrent. The following morning he was given a note from his father which read *Illium crimen horribile quod non nominandum* – the horrible crime which is not to be named.

> '**I don't quite know how he is going to fortify his soul against the ravages of this "fairy". Perhaps he should now play a plumber by way of antidote.'**
>
> **Drama critic** on an actor playing a gay role

BEVERLEY
NICHOLS IN HIS
GARDEN

Frith's theatrical career coincided with the tail end of the Wilde backlash. Conservatism ruled the day and the Wildean urge to push theatrical barriers and fill the scripts with gay references was severely frowned upon. Equally beyond the pale were Wilde's dandified heroes. In their place there were virile characters often played by Gerald du Maurier (the father of the novelist Daphne du Maurier), the leading actor-manager of his day. Throughout the Twenties, du Maurier had reigned supreme. In 1924, when Noël Coward's play, *The Vortex* – a melodrama about the love/hate relationship between a son and his mother which has many oblique references to homosexuality – was produced, du Maurier was furious about the indecency of the subject matter and condemned the play as 'filth', referring to it as 'dustbin drama'. Ironically, several decades later, Noël Coward displayed much the same attitude towards the next generation of iconoclastic young dramatists wanting to break the grip of the clever drawing room comedy that Coward exemplified. In a series of three articles published in the *Sunday Times* in 1961 he rubbished John Osborne in much the same terms with which Du Maurier had denounced *The Vortex*.

What du Maurier was implicitly objecting to was that the characters

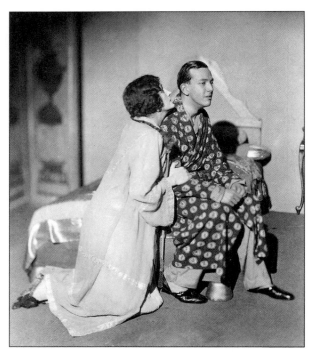

NOËL COWARD
AND LILIAN
BRAITHWAITE IN
THE VORTEX
IN 1924

in *The Vortex* were sympathetically portrayed. Characterizations of gay men during du Maurier's day were invariably painted with a brush dipped in vitriol, if they existed at all. One of Frith's friends had appeared in a play by Frederick Lonsdale called *Spring Cleaning* in an obviously gay role in 1925. The critics were scandalized and even suggested that the actor would be corrupted by playing such a role. In his stage directions for *Spring Cleaning* – a piece about sexual sophisticates – Lonsdale described the character of Bobby Williams as an overdressed, effeminate young man of twenty-two. Bobby exclaims over the exquisite 'sweetness' of the cushions and recounts a row he has had with his hosier about obtaining under-wear in a particular shade. The female characters in the play describe him as a 'powder-puff' and a 'fairy' and the other male characters despise him.

'He [Frith's friend who played Bobby] was asked what he thought of these young men in real life and it was very difficult for him . . . Of course he couldn't say I am one of them . . . A very famous critic of that period said, "I don't know how he is going to fortify his soul against the ravages of this 'fairy'. Perhaps he should now play a plumber by way of antidote . . ." Why should an actor have to fortify his soul against a part he is playing – I mean do we have to have every Macbeth fortifying his soul in case he should feel like murdering somebody? And the idea that he should now play a plumber by way of antidote – as if a plumber couldn't possibly be homosexual. I dare say we've all known a few homosexual plumbers . . . Sadly, in the end he killed himself, couldn't face himself really.'

By the time Frith did his first West End play in 1933 – ten days after leaving RADA – du Maurier was an old man and his hold was fading. A new generation was gaining supremacy in the theatre – Noël Coward was reaching the apex of his career as writer, actor and impresario with plays written in a clipped, epigrammatic style which epitomized the brittle campness that informed haute bohemia. That was the year that Coward's play *Design for Living* was premièred which has as its centre a menage à trois in which each individual loves each of the other two. Unlike *The Vortex*, written years earlier, the subject is dealt with directly rather than metaphorically and there is no angst about it – the problematic aspects of the arrangement being the essence of the comedy. In addition to Coward, there was his great friend Binkie Beaumont who also produced plays with gay subtexts. Cecil Beaton, the designer and photographer, was the most sought-after portraitist of the day, for his arch, baroquely camp images which were in complete contrast to the stiff studio portraits of the preceding years. Beaton's subjects ranged from other gay men like Stephen Tennant to eccentrics like the Sitwells to the royal family.

By the Thirties, among those who liked to think of themselves as bohemian, there was an element of chic attached to being gay. Students, who in every age have felt the need to break convention, therefore embraced it wholeheartedly although how many of them were genuinely gay and how many were simply putting it on is difficult to say. '[Homosexuality was] very largely the particular form which the revolt of the young took at the universities at that time,' says Goronwy Rees, a prominent journalist who worked on the *Guardian* and the *Spectator*, and was at Oxford in the Thirties. 'Among undergraduates and dons with pretensions to culture and a taste for the arts [it was] at once a fashion, a doctrine and a way of life.' This was further confirmed many years later during the House of

NOËL COWARD (centre) ARRIVING AT A GARDEN PARTY WITH THE DUKE AND DUCHESS OF KENT IN 1937

FRITH BANBURY
AS A YOUNG
ACTOR IN 1935

FRITH BANBURY

The Apprentice in " THE HANGMAN "
—*Duke of York's Theatre*

John Gielgud's " HAMLET "—*New Theatre*

Barry Green in
" THE DARK TOWER "
—*Shaftesbury Theatre*

Montague in " RICHARD of BORDEAUX "
—(First Tour)
RICHARD at the King's Theatre, Hammersmith,
during the indisposition of Glen Byam Shaw

Height 5 feet 11 inches   *Houston Rogers*

FRENCH.   GERMAN.   PIANO.

38, Abercorn Place, N.W. 8   MAIda Vale 4897

Lords debate on decriminalizing homosexuality when the Bishop of Rochester recalled his time at university and the presence of what he called 'sodomy clubs'. 'There was one in Oxford between the wars and I am informed that there was another in Cambridge which even shamelessly sported a tie,' he fumed.

Frith, who was also at Oxford during this period certainly found that there were a lot of people who shared his sexual preferences. 'I got in with a lot of people who had similar tastes. It was the moment of the aesthetes and the hearties and I naturally was an aesthete . . . who were the intellectuals, who were going to be artists and writers. The hearties were the rowing blues, the rugger players and all the other sporting chaps. The self-consciousness of the aesthetes irritated the hearties who used to dowse them in the river. One chap I know got thrown into the Cherwell for growing his hair too long.'

When they came down from Oxford, the hearties, no doubt, ended up in the civil service or doing their duty in various corners of the empire whereas the aesthetes went into the arts. As a result, fashion, photography, film and music were all informed by a gay sensibility – but there was an unwritten code about how far one could go. So when Noël Coward wrote 'Mad About the Boy' – whose lyrics to modern ears seem a straightforward declaration of Coward's sexuality – it would have been considered scandalous for Coward to sing the song himself. It had to be sung by an actress.

This is emblematic not only of Coward but of almost all the other gay people in his circle. Their sexuality was tacitly accepted in their own milieu but it would have been unthinkable to be open about it. The same applied to their work which was full of hints and allusions but Coward was as likely to make a direct reference to his sexuality as he was to goose the King. Coward did, however, have the opportunity of friendship with the King's brother, the Duke of Kent, whom he first met in Paris in 1923. According to a friend of Coward, Michael Thornton, in 1969, twenty-seven years after the duke's death, Coward told a small party of friends at his suite in the Savoy that he had had a special relationship with Prince George, the current Queen's uncle. 'It didn't last long and we were both very young at the time. He was absolutely enchanting and I never stopped loving him.'

The journey from Mayfair to Mile End was a matter of miles but in cultural terms there was a yawning gap between the West End and the East End. The closest that Terry Gardener and his friends got to coronets and tiaras were the ones they bought from costume jewellery shops, but they wore

A GLAMOUR SHOT OF TERRY GARDENER TAKEN AFTER THE WAR

them with as much pride as any duchess. The other difference between the two places was that, in the East End, people who were gay were allowed to be much more open about it. They could hardly claim they were straight when their working lives consisted of putting on frocks and delivering a patter which constantly hinted at their own sexuality. Terry's drag career started while he was still at school when he took the lead role in *Mrs Mason's Homely Kitchen*. 'In one of my mother's work dresses and the hair, which was very lustrous and curly, piled on top of my head in an elastic band, I became Mrs Mason. It was such a success that this teacher asked permission from my mother if I could do it at a local club, which I did. That told me I could go on stage dressed as a woman and make people laugh. Even if they were laughing at me it didn't matter as long as I was part of it.'

Acquiring costumes and make-up was as easy as anything for Terry. 'In the East End there were lots of second-hand shops and for one-and-six one could buy a beautiful evening gown which I did frequently . . . One only went to Woolworth's for a stick of make-up which was threepence a stick. If you were posh you bought Leichner powder which was sixpence. A threepenny stick of make-up and a sixpenny box of powder and I was equipped for anything. I often think about it and wonder if he [the teacher] knew what the future was going to be for me.' Terry's teacher could hardly have known that his precocious pupil would go on to entertain the troops during the Second World War, tour in one of the ex-servicemen's drag revues that became popular in the post-war period and end up one of the veteran drag queens of the London gay scene.

'Darling you're **divine**. I've had an affair with your husband. You'll be next.'

Tallulah Bankhead on being introduced to Joan Crawford

While cross-dressing men were only sanctioned in very specific circumstances – East End entertainments at one end of the social scale and Oxbridge student revues at the other – women in men's clothes were much more acceptable in some ways.

As early as the turn of the century, the music hall singer Vesta Tilley had made cross-dressing a trademark when she donned a dinner jacket to sing her signature tune *Burlington Bertie*. Decades later in Robert Aldrich's seminal lesbian film, *The Killing of Sister George*, Beryl Reid, in a tribute to Tilley, sings *Burlington Bertie* also dressed up in a dinner jacket. Pre-World War One postcards of women dressed in masculine clothes show that the phenomenon was far from unknown. One of these pre-war postcards – dating from 1905 – depicts a woman in mannish hat, tweed jacket, stiff collar and bow tie, holding a stick in one hand and bulldog at the end of a leash in the other. The verse beneath it reads:

> *She is mannish from her shoes to her hat,*
> *Coat, collars, stiff shirt and cravat,*
> *She'd wear pants in the street,*
> *To make her complete,*
> *But she knows the law won't stand for that.*

VESTA TILLEY, THE MUSIC HALL SINGER, IN HER 'BURLINGTON BERTIE' COSTUME

The major difference between cross-dressing women before and after the First World War was that post-war women found themselves regarded as chic. Marlene Dietrich spent much of the Twenties attending Berlin parties in clothes which could just as easily have hung in the wardrobe of a fashionable young man of the day according to her latest biographer, Donald Spoto, who also reveals that she started the first of many sexual relationships with women at this time with a writer called Gerda Huber. Film stars who may not have defined themselves as lesbian, but who alluded to relationships with other women were not considered out of bounds by the public. Indeed, it gave them an air of rebellion which added to their allure. One such was the American actress Tallulah Bankhead who arrived in Britain in 1923. 'She ruled London. Never a day went by without the papers making remarks on her antics . . . she professed to be a lesbian,' recalls Quentin Crisp. 'And she had a friend called Miss Maurice and they were talked about and people made fun of them and that's exactly what Tallulah Bankhead loved, of course, anything that could make her seem scandalous. And the people came to see her shows to see how anyone so wicked could still move and speak.'

They found out that she could move and speak with great agility – a discovery made by any number of movers and shakers on both sides of the Atlantic. Beverley Nichols, among others, recalls that Bankhead was not only skilled in delivering epigrammatic lines in the roles that she played, she was equally adept at coining them. On being introduced to Joan Crawford with her new husband, Douglas Fairbanks Jr, Bankhead said: 'Darling you're divine. I've had an affair with your husband. You'll be next.'

In Paris, a lesbian salon had been set up largely peopled by expatriate American women led by Gertrude Stein and her lover Alice B Toklas and

their friends Romaine Brooks and Natalie Barney – 'the wild girl from Cincinnati' as she was called. The archetype of the Twenties' lesbian owed its origin to this coterie of Parisians as much as anything else. The stereotype was of wing-collared women wearing monocles, jodhpurs and boots set off by silver-topped canes.

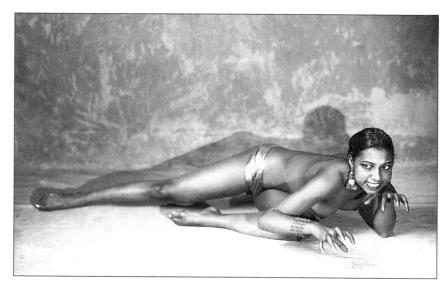

Natalie Barney's house in the Rue Jacob was where the *beau monde* gathered for masquerade balls and pageants which took place in the drawing room till the architect warned that the floor of her 300-year-old mansion was in danger of collapse. Paris in the Twenties became a centre for everything that was deemed exotic – Josephine Baker whose dances were considered too risqué in America emigrated to Paris and found herself embraced and exalted. While wealthy American lesbians and gay men came to Paris for its

louche atmosphere, Afro-Americans came because it was comparatively less racist than the United States where segregation was still the norm not only in the south but also in supposedly enlightened places like Manhattan. Many jazz musicians, for instance, resented the fact that the New York night-clubs they played in, didn't welcome black people as patrons. In Josephine Baker's case Paris was the place to be for both these reasons – not only was it more tolerant of black women who wanted to control their own lives but it was also more receptive to her highly sexualized dance performances.

In Britain too there were plenty of women who were blurring the outlines between male and female dress. As early as 1918, Vita Sackville-West and her lover, Violet Trefusis, went to Hyde Park Corner with Vita passing herself off as a man. She then walked down Piccadilly on her own and was delighted to find that nobody guessed her secret. She bought a newspaper

and found herself addressed as 'sir' by the paper boy. She was even accost-
ed by prostitutes. She repeated the exercise again in Paris when she was visiting with Violet. The pair strolled along the boulevards with a khaki
bandage tied around Vita's head to hide her hair. Being immediately after
the First World War this was not an uncommon sight. In her unfinished
autobiography which made up part of her son's portrait of his parents' marriage, Vita describes herself in this guise as 'a rather untidy young man, a
sort of undergraduate, of about nineteen. It was marvellous fun, all the more
so because there was always the risk of being found out.' This sense of illic-
it pleasure was the essence of Vita's enjoyment in cross-dressing. She loved
passing herself off as a man for a prank. In ordinary life she switched from
corduroy trousers to red silk dresses with hats to match according to how the
mood took her. Vita Sackville-West had been a cause célèbre in 1920 when
she and Violet eloped together. Their respective husbands came chasing
after them in a highly publicized case of the time. She was also known for
her writing and for her horticulture, having defined garden design in the
grounds of Sissinghust Castle in Kent between the wars. From the Twenties,
her customary costume when gardening, was breeches bought from Simp-
sons in Piccadilly, high boots which were custom-made for her, and a jerkin
over a blouse all set off by pearls and dangly earrings.

> '**Una and John both wore monocles, and at one point I had a monocle, too – but I didn't need one – so it was plain glass.'**
>
> Evelyn Irons

While Vita Sackville-West's sartorial style owed something to the Parisian school of stereotyped lesbian it was essentially individualist. The most prominent exponent of the Paris style in Britain was Radclyffe Hall, the novelist, who was to go on to become the twentieth-century's most famous lesbian. Along with her lover Una Troubridge, Radclyffe Hall was a frequent visitor to the Parisian salons of Romaine Brooks and Gertrude Stein.

Evelyn Irons was also affected by the fashion for a while. She started dressing in men's clothes in an artless way when she was still very young and went on to perfect her style when she met Radclyffe Hall. Evelyn's early experimentations were made easy by the fact that she could borrow her father's clothes. 'My father wasn't a very tall man and his clothes fitted me all right . . . There was one particular friend I had whom I used to go out with quite a lot, we used to go to the movies and things like that together but I always wore plus-fours . . . and a shirt, of course, and a collar and tie. The whole outfit [even] his shoes fitted me.' However, parading around in her father's clothes and going to the cinema was as unsophisticated as a children's dressing-up game compared with the finery that Evelyn wore to West End premières after she and her partner at the

RADCLYFFE HALL
IN 1934

time, Olive Rinder, became friends with Radclyffe Hall and Una Trou-bridge. Radclyffe Hall – who liked to be called John among her own circle of friends – was well known around London for her dashing mode of dress, made all the more distinctive by her mien. She had a full-square face with a direct, intelligent gaze. Writing after their first meeting in 1915, Una Troubridge describes Radclyffe Hall as having a 'curiously fierce, noble expression that reminded me of certain caged eagles at the Zoological Gardens.' She and Evelyn must have been a wondrous sight as they cut a swathe through London's fashionable spots.

'It was really outrageous because John and I – of course Radclyffe Hall was always called John – always wore dinner jackets and skirts with striped braid down the side, not trousers,' Evelyn recalls. 'And I had a shirt and black bow tie and she always wore jabots and ruffles which I thought was rather effeminate. Then we had Spanish cloaks, a very dramatic sort with scarlet linings which you flung around you. Una and John both wore monocles, and at one point I had a monocle too but I didn't need one, so it was plain glass. I didn't wear it all the time because I did think it was a bit silly.'

Beverley Nichols recalls how all heads turned when Radclyffe Hall swept in: 'Her entry into the theatre always caused a minor sensation and whenever I saw her striding towards me I used to beat a hasty retreat into the one place, ironically enough, she was unable to follow me.'

Evelyn encountered Radclyffe Hall not through other lesbian friends but through work. Evelyn had been trying to make a living by writing short stories which were published in *The Lady* – a magazine which, as its title suggests, was genteel and restrained and remains so today. The editor of *The Lady*, Nora Heald, gave Evelyn an introduction to the editor of the women's page of the *Daily Mail*. Even though both women's pages and the *Daily Mail* were anathema to Evelyn, the five pounds a week that she would receive for the work was very welcome. One of the first ideas that she put forward was a series of articles entitled 'How Other Women Run Their Homes' which was taken up with enthusiasm.

Evelyn's next problem was to think up candidates for the series. She first alighted on an artist living around the corner from her in Chelsea called Gluck who, Evelyn says, 'was certainly not the sort of girl to run a home of any sort'. The painter, Hannah Gluckstein – who preferred to be known as just Gluck because it carried no gender connotations – was a well-established, between-the-wars painter who had a series of female lovers. She was the daughter of a prominent Jewish family who owned the chain of Lyons tea shops which, ironically, were one of the major meeting places for gay men in the Twenties and Thirties. Gluck also happened to be a lover of Edith Shackleton Heald, sister of Nora Heald who had given Evelyn her

RADCLYFFE HALL
(right) WITH HER
LOVER UNA
TROUBRIDGE
c. 1927

introduction to Fleet Street. Next in the series about other women's house-keeping arrangements was Radclyffe Hall.

Radclyffe Hall was a very different proposition compared with Gluck. She was publicity conscious in a way that the more unworldly Gluck just wasn't and was much more willing to enter into the game which required more than a little subterfuge. While Radclyffe Hall was keen to participate in Evelyn's series of articles, the problem was that she had no direct experience of housekeeping. Hall's relationship with Una was run very much along the lines of a heterosexual marriage with Una playing the wife. Hall only ever lifted a finger on the domestic front to ring for the maid. 'I said, well this article can't be about that because most people don't have maids,' Evelyn explains. 'So she was quite willing to enter into my ploy.'

When the article appeared it made the Bayeaux tapestry look like a piece of minor embroidery. It talked about how Radclyffe Hall was a meticulous housekeeper with a 'perfect mania' for home-making who liked nothing better by way of relaxation than waxing and polishing her collection of antique oak furniture. This must have caused much mirth in Radclyffe Hall's circle of friends who were well aware of her horror of household management. Beverley Nichols, in his memoir of the Twenties, recalls the pride Radclyffe Hall took in her lack of domesticity. 'I can see her now standing in front of the fireplace . . . doing what some of us called her British policemen act. This is the symbolic gesture associated with the conventional music hall cop . . . hands clasped behind the back, chin thrust up, knees bent and jerked outward in a springy . . . motion. While indulging in these callisthenics, she would discourse intelligently on the latest novel. It was her boast that she knew nothing about housekeeping. She must have regarded this innocence as a sign of virility because she so often referred to it. "Can't boil an egg," she would proclaim gruffly jerking out her knees with extra gusto. "Can't light a fire, couldn't dust a chimneypiece."'

Even though Radclyffe Hall's private life was known about, she was accepted by the press. Evelyn's article about Radclyffe Hall, which made her sound like the patron saint of domesticity, passed without comment and her flamboyant appearances at first nights and gallery openings were seen as entertainingly eccentric rather than shocking. 'The gossip writers in the *Daily Mirror* and so on used to write about how Radclyffe Hall and her amusing entourage would appear at the first night. It was all very amusing and . . . it gave them something to write about . . . there was not a word of criticism until *The Well of Loneliness* came out.' And then the world came crashing in around Radclyffe Hall's Eton-cropped head.

'The life from **infancy** to maturity of a congenital invert . . .'

Radclyffe Hall on her forthcoming book

If Radclyffe Hall had not existed someone would have had to invent her. Indeed, to some extent the public Radclyffe Hall was an invention – of herself. She had been born Marguerite Radclyffe Hall in 1880 and put the name to seven volumes of poetry before dropping the Christian name for her subsequent seven novels. She was the daughter of the curiously named Radclyffe Radclyffe-Hall from whom she inherited a fortune at the age of twenty-one allowing her to live a life of letters and considerable leisure. She had a house in Kensington and another in the country and was able to indulge her literary impulses and her taste for antique furniture.

By the mid-Twenties she was a novelist of some repute having published three novels and achieved great acclaim in 1926 with *Adam's Breed* which won her a clutch of trophies. The book was awarded both the Prix Femina Vie Heureuse and the James Tait Black Memorial Prize – a double victory which had been accomplished only by *A Passage to India* up to that point. The book was that rare thing, both a commercial and a critical success. The public bought it in good numbers and the reviewers were also keen on it, not to mention members of the literary establishment – Thomas Mann wrote to Radclyffe Hall to congratulate her on the book.

As Evelyn Irons has described, she was a fashionable fixture on the London scene and although she wasn't out of the closet in any modern sense, neither did she tell any major lies. The nature of her sexuality was well known in artistic and literary circles and she never made any bones about the fact that she shared her home with Una Troubridge. Radclyffe Hall was a keen self-publicist and the newspapers lapped it all up as entertaining copy. There was hardly a hint of censure.

Given her popularity as a writer, the esteem she was held in by the critics and the indulgence of the gossip columnists, Radclyffe Hall felt that the time had come for her to tackle something a bit more meaty. She had been friends with the sexologist Havelock Ellis for a number of years and was a convert to the theory he had expounded in his book, *Sexual Inversion*, that homosexuality was innate. Radclyffe Hall's new project, as she described it to Ellis, would be 'the life from infancy to maturity of a congenital invert, treating inversion throughout not as a perversion or an unnatural occurrence but as a condition, which, since it occurs in nature, must, even if unusual, be recognized as a natural fact.' That sums up the appeal that the congenitalist theory had for Radclyffe Hall. During the Twenties, as homosexuality moved from being regarded as a vice to a disease, there were two schools of thought about what kind of disease it was. The congenitalist theory – advanced by Ellis and his colleagues – argued that it was caused by 'defective' breeding. Opposing them were the behaviouralists – led by the relatively new, and rather fashionable, psychoanalysis movement which argued that homosexuality was conditioned by childhood experiences. Radclyffe Hall embraced the congenitalists, not least because if you accept that homosexuality is learned behaviour then there is the possibility of 'treatment'. However if it is innate then nothing can be done about it and therefore to disparage homosexuality was as illogical and pointless as discriminating against albinos. *The Well of Loneliness* was going to argue the inverts' case with all the force and emotional impact that a novelist could muster.

In an unpublished letter to Havelock Ellis, now at the Humanities Research Centre at the University of Texas, Radclyffe Hall says that her purpose in writing the book was to convince society that lesbians deserved 'merciful toleration'. So, what she wanted wasn't acceptance of lesbians as women who were happy in their chosen lifestyle, but as a group who were trapped in a situation by happenstance whom society should feel sorry for. Her private view was that in a sexually illiberal society homosexuality would only be acceptable if it was generally accepted that homosexuals had no choice but to be who they were.

She created a heroine called Stephen Gordon – so-called because her parents had longed for a son. Stephen's childhood and adolescence are filled with the kind of incidents that would give Freudians a field day – Stephen's rejection by her mother, her love of dressing up as a boy, her horror of menstruation – but Radclyffe Hall also added those characteristics that were supposed to make it clear that Stephen was a product of nature rather than nurture. Stephen was a 'tadpole' of a child with broad shoulders and narrow hips who instinctively wanted to behave like a boy. The purpose in writing the novel was twofold. The first objective was to make it clear that homosexuals were well aware of their own shortcomings and that theirs was a pitiful state that ought not to be despised. She does this by references to 'the terrible nerves of the invert' and 'those haunted tormented eyes of the invert' as well as by straightforward polemic. So, she describes lesbians thus: 'there are so many of us – thousands of miserable unwanted people . . . hideously maimed and ugly – God's cruel; he let us get flawed in the making.' The second objective was to demonstrate that apart from this one 'defect' lesbians are upstanding members of society who have much to contribute. To this end she makes Stephen into an upholder of traditional rural values with a concern for maintaining property and managing livestock with a conservative, chivalrous view of life that was almost Victorian. In order to make sure that nobody would be in any doubt about where she stood on these matters, Radclyffe Hall gave an interview to her friend Evelyn Irons, who worked on the *Daily Mail*, on the eve of the publication of *The Well of Loneliness*.

The article, published on 26 July 1928, opens with the words: '"You will doubtless consider me old-fashioned," said Miss Radclyffe Hall, "but I do think that, generally speaking, the woman's place is in the home. Nothing

is more stupid in the modern young woman of intelligence than her tendency to a superior attitude towards the domestic arts. To be a good wife and mother is the finest work a woman can do. And given the attention it deserves, it will occupy her life.'" Radclyffe Hall does concede that there may be circumstances when a woman wants to work – perhaps after her children are grown – in which case she would be most suited to social work or some form of 'domestic science'.

Evelyn explains: 'She told me the woman's place was the home . . . and the active member of the couple should go out into the world and work and bring home the salary . . . The article appeared the day before *The Well of Loneliness* came out . . . and it described how she liked women to stay at home and do the little woman bit so . . . in that way she got over a different picture of herself from what came out in the court case.'

> '**You** are going to tell the whole **world** that there is such an offence, to bring it to the notice of women who have never heard of it . . . '
>
> **Lord Desart** on why sexual acts between women
> should not be criminalized

On 27 July 1928, *The Well of Loneliness* was published by Jonathan Cape, a young and adventurous new firm which had only been set up in 1921 with the intention of publishing vigorous new writing from the likes of Ernest Hemingway, Sinclair Lewis and, of course, Radclyffe Hall. *The Well of Loneliness* has been credited with creating the archetypal fictional lesbian. It was translated into twelve languages within a few years of first publication and for four decades it was regarded as the emblematic lesbian novel. It has also earned an undisputed role in the history of literary censorship for being prosecuted for obscenity, with the trial creating the kind of public debate about literature which has only been seen twice in our century. It didn't happen again until the Lady Chatterley trials in 1960.

For a book that has achieved such iconic status, *The Well of Loneliness* was far from being completely original in its subject matter, nor was it received with immediate opprobrium, as is generally assumed. Ten years before *The Well of Loneliness*, there was *Regiment of Women* which described the relationship between two teachers and one of their pupils. Radclyffe Hall knew the author and she was certainly familiar with the book because there is a record of Una having read it aloud to her. The difference was that *Regiment Of Women* was written by Winifred Ashton, under the pseudonym Clemence Dane, and she kept herself very much to herself. Little was known about her private life. The reason why Radclyffe Hall attracted the anger that she did with *The Well of Loneliness* was that she was a public figure.

Gay men and lesbians in the public eye were tolerated – fêted even – as long as they didn't draw too much attention to their sexuality. It was a lesson that had been well absorbed by Noël Coward and his circle whose work was suffused with campness but who none the less maintained a public façade of heterosexuality – or at the very least a sort of sexual neutrality. As Frith Banbury who moved in the same circles as Noël Coward recalls: 'It was something that they didn't want to know about – you found him entertaining when you went to see him, loved his plays, liked his shows and looked the other way when it was inconvenient . . . a lot of these people chose to ignore what his predilections were.'

What the establishment objected to more than the 'crime' itself was any mention of it. This had been amply demonstrated in 1921 when an attempt was made to include sexual acts between women within the sphere of the law for the first time in British judicial history. The House of Commons passed the amendment to the Criminal Law Amendment Bill which moved on to the House of Lords where it was rejected. Lord Desart warned in ringing tones about the danger such a law posed. 'You are going to tell the whole world that there is such an offence, to bring it to the notice of women who have never heard of it, never thought of it, never dreamed of it. I think that is a very great mischief.' He was not alone in that opinion. The Lord Chancellor at the time, Lord Birkenhead added his voice to Desart's. 'I would be bold enough to say that of every 1,000 women . . . 999 have never even heard a whisper of these practices. Among all these . . . the taint of this noxious and horrible suspicion is to be imparted.' In other words the best way of dealing with lesbianism was not to talk about it.

Radclyffe Hall not only talked about it, she published it in the form of a popular novel. On the night before publication, she went for a walk and made a point of seeing how the publicity was going and was delighted to note that W H Smith had displayed a whole row of copies in the window. Radclyffe Hall fans bought it in large numbers – within a week, the first edition of 1,500 copies had sold out and Jonathan Cape ordered a second edition. The book got lukewarm reviews not so much for its subject matter as for its literary merit. Virginia Woolf's husband, Leonard, in his review for *The Nation*, was a touch sniffy about Hall's writing, and Vera Brittain, in a review for the magazine *Time and Tide*, was sceptical about Hall's theory and its reliance on stereotypes of male and female behaviour. She was particularly doubtful of the assumption that the young Stephen's fondness for tomboyish pursuits was a sure sign of her adult sexuality. 'In describing the supposedly sinister predilections of the child Stephen Gordon, much ado is often made about nothing; so many of them appear to be the quite usual preferences of any vigorous young female who happens to possess more vitality and intelligence than her fellows,' she wrote.

Radclyffe Hall was most disappointed by the reaction. She had been planning *The Well of Loneliness* for a very long time, as she told Evelyn Irons. 'She had *The Well of Loneliness* in her head for years,' Evelyn recalls. 'I knew

EVELYN IRONS
WEARS 'THE RING'
ON HER LITTLE
FINGER

THE DAY AFTER
THE *SUNDAY*
EXPRESS
ATTACKED
RADCLYFFE HALL,
ITS SISTER PAPER
CONTINUED THE
CAMPAIGN

NOVEL TO BE SENT TO THE HOME OFFICE.

SEQUEL TO ATTACK IN THE "SUNDAY EXPRESS."

PUBLISHERS' REPLY.

"THE Well of Loneliness," the new novel by Miss Radclyffe Hall, published recently by Jonathan Cape, Ltd., which was condemned by the Editor of the "Sunday Express" in yesterday's issue of that newspaper, is to be sent by the publishers to the Home Office and the Director of Public Prosecutions for examination.

Miss Radclyffe Hall.

The Editor of the "Sunday Express" appealed to the Home Secretary to set the law in motion against the book, which deals with a form of sexual perversion. He described it as "an intolerable outrage," and said:—

" The adroitness and cleverness of the book intensifies its moral danger. It is a seductive and insidious piece of special pleading, designed to display perverted decadence as a martyrdom in

from the time I met her that she was going to write a book on the subject and it was very much a question of being a pioneer – she used the word "pioneer".' The problem is pioneers only become pioneers if the territory they have claimed is recognized by others and so far it hadn't been. Radclyffe Hall had wanted to smash the 'conspiracy of silence' but her voice had not been heard. She had been anticipating 'the shipwreck of her whole career' and instead she found herself becalmed – and bored.

If it was excitement she sought, however, she didn't have to wait long to get all too much of it. About three weeks after *The Well of Loneliness* came out, the *Sunday Express*, on 19 August 1928, ran an article by James Douglas about the book and its author under the headline 'A Book that Must Be Suppressed', accompanied by a photograph of Radclyffe Hall looking particularly butch. Now that Radclyffe Hall had articulated what the House of Lords believed was best left unsaid, James Douglas felt it was open season. 'Perhaps it is a blessing in disguise . . . that this novel forces upon our society a disagreeable task which it has hitherto shirked, the task of cleaning itself from the leprosy of these lepers and making the air clean and wholesome once more.' Douglas added that in his opinion, it would be preferable to give a healthy boy or girl a phial of Prussic acid rather than a copy of *The Well of Loneliness* because 'while poison kills the body, moral poison kills the soul'. Many people were prepared to take that risk – on the Monday following the appearance of Douglas's article, one London library received 600 inquiries about the book.

The tabloids had scented blood and now they pursued what they perceived to be an easy target. No doubt an important factor in this was the time of the year. It was August – the traditional silly season when Parliament is in recess, half the country is on holiday and the British press finds stories hard to come by. The *Sunday Express* article was followed by pieces in the *People* and the *Sunday Chronicle* which claimed, wrongly, that Scotland Yard was examining the book.

Jonathan Cape, alarmed by all this publicity, wrote to the *Sunday Express* defending the book and adding that copies had been sent to the Home Secretary and if it could be shown that it was against the public interest, it would be withdrawn. This was a huge tactical error. The Home Secretary at the time was Sir William Joynson-Hicks a devoutly religious man and a leading light in the zealously Christian Zenana Bible Mission. Joynson-Hicks's response was the only one that could have been expected of such a man – he asked for the book to be withdrawn. Jonathan Cape cancelled the third edition but decided on an alternative strategy since demand was still quite high. The book could be printed in Paris from where British booksellers could order copies. The printing moulds were sent over to Paris where *The Well of Loneliness* was published by Pegasus Press. Soon the book was available in London again although in smaller numbers and in more furtive circumstances. This outraged the *Sunday Express* even further – it tipped off Customs and Excise which confiscated a batch of 250 books on their way to London. It wasn't long before the Home Secretary raided Jonathan Cape's offices, all copies were seized under the Obscene Publications Act of 1857 and the distributors were summoned to appear in court.

> '**Instead of offering to reprint the masterpiece, we are already beginning to wish it unwritten.**'
>
> **Virginia Woolf** on THE WELL OF LONELINESS

Radclyffe Hall's book, and therefore the author herself, were going to have a floodlight shone upon them, and she wanted her friends and supporters lined up next to her. However, for many people standing in that harsh glare was difficult for a variety of reasons. For Evelyn Irons it was a question of livelihood. As Evelyn was a writer on the women's page of the *Daily Mail*,

Radclyffe Hall expected her to take up the cudgels, journalistically speaking. 'I felt she wanted me to do an article in the paper supporting her but . . . if I wrote about it at all, I would have [had] to align myself against the book and I wasn't prepared to do that. I was prepared to keep quiet and she couldn't understand this. I think she thought I ought to go marching . . . and one wasn't prepared to go to the stake and be a martyr and suffer all this and be fired – instantly be fired from one's job which was a real danger then.'

There was much concern among prominent British writers about the precedent set by the prosecution brought against *The Well of Loneliness* but they too found it difficult to defend Radclyffe Hall unreservedly. Since most of them were well established in their careers their cavils were more to do with literary merit than fear of losing their livelihoods.

E M Forster and Leonard Woolf organized protests which included collecting signatories to an open letter which defended the book on principle. At one point the Woolfs, who ran the Hogarth Press, were even considering reprinting the book themselves but came across an obstacle when Forster and Leonard Woolf went to visit Radclyffe Hall in Kensington. In a letter to Vita Sackville-West dated 30 August 1928, Virginia Woolf wrote that Radclyffe Hall was insisting that any letter of support for *The Well of Loneliness* must 'mention the fact that it is a work of artistic merit – even genius and now we must explain this to all the great signed names – Arnold Bennett and so on, so our ardour in the cause of freedom of speech gradually cools and instead of offering to reprint the masterpiece, we are already beginning to wish it unwritten.' Writing in her diary the following day, Virginia Woolf was even more forthright in her account of the meeting between Radclyffe Hall, E M Forster and her husband. She called the book meritorious and dull and described Radclyffe Hall as 'screaming like a herring gull, mad with egotism and vanity. Unless they say her book is good she won't let them complain of the laws.'

As Evelyn Irons recalls, although Virginia Woolf, Vita Sackville-West and Radclyffe Hall represented the three most progressive and gay-friendly authors of their time, there was no love lost between them. 'Vita Sackville-West and Virginia Woolf were the twin deities then as far as a lot of people were concerned. And quite a different class of author, incidentally, from Radclyffe Hall whom they rather despised . . . It was awful really because both Vita and Virginia volunteered to give evidence if required at the trial for *The Well of Loneliness* but they did not approve of all the publicity for *The Well* and they certainly did not approve of Radclyffe Hall's writing.'

In actual fact, Virginia Woolf did not agree to appear in court unconditionally. According to defence counsel documents she only agreed to do so on the condition that she be the last to be called and only if it was absolutely necessary, but at least she agreed – there were plenty who refused to do even that. In a letter to her nephew Quentin Bell, Virginia Woolf wrote: 'Most of our friends are trying to evade the witness box for reasons you may guess. But they generally put it down to the weak heart of a father or a cousin who is about to have twins.'

The list of those who refused to appear in court to support Radclyffe Hall includes John Galsworthy, Evelyn Waugh and Rebecca West. They needn't have worried: when the trial opened on 9 November at Bow Street before the chief magistrate, Sir Chartres Biron, he declared that the question of obscenity was for him, and him alone, to decide and that evidence of literary merit was inadmissible. The court was full long before the trial began and one report notes that most of the public seats were occupied by women. Radclyffe Hall appeared in court wearing a Spanish riding hat and a leather motor coat with Astrakhan collar and cuffs to match. The judge referred to 'these horrible practices' and 'acts of the most horrible, unnatural and disgusting obscenity' which gives an indication of his personal views. On 16 November, he pronounced the book obscene, fined Jonathan Cape twenty guineas and ordered all copies to be seized and destroyed.

As Radclyffe Hall emerged from the court the women who had been occupying the public seats rushed to shake hands with her. At the

SIR WILLIAM ARBUTHNOT, RADCLYFFE HALL AND UNA TROUBRIDGE AT A FOYLES LITERARY LUNCHEON IN 1932

subsequent appeal, which she also lost, some female fans stepped forward and kissed her hand. This sudden surge of friendship made Radclyffe Hall even more keenly aware of those friends who hadn't done as she wanted and she broke off relations with them. One of them was Evelyn Irons. 'She used the word "pioneer" a lot and the trouble was she expected her friends to be pioneers and martyrs too. So poor John was let down by a great many people, including myself, who she took for granted would come out of the closet and confess themselves on her side and would support her in every way. But there wasn't a big scene or anything like that – it just so happened that one eased off a bit.'

Even though Radclyffe Hall had lost the trial, she had succeeded in making the issue as difficult to ignore as Nelson's column. Until then lesbianism was very much a thing that the smart set in London might talk about, but as Evelyn discovered, after the prosecution of *The Well of Loneliness* it became something that everybody was aware of – even Evelyn's mother up in Scotland. During the course of the trial, Evelyn went up to see her mother for a holiday who raised the subject one day: 'I've never forgotten this scene – we were making a bed and my mother stopped and said: "You're a friend of Radclyffe Hall's, aren't you?" and I said "yes" and she said: "Well that sort of thing can carry on in Paris but certainly not here", and we went on making the bed. And there I was in collar and tie and everything – dressed in the uniform – and she didn't realize what the hell it was about.'

If Evelyn's mother chose not to realize that it was everywhere, plenty of other people did. For many lesbians it was an affirmation of their existence. There were, no doubt, isolated lesbians who had no idea that there were other women who shared their feelings and the book made it clear that they were not alone. For others it meant that a subject that had been taboo was suddenly out in the open and to be visible is always better than to be ignored. During the course of the trial, Radclyffe Hall received 5,000 letters – a large proportion of them from women thanking her for writing the book – and only five of them were abusive. For years afterwards, *The Well of Loneliness* became a source of inspiration for lesbians.

Barbara Bell remembers first coming across a copy in the Thirties. 'It was a revelation, I thought well I must join this club, I'm all for this – sounded like just what I was wanting and needing,' she recalls. 'Now of course I've got one on my shelf . . . but then it was so secret, you'd pass it in a paper bag to somebody if you wanted to give it to them.'

Certainly copies of *The Well of Loneliness* were more difficult to come by after its successful prosecution, but Jonathan Cape had arranged for it to be published in the United States and visitors from America kept a steady flow of copies coming into the country. An even greater source of supply for British readers was Paris where *The Well of Loneliness* was prominently displayed on bookstands at the Gard du Nord so British visitors, about to board their trains, could stock up before crossing the Channel.

> '**Well** it was **wonderland** . . . in my wildest imagination I didn't know such a thing existed.'
>
> **Barbara Bell** on her first visit to a gay bar

Paris, which had always been a by-word for all that was permissive, became even more so now. Barbara Bell knew she had to get herself there so she booked a holiday through Thomas Cook – but once in Paris, how to find the lesbians? What she did have was the name of an area of Paris where lesbians were known to congregate, so she hung around in a square where eventually a tout for a gay club recognized her intent and led her and her friend to a place called Le Monocle.

'He took us to this insignificant looking door and gave his signal. The door was opened and in we went and negotiated our way round a red curtain in a sort of crescent shape. Well it was wonderland . . . in my wildest imagination I didn't know such a thing existed. There were these masculine-look-

ing women sitting on stools around the bar with little tables and chairs around the wall with their feminine counterparts – very beautiful looking women . . . and the women wore ties – bow ties mostly because it was evening dress and I had a black silk shirt and a black silk jacket to match. They chatted and made a great fuss of us . . . I don't think

BARBARA BELL IN HER YOUTH

they even let us pay for the drinks because they were so pleased to see this English couple around the bar.'

However Paris wasn't just thought of as a place with a *laisser-faire* attitude to homosexuality – in Britain it had a reputation where anything could happen. Hallam Tennyson went there as a schoolboy in the Thirties and in an attempt to prove to himself that he was straight he decided to visit prostitutes. 'They were quite amusing experiences if amusing is the right word because after all these women were being terribly exploited,' he explains. I remember in Paris approaching a lady standing outside the Gard St Lazare and she told me she had *belle faux dents* and I didn't understand the reason why she was telling me she had good false teeth, I didn't understand at all why that was an attraction – it seemed to me something which one wouldn't be terribly proud about. Of course it wasn't till years later I learned [she was talking] about oral sex. I think in the Thirties only the French knew about oral sex.'

If oral sex was still seen as an exotic practice which only foreigners engaged in, other aspects of gay and lesbian sexual identity were becoming

MARLENE DIETRICH WITH CROSS-DRESSING CHORUS GIRLS IN 1959

more widely practised in Britain. Radclyffe Hall's blurring of lines between what was considered male and female attire – which had largely been something that fashionable women in Paris, Berlin or London might have done, began to gain a wider currency helped no end by the influence of American movies. Hollywood catered for mass audiences and they in turn wanted to imitate what Hollywood showed them on screen.

Dietrich, who had cross-dressed in Berlin throughout the Twenties, moved to Hollywood in 1930 and her first venture there was *Morocco*, a film dripping with sexual ambivalence with cross-dressing women and men who wafted themselves with fans, wore earrings and tucked flowers into their hair. In one of her first appearances in the film, Dietrich saunters through a crowded night club, wearing a top hat, white tie and tails, to a table where a beautiful woman is sitting. Dietrich plucks the flower the woman is wearing in her hair, sniffs it and then kisses the woman full on the lips. The director Josef von Sternberg wrote in his autobiography that he got the idea for the scene from Dietrich's lifestyle in Berlin.

She didn't feel any need to make a change when she arrived in Holly-wood. In 1933 the *LA Times* noted that Dietrich was rarely seen in public wearing women's clothes – tweed suits, ties and beret were her preferred garb – and called her the best-dressed man in Hollywood. And she wasn't the only one. In 1931, a newspaper photographer had snapped Garbo strid-ing across Hollywood Boulevard in men's clothes with the noted lesbian Mercedes de Acosta a few paces behind her. It appeared under the head-line 'Garbo In Pants'. Garbo, too, made films in which she cross-dressed. Originally she wanted to play Dorian Gray in an adaptation of Oscar Wilde's novel *The Portrait of Dorian Gray* – an allegory about homosexuality in which the handsome hero is tormented by a putrefying portrait of him-self which he keeps hidden in a dark corner of his house. However, the stu-dio boss Irving Thalberg hated the idea. Instead Garbo made *Queen Christina* in 1933 which, if anything, went even further than *Morocco*. Just before the release of the film, a new biography of the seventeenth-century Swedish monarch had been published and a review in the *New York Herald Tribune* posed the question that must have been in many minds: 'The one persistent love in Christina's life was for the Countess Ebba Sparre . . . the evidence is overwhelming but will Miss Garbo play such a Christina?'

No, not quite, but she managed to get as near as the strictures of Thir-ties Hollywood allowed. There is a scene with the Countess Ebba (played by Elizabeth Young) where the two kiss on the lips and, when asked by a nobleman whether she intends to die an old maid, Garbo's response is, 'I shall die a bachelor.' Of course this situation had to be remedied if Holly-wood bosses were to sleep soundly and Christina soon meets a proper man

in the guise of John Gilbert's Spanish ambassador who falls in love with her although he first mistook her for a man. There was no need to spell it out. For gay men and lesbians in the Thirties these hints were as good as a twenty-foot hoarding and they flocked to see Dietrich and Garbo.

'Greta Garbo was my big favourite,' exclaims Barbara. 'And Marlene Dietrich because she had a deep husky voice and long legs and she had beautiful eyes – ooh, made me belly turn over! Never failed to tickle my fancy when I saw her and I would always go a long way to see Greta Garbo films.' However, although gay men and lesbians picked up the subtext in these two movies, there was no hint of the fact that both women had affairs

QUENTIN CRISP
(1996)

with other women. In her memoirs, Mercedes de Acosta talks about her sexual relationships with both Dietrich and Garbo and in May 1960, Alice B Toklas wrote in a letter to Anita Loos: 'You can't dismiss Mercedes lightly – she has had the two most important women in America – Garbo and Dietrich.' Interestingly, Garbo and Dietrich weren't great friends and didn't even meet till the end of the Second World War. Dietrich's only recorded comment after the meeting was: 'Her feet aren't as big as they say.'

Just as any overt expression of lesbian sexuality between the wars was marked by a masculinization in dress and outlook – as it was with many of the Paris salon, Radclyffe Hall and Evelyn Irons, Garbo and Dietrich – the gay male equivalent was subject to an equal and opposing pull towards feminization. In an era where gay men and lesbians could only define themselves in terms of the heterosexual world, the ones who were relatively open about their sexuality felt that they had to present themselves as parodies of that world.

'The roughs were the boys who pretended to be more masculine than they were and the bitches were the boys who pretended to be more feminine than they were,' explains Quentin Crisp. 'And in this way we parodied the masculine/feminine – it was a pseudo-normal life. We couldn't imagine a life in which two women who are fond of one another live together – it had to be that one was a pseudo man and one was a woman. And it was the same with the boys – we had to have a pseudo-normal relationship.'

Quentin, naturally, was one of the 'bitches'. Any man who wore a velvet suit in those days, hennaed his hair and applied lipstick had to align himself with the femmes and that's exactly what Quentin did. Their most regular meeting place was a café called the Black Cat in Compton Street which was like any number of similar establishments in Soho with a long bar, black-and-white checked linoleum and mirrors. The difference with the Black Cat was that it tolerated camp young men which few others did. Quentin and his friends would sit and gossip in the Black Cat, tell risqué jokes, comb their hair and try on each other's lipsticks. However, in order to stay there they had to keep drinking and so a cup of tea would be made to last the length of a four-course meal by dint of taking only the daintiest of sips. Of course, in an age where even this sort of innocent fun was considered a form of depravity, it couldn't be allowed to go on unchecked. 'After a bit the police got to hear about the Black Cat and raided it. And then we would all go to another café and congregate there. What the proprietor had to do was decide whether he would let the first of us in knowing the others would come or whether he would get rid of the first ones so that he was never accused of running an immoral place.'

Even among his own set Quentin was considered outrageous. John, who was part of that set, is quoted, in Jeffrey Weeks and Kevin Porter's oral history of gay men in this century, as saying that sometimes he used to hide or cross the road when he saw Quentin coming because he was so much more extreme than anybody else. Of course the majority of gay men and lesbians led closeted lives and as such cross-dressing or overt signs of effeminacy in men were completely out of the question. Women found it easier to adopt certain male characteristics as long as they appeared to be happily married with children. A prime example of this was Vita Sackville-West. By the Thirties, her elopement with Violet Trefusis and the ensuing scandal had been all but forgotten. Her husband, Harold Nicolson was by now in the

HAROLD
NICOLSON AND
VITA SACKVILLE-
WEST IN THE
TOWER AT
SISSINGHURST
CASTLE

diplomatic service and was interested in entering politics. Outwardly they had a conventional monogamous marriage – they even gave radio broadcasts on the BBC in the Thirties on the subject of marriage and happiness with each other. No mention was made, publicly, about the fact that, privately, their happiness depended on a sexual frankness and absence of monogamy. Both Vita and Harold had frequent affairs with members of their own sex – the only condition was that they should be kept discreet.

> **'Vita didn't like the butch get-up at all.'**
>
> Evelyn Irons on Vita Sackville-West's sartorial preferences

One of Vita Sackville-West's lovers was Evelyn Irons and, as with Radclyffe Hall, Evelyn's introduction to Vita came through work. Evelyn was attending a public reading of excerpts from *The Land* – Vita Sackville-West's epic book in verse, which had received the Hawthendorn Prize for poetry – and stayed on to ask Vita a few questions with the thought of writing an article about her for the *Daily Mail*. 'Then I left and started to walk along the street with my head in the air, rather, and heard footsteps behind me and here was the author herself pounding along the pavement,' says Evelyn. 'So she asked me if I'd like to come to lunch . . . with her. Would I! It was a great privilege in those days to consort with Vita Sackville-West . . .'

And consort she did. Evelyn and Vita became lovers and Vita wrote some of her most passionate poetry addressed to Evelyn who, by now, was no longer the butch young thing who attended first nights with Radclyffe Hall. She covered events like Ascot and the Paris couture shows and had to

VITA SACKVILLE-
WEST IN THE
GARDEN AT
SISSINGHURST

dress appropriately. Vita Sackville-West was particularly fond of Evelyn's Ascot dress which she thought 'absolutely ravishing'. 'She wanted me to wear that dress all the time . . . Vita didn't like the butch get-up at all – I think I got out of it pretty well before I met her. And she didn't care for Radclyffe Hall and . . . she certainly didn't like demonstrations or publicity of any sort. In fact she liked this sub-culture business,' Evelyn explains.

It wasn't all fabulous frocks – during the course of 1931 and 1932, when Evelyn's relationship with Vita was at its most intense, Vita was in the process of doing up Sissinghurst Castle and most particularly its grounds. On her visits to see Vita, the pair spent a lot of time throwing old bicycles and prams out of the moat and Evelyn would be given a patch of path to weed – she wasn't trusted with the beds because of her difficulty in telling flowers from weeds. Her other job was to bring buckets of water to fill the watering cans and Vita inscribed one of her books for Evelyn with the words 'for the Waterboy'.

But Vita also had another, less flattering, nickname for her. When Vita's friends heard of her dalliance with Evelyn they described her as having got into a scrape. Vita therefore decided to call Evelyn 'Scrape'. 'She looked it up in an encyclopaedia and it's a disease of sheep she was delighted to tell me,' recalls Evelyn. Until the year before her death in 1961, Vita was still writing letters to Evelyn addressed to 'Darling Scrape'.

Although Vita was the soul of discretion publicly, she did enjoy in-jokes where the private meaning would provide an added piquancy to the few who understood it. In a whimsical article she contributed to the *New Statesman* in 1931, for its 'Country Notes' column, she decided to write about scrape – the sheep's disease – making oblique allusions to Evelyn and the fact that she was Scottish. She wrote that scrape was 'nothing less than homesickness; it occurs only in sheep pining for their native land. The native land in this case happens to be the highlands of Scotland . . . The only remedy, according to my friend, is to cross the breed with a southern ram, when the North apparently agrees to settle down comfortably with the South.'

There were many thousands of gay men and lesbians who, like Vita Sackville-West, led discreet lives where they had affairs with members of their own sex but, unlike Vita Sackville-West, did not have the connections to meet them with ease. So there were certain signs and signals which let gay men and lesbians recognize each other in public places. For a period during the Twenties and Thirties, brown suede shoes were considered a sure mark of a gay man, but as these passed into the mainstream new ways had to be devised of distinguishing gay men from the common herd.

Barbara Bell used to go around with a group of gay men and some Saturdays they would catch the train from Blackburn to Blackpool for a drink at the Tower Bar which was known as a place where gay men congregated. This gave Barbara the perfect opportunity to observe the salient fashions which gay men used to signal their sexuality to each other. 'I remember vividly one year it was pink shirts. Nobody ever had pink shirts so if you wore a pink shirt you definitely signalled that you were a gay boy,' she recalls.

A more enduring sign for gay men but, more particularly, for lesbians was the wearing of rings on the little finger. It is interesting to note that in almost very photograph of Radclyffe Hall one can spot the signet ring on her little finger. 'You'd recognize the lesbians by . . . their little finger ring. So you'd plenty of chances for making passes if you were standing on the Underground or waiting at a bus stop and there was always this lovely glance of recognition and it was a lovely warm feeling to think, well you weren't the only one – there were hundreds. And if you "married" – you swore that you would be together forever – you would exchange rings and wear them on your third finger,' Barbara recalls. 'It was a good idea . . . it's like wearing a badge. I wore a little finger ring until the last two years but my fingers have got so thin now I can't keep one on.'

Although there was no such thing as a gay bar which could advertise itself as such, there were plenty of places where gay men and lesbians could meet and not be ejected – provided they weren't too outrageous. Since the theatre had a great reputation for being gay friendly – both on- and off-stage – it became a place where gay men went to meet other like-minded people who might also be in the audience. Of course it was difficult to do this if you were stuck in a seat so the idea was to stroll around in the gallery rather than reserve a seat. 'The King's Theatre at Hammersmith had a huge gallery then – all the men stood at the back, however full or empty the place was – where presumably things went on,' says John Beardmore.

There were also a number of pubs which were known to attract gay people like the Trocadero and the Cavour Bar in Leicester Square – the former had a sweeping staircase which was much admired – the Golden Lion in Soho and the Running Horse in Shepherd's Market in Mayfair which had a reputation for attracting people after they'd dined in the gentleman's clubs round the corner in Piccadilly or across the park in Pall Mall. There were other pubs where Thirties bohemia gathered which meant that gay people felt at home there. Gerald Dougherty remembers visiting one such place called the Fitzroy: 'It was just like any pub but if you looked underneath the surface a bit you realised that there was something different . . . It was used by straight people like Augustus John and his models but there was also a lot of the fringe of the gay world there. It wasn't like the Cavour which was entirely queer – this was a mixed bar with a lot of women there.'

THE LYONS
CORNER HOUSE
IN LEICESTER
SQUARE, A GAY
MEETING-PLACE
FOR OVER THREE
DECADES

THE LYONS CORNER HOUSE IN LEICESTER SQUARE, A GAY MEETING-PLACE FOR OVER THREE DECADES

The one place that almost every gay man who had contact with other gay men, went to at one point or another was the Lyons Corner House in Leicester Square. It became an unofficial headquarters for London's male gay population whose nickname for the place was the Lilypond – possibly because at one point it had a mural of lilies on one of its walls. There was another branch at Marble Arch which Terry Gardener recalls people went to if 'one was having a posh night out', but the most popular one was in Coventry Street, just off Leicester Square, which was larger and also much nearer other gay venues.

'There were a number of restaurants there and there was an orchestra,' explains Gerald Dougherty. 'People often went at teatime and there was one side of the place which was always used by gay people. There was nothing to say it was different but the waitresses all knew and [they] wouldn't let a woman sit anywhere near: "No, not this table, it's reserved."'

It wasn't just unsuspecting matrons who were steered away from the unofficial gay section of the Lilypond – gay men who weren't deemed appropriate were also kept away. One such was Terry Gardener. 'I was asked to leave once . . . I remember being terribly embarrassed and being escorted to the door by a big overpowering doorman and told not to come back. I did.'

Quentin Crisp and his crew who sported lipstick and called each other names like Greta and Marlene found it difficult enough to get into small cafés in Soho but this never deterred them from trying the Lyons Corner House from time to time: 'They tried to keep us out but the place was so large and [had] so many entrances . . . people were always creeping in.'

Although meeting people was easy enough, making contact on a more intimate level was still difficult for a lot of people. Quentin Crisp makes much of having to make do with dark doorways and although for other gay men and lesbians things were a bit better it was merely a matter of degree. In an age when homosexuality didn't figure much in the minds of the majority of the population it was possible to share a room – and sometimes a bed – with another member of the same sex if you were living at home or in digs, but such opportunities were few and far between.

Everything changed in 1939. With the declaration of the Second World War, mobilization meant that men and women from different parts of the country were thrown together in a way that they could never have foreseen. There was however at least one gay man in Britain who anticipated what the war would mean and made preparations for it. 'The day war was declared I went out and bought two pounds of henna and I did right because it became very scarce,' says Quentin Crisp.

PART TWO THE WAR

'When the **black-out** came,
London became a vast double bed.'

Quentin Crisp

On 13 May 1940, in his speech to the House of Commons on becoming Prime Minister, Winston Churchill told the country that he had nothing to offer but blood, toil, tears and sweat but there was no mention of other body fluids which were to flow just as freely during the war. The start of the Second World War and mobilization meant that men and women who had never spent a night away from home suddenly found themselves miles away, among people of their own age, responsible to nobody but themselves. The idea that death might be imminent – both for civilians who were vulnerable to bombing and for combatants who faced a much more immediate threat – led to a devil-may-care attitude. People plunged feet first into activities they would have been frightened to dip a toe in before the war began. If you were going to die tomorrow, you might as well do what you desired today – you may never have the chance again.

The problem about not thinking about tomorrow was, of course, a huge rise in unwanted children and a corresponding increase in cases of sexually transmitted diseases. The number of illegitimate births more than doubled from 26,574 in 1940 to 64,174 in 1945 and much the same happened to the incidence of venereal disease which rose by seventy per cent between 1939 and 1942. Many people believed however that this was an underestimate. The MP, Dr Edith Summerskill, argued that the official numbers – 70,000 cases – reflected less than half the number of cases and that the figure was nearer 150,000. If Dr Summerskill's figure is correct then it puts the number of people with the clap higher than the number of Blitz casualties.

These dry official figures give no inkling of the sense of liberation people felt. That feeling was true for straight people as well as gay men and lesbians but not in equal measures. By the end of the Thirties information on heterosexual sex had become easier to acquire and, of course, such sex was condoned and encouraged within certain parameters, but homosexuality had remained taboo which meant that the relative relaxation of mores seemed like an immense liberation to gay people. The segregation of the sexes when it came to living quarters also helped. In short, gay men and lesbians had what could be called a 'good' war although goodness, as Mae West might have said, had nothing to do with it.

Frith Banbury recalls how sexual licence was very much to the fore during the war. 'Let's face it, people were in different circumstances, away from their families so the what-will-the-neighbours-say factor didn't come into it. And there were lots of foreigners – Poles, Czechs, the French – all round the place so there was a good deal of sex to be had from people who were on the loose. I know of a respectable clergyman who came from Canada and he had the time of his life even though he had a wife and four children at home. When he went back after the war, the marriage broke up in three months. And later the poor chap came back to London hoping and thinking it would be like it was during the war and of course it wasn't.'

Not only did people feel that they were able to indulge themselves in areas that had previously been taboo, the blackout provided the opportunity for them to do so. In most cases people were either living in communal barracks or in digs and bringing somebody back to share your bed would have been considered as unspeakable as saying Adolf was your best pal. However, when the whole of the country was plunged into darkness, a corner of a cul-de-sac or the edge of a park was as private as anywhere. Indeed there are even some reports of sexual goings-on in Trafalgar Square although on the whole people were not quite so brazen.

For Gerald Dougherty the first night of the Blitz provided just such an opportunity so that the earth moved both literally and metaphorically for him that evening. On 7 September 1940, Gerald went to the Proms at the Queen's Hall with some friends when the programme was interrupted by an announcement that German planes were on their way. After all the frights and false alarms of the previous year, this was finally it. Gerald dutifully filed out of the hall intending to go home to his parents who he assumed would be worrying about him. As he emerged from the Queen's Hall, 'the sky was absolutely scarlet and the noise of the aeroplanes and the guns was everywhere'. Rather than go home immediately, Gerald decided to visit a gay pub called the Fitzroy. 'I thought I may die tonight, I'm going to see what it's like.'

Getting to the Fitzroy involved walking down Oxford Street and, to his amazement, Gerald found London's main thoroughfare, which was usually throbbing with cars and buses and people, completely deserted. 'I thought I'm mad walking down Oxford Street because of all the glass windows which could have broken and killed me. Anyway I got to the Fitzroy and it was magic inside with lights and music and gaiety and I thought I'd rather die here than in the streets.' On his way out of the pub, Gerald found himself in the company of another man and discovered that they were both on their way to Charing Cross which meant negotiating their way through Soho down to the Strand. 'We ran dodging from door to door because the shrapnel from the guns was sparking on the pavement and could easily have killed us.' When they reached their destination, Gerald and his companion discovered that there were no trains anyway and so neither of them could get home. The other chap, however, had a bright idea and bundled Gerald into the first-class compartment of a stationary train. 'It was most exciting with the bombs dropping and the glass shattering and I thought this is the way to spend the first night of the Blitz – in the arms of a barrow boy in a railway carriage.' Gerald and his friend were lucky – the collective damage caused by the raids that

night and on the next night was immense. About 350 people were killed and 1,300 seriously injured. Dock warehouses were set on fire and the fires, still smouldering, guided the raiders back to their targets again the following night. In fact until 1942, the number of civilians killed by Hitler's bombers was higher than the forces' casualties in actually fighting the enemy.

> ## 'Overpaid . . . oversexed and over here.'
> ### Tommy Trinder

While barrows boys were very nice it was North Americans and Canadians in particular that Gerald had contact with during the Second World War. Having met one Canadian, Gerald found himself being introduced to a whole succession of them who would look him up when they came to England and this continued till well after the war. 'I used to make this joke about myself and say I was the Canadian tart,' he says.

North American soldiers were the largest group of foreign militia stationed in Britain and their free and easy ways with chewing gum, chocolate and tights caused resentment among heterosexual British men with the wartime comedian Tommy Trinder popularizing the phrase 'overpaid . . . oversexed and over here' to describe all the things that were wrong with GIs. These were exactly the attributes that endeared American soldiers to gay men and the feeling was mutual despite the best efforts of the authorities.

The United States Army had taken great pains to eliminate homosexuality from among its ranks. Psychiatrists in induction station interviews used to try and detect gay men either by their 'effeminate looks or behaviour or by repeating certain words from the homosexual vocabulary and watching for signs of recognition'. Alas, it is not recorded what these words from the 'homosexual vocabulary' were. The problem then arose that men who didn't want to fight would fake homosexuality in order to get out of the Army. The United States Army therefore decided that it had to divide the men who were genuinely gay from camp followers.

Accordingly, diagnostic tests were devised including one by Nicolai Giosca, published in the *American Journal of Psychiatry* after the war, which came up with the ludicrous notion that homosexual men did not display a gag reflex when a tongue depressor was put down their throat. An even more absurd study was conducted by A C Cornsweet, a commander in the US Naval Reserve, and Dr M F Hayes an army physician who concluded, after conducting a survey among 200 gay men, that they had discovered a specific reaction common to all those 'confirmed to the practice of sexual oralism'. This constituted a localization of pleasure which could only be described by the true homosexual. He assumed that this would also be true of heterosexual women who indulged in oral sex but no mention is made of lesbians. Indeed while the United States Army did all it could to weed out gay men it seems to have been much less concerned about lesbians in the forces. A urinary hormone secretion test had also been developed but this proved to be too 'uncertain and expensive'. Not that the others were sure-fire successes.

If these diagnostic tests failed – and the chances of them succeeding seem infinitesimal – then there was a 'fail-safe' final check. During enlistment for the Second World War men were asked, for the first time in the history of the United States Army, if they had ever had homosexual feelings or experiences. However, any men who wanted to serve in the Army could easily evade this screening. Bob Ruffing who enlisted in the Navy recalls being interviewed by an officer dripping with gold braid. 'He was a queen if ever I saw one and he asked me the standard questions ending with, "Did you ever have any homosexual experiences?" I looked him right in the eye and said, "No." He looked right back and said, "That's good." Both of us lying through our teeth.' An indication of exactly how futile this exercise was came at the end of the war when *Newsweek* published an article in June 1947 on the United States Army's own figures on homosexuality that had just been tabulated. During the course of the Second World War, between 3,000 and 4,000 men were discharged for this 'abnormality' and an unspecified number were released as 'neuropsychiatric cases'.

Of course for every GI that was caught and court-martialled there must have been several who weren't and Britain's gay population was immensely grateful for them. American soldiers, when compared to their Limey counterparts, seemed incredibly glamorous. How could they not be when their number included the band leader Glenn Miller and the actor James Stewart. Quentin Crisp, never one who would fail to notice the cut and the cloth, remembers that for a start their uniforms were made of a finer fabric and that they fitted better than the baggy kit issued to British soldiers. This intrigued him so much that one day when walking behind a GI, Quentin couldn't help but blurt out the question: 'How do you fight in that uniform, it looks too tight?' Quentin called the GIs stationed in Britain 'the army of no occupation because they had nothing to do but whistle at the girls and talk to the boys'. The fascination that British gay men had for American soldiers was reciprocated. Many GIs had never travelled outside their home state before, let alone been abroad, and their eyes were wide with fascination at the sights Europe had to afford and must have almost popped out of their sockets when they clapped sight of Quentin Crisp.

'They simply couldn't believe what we were like because they hadn't all come from New York, you know,' Quentin remembers. 'They'd come from Maple Leaf, Missouri and places like that and so when they saw us they simply couldn't believe it.' Quentin with his hennaed hair, painted face and varnished nails must have seemed as exotic as the Queen of Sheba: 'They would seize my hands in which the nails were more off the finger than on and they'd say, "Come here Hank, look at his hands." And then your voice fascinated them. They said, "Say something." And whatever you said was wonderful, just the sound of it. So we thought this is wonderful – I'm the toast of the regiment!'

As Quentin discovered, however, the GIs didn't just want to talk. 'It was wonderful because they were away from their wives, away from their teachers, away from their preachers and anything went.' According to Quentin, the superiority of the Americans didn't stop at the cut and quality of the uniforms they wore – indeed it went far deeper than a few millimetres of blue serge. 'GIs were more natural in their sexual behaviour than Englishmen. Englishmen pretend nothing has happened – you have a wild affair with an Englishman and when it's over he talks about the weather or politics or something like that exactly as though nothing had happened. But American soldiers discussed their sex life and your sex life.' Quentin also found that the American soldiers he met were more willing to be seen with him than their British counterparts who would 'walk slightly ahead of you or slightly behind but they were never really with you. But the Americans walked beside you and stared at you. They'd walk crabwise so as not to miss anything you said.'

Apart from making the necessary adjustment to accommodate the arrival of Americans and the opportunities they afforded, Quentin refused to let the war inconvenience him in any other way. He didn't even take any notice of air raids. 'I never went into an air-raid shelter. If I was invited out whether there was an air raid or not, I went. The sky was pink with doom because buildings were burning and you could hear the shrapnel falling through the branches of the trees and tinkling on the pavement. Of course, if it landed on you, you would be killed but it was no good standing still so you might as well walk on. So we behaved exactly as though nothing had happened which was wonderful.'

> '**All conscientious objectors should be shot,**
> **but not you, my dear . . .**'
> **Old actress** to Frith Banbury

One of the things that made it possible for Quentin to behave as though nothing had happened and process through London in stately fashion, come rain or raid, was that he hadn't been forcibly enlisted. When he went for his physical examination, Quentin was asked whether he was gay. This was at a time when the British forces found the very idea of an admitted homosexual abhorrent, let alone an admitted homosexual within their own ranks. They none the less examined him which caused great consternation among the medics. 'All the doctors were in a terrible state when they saw me. They were terribly flustered, rushed about and talked to each other in whispers.' Despite the fuss there was no dispute that Quentin didn't belong in the army and he was given his exemption papers on which it stated that he suffered from sexual perversion.

There were other gay people who also refused to fight but on the grounds of pacifism. Frith Banbury did not believe in war as a solution and while a schoolboy at Stowe he had refused to join the Officers' Training Corps, a ritualistic form of army training and square-bashing which was standard in British public schools until well into the Sixties. Frith had come across the Peace Pledge Union, set up by the Reverend Hugh Richard Lawrie Shepherd who had become famous in the Twenties for radio broadcasts from his church, St Martin-in-the-Fields on Trafalgar Square – probably London's most distinguished church after St Paul's. In October 1934, the Reverend Dick Sheppard, as he was universally known, wrote open letters to the papers urging men who shared his pacifist views to send him a postcard on which they had written: 'We renounce war and never again, directly or indirectly, will we support or sanction another one.' To his astonishment, 2,500 cards landed on his doorstep in the next couple of days and within weeks the pile numbered 50,000. The momentum gathered until 22 May 1936 when Sheppard officially launched the Peace Pledge Union whose founder members included such luminaries as Siegfried Sassoon, Bertrand Russell and Aldous Huxley, later to be joined by Benjamin Britten (who wrote the rather oxymoronically titled 'Pacifist March' for the organization), Vera Brittain and Sybil Thorndike. In total 50,000 men and 2,000 women registered as conscientious objectors. Frith became part of that number in 1937, so when it came to registering for military duty after the Munich Crisis, Frith put himself down as a conscientious objector and continued with his career in the theatre. In the autumn of 1940, however, he was asked to appear before a tribunal and justify his decision not to fight.

Frith had his case well prepared. He had attended other people's tribunals and seen young men of sixteen or seventeen argue rather naively that the reason they couldn't go to war was because the Lord had said: 'Thou shalt not kill.' Whereupon the tribunal would quote back another section of the Bible which contradicted or qualified the sixth commandment, leaving the poor appellant rather stuck for a response.

'I realized that this was not on and by that time I was a non-believer anyway,' says Frith. 'So I said on ethical grounds and these eight august gentlemen, who were rather bored, sat up thinking this is different.' Frith clearly acquitted himself well before the tribunal which then asked him what he was prepared to do, to which Frith replied that he could not countenance any work that was under military law. 'So they then said, "Are you prepared to do farm work?" and I said, "Yes, prepared but not equipped." So they then consulted and registered me on condition that I went on being an actor.' Frith could not have hoped for better since that was exactly what he wanted to do.

Pacifists who refused to fight on a matter of principle were disparagingly called 'Conchies' and faced hostility everywhere except among the intelligentsia who could see that being a conscientious objector was far from being an easy option. A Mass Observation Survey carried out among RAF conscripts in April 1940 said: 'Many dismiss them [conscientious objectors] all as unnatural and meet to be shot. The more thinking concede that it requires a good deal of guts to be a conscientious objector and that we have taken the easy way out by following the crowd.' Because Frith worked in the theatre, things weren't as hard as they could have been. 'Although one marvellous old actress who shall be nameless said to me, 'All conscientious objectors should be shot, but not you, my dear, you're sincere.''

'There's an **opening** for you in the Navy.'
Slogan on recruitment poster

Other gay men went to their medicals never expecting to get through and found themselves in, to their astonishment. One such was Terry Gardener who had been an enthusiastic drag queen in the years leading up to the war. When he was called up his friends gave him some advice. 'The two queens I'd worked for said: "Now dear, if you don't want to go into the forces, when you go up for your medical be really outrageous – be yourself – and you won't get called up."' It didn't work. Terry passed his medical and was sent through for the interview where he was asked what he could do. 'I said: "Well nothing really although I can cook." So they said: "Right, cook in the Navy," and I was in.' Terry was quite prepared to do his bit but his friends were worried that while Terry might not mind being in the Navy, the Navy might mind Terry. His friends in the drag act had some further advice for him. '"Now listen, dear," they said. "No one's ever going to mistake you for a man so if you really want to be a success in the Navy just be an outrageous theatrical and you'll find that you'll either be kicked

TERRY GARDENER
AND ALAN
HAYNES DOING
THEIR ACT

TERRY GARDENER AND ALAN HAYNES DOING THEIR ACT

out or you'll be welcomed with open arms.'" This time their advice worked.

The opportunity for Terry to show his true colours – in all their vivid gorgeousness – came quite quickly. He was sent to a Butlin's camp in Skegness which had been requisitioned for training. Needless to say an out-of-season holiday camp with acres of mud and poor living conditions rather destroyed Terry's image of the glamorous Navy life, but all was not lost. He had brought his own little bit of glamour with him. He'd managed to take

a little cigarette tin of make-up, a wig and an old frock and when, a couple of weeks into training, a 'go-as-you-please' entertainment was announced in the mess, Terry spotted his chance. He put on the slap, pulled on the wig, shimmied into the frock and schlepped down to the canteen theatre where, to everyone's amazement – not least his own – Terry tore the place apart with a couple of songs and few dirty jokes. 'I'll never forget coming back to my chalet to find a queue of boys all anxious to get to know the woman that had been on!'

Terry realized that this could be his métier in the Navy. When he was drafted after the five-week training course was complete, he found himself in Chatham Barracks where he quickly sought out the person in charge of entertainment and was referred, curiously, to the padre. Soon he was a permanent entertainer at Chatham Barracks and could have stayed there for the rest of the war, but Terry wanted to find out what life at sea was like and became a cook in the officers' mess in a ship that plied the route between Britain and Gibraltar, carrying goods and personnel. Because of the danger of attack, the ships travelled in convoy and it often took a fortnight to complete a journey that ought to have taken two days. However, Terry didn't hang up his wig permanently when he swapped it for a chef's toque. While serving in the Navy, he got permission from the Admiral of the Fleet, no less, to take part in the Army concert parties at Gibraltar.

There were other gay men in the Navy who managed to get away with it through sheer chutzpah. John Beardmore recalls a coder on his ship, who had been a chorus boy in peace time, whose action station was to relay the messages from the captain to the forward guns. During moments of high drama he sometimes defused the tension by camping it up. So when the captain issued orders to open fire, he simply repeated, 'Open fire, dear,' which would crack up the troops. 'He was called Freddy and was immensely popular on the ship – everybody loved him and he loved everybody else,'

John recalls. 'He often wrote letters home for those who couldn't write and was greatly admired.' However, it wasn't all plain sailing even for people like Freddy and Terry. Inevitably some of the men took exception and the only response was to give as good as you got, and Terry, while he may not have been a champ with his fists, could give a tongue lashing that could be just as bruising as several rounds with Mike Tyson. If people objected to him he didn't mince any words, telling people who challenged him: 'What goes up my fucking arse won't give you a headache.' Looking back on it now, Terry is surprised at his own audacity. 'I had the cheek not to let anybody take advantage of me so if anyone said "Are you queer?" I would say, "Yes! So what?" I can only say that I was very green. I didn't really know what I was doing and sometimes there is a guardian angel that watches over people that are very stupid.' Terry adds, though, that hostility was the exception rather than the rule and, for the most part, he managed to get on with the other men who positively enjoyed having him around rather than merely tolerating him. 'I could be very entertaining,' says Terry. 'Everybody loves to laugh whatever the circumstances, and believe me there were some dreadful, dreadful circumstances especially on the Western approaches. People were just thankful to get through the day and, of course, if I was around to give them a laugh, it was a bonus, wasn't it?'

> '**The captain** occasionally used to squeeze my arse.'
> John Beardmore

Sexual contact between people of the same sex appears to have been as common as khaki in the forces although it was always furtive and secret since being caught meant a certain court martial and subsequent disgrace, not only for having committed the supposed 'crime' but furthermore because the ejection from the post meant that the individual wasn't doing his or her bit. In actual fact, though, servicemen and women in all three forces had sexual relationships with other members of their own sex as long as that relationship was kept securely zipped up and out of sight at all times.

In some instances relationships which, it was tacitly accepted, might involve a sexual element were enshrined in the structure of the Navy. John Beardmore who joined the Army in 1939 at the age of nineteen says, 'The captain must have known I was gay because occasionally he used to squeeze my arse.' John remembers a system of 'wingers' and 'oppos'. A 'winger' was a senior officer who would take a new recruit under his wings and show him the ropes while an 'oppo' was a seaman of the new recruit's own age and rank, often on the same watch and the pair were expected to be pals, go ashore together and generally keep an eye on each other. As soon as John went aboard, he became a target for young married men who were mostly active service and petty officers who wanted him to become his 'winger', with a motive that was more sexual than philanthropic. In the nine months that he was on his first ship, before he was sent to officers' training college, John fought a losing battle against this. The relationship between oppos was more equal. 'You shared duties and he looked after your tot when you were on duty and put you to bed when you came back from shore pissed. It was largely platonic but in some cases it developed into a sexual relationship which went on after the war ended. I know of fellows who were oppos and who were having affairs at the time who went on to become godfathers to each other's children.'

John was no exception. He and his oppo, when they were given leave, would check in at the Union Jack Club near Waterloo where volunteers provided food and drink for servicemen and women. Even more inviting than the tea and sandwiches was the fact that for a shilling you got your own little cubby hole for the night which helped no end at a time when privacy was considered as much of a luxury as bananas. 'We'd go dancing and try to get off with girls, usually unsuccessfully, so we'd return to the Union Jack Club and end up in the same bed together. I met this man again some fifty years later, now a grey-haired grandfather, and he came up and recognized me and said, "My goodness, Lofty, I still remember those nights at the Union Jack Club," which is something that most men would prefer to forget.'

For the men to lend each other a hand was not considered at all unusual on John's ship. 'Sailors were a fairly randy lot and masturbation was not at all uncommon,' John recalls. 'You could go down in the middle watch which was twelve midnight to four and hear a whisper come from a hammock, someone saying, "Give us a wank," which was just completely accepted by the lower deck ratings.' The crucial point about all this, of course, was that these people regarded themselves as heterosexual even though they were having sex with other men. According to John, married men were often more active in having sex with other men 'because they were missing it all the time and they thought at least if they went with another man. It wasn't an infringement of their marriage vows, which it would have been if they had gone with another woman.' Indeed, sailors coming back from shore leave sometimes boasted of having gone back with a gay man whom they disparaged as if the story had no implication for their own leanings. 'When you went ashore and you met somebody who took you home for five bob or so many pints of beer you would say: "I went with a brown hatter last night." That was the common term which I believe originates because during peace time gay men used to go down to Portsmouth to pick up sailors and in those days brown trilby hats were very fashionable. In point of fact, though, it also has a rather salacious reference,' John laughs.

> '**I** was standing **shivering** in this cupboard, hoping to God **I** wouldn't sneeze.'
>
> Chris Gotch

While the Navy has had an enduring reputation for same sex liaisons – or 'rum, bum and concertina' as George Melly put it – the other forces were far from being havens of heterosexuality, as Chris Gotch discovered when he joined the Air Force. Chris's father, who had been a sapper in the First World War, was keen for Chris to follow in his footsteps but Chris had other ideas.

While still a schoolboy at Marlborough, Chris had an enormous crush on a chap named Jimmy with whom he eventually ended up sharing a study. Jimmy had decorated the walls of their study with pictures of Spitfires and Hurricanes, and when it came to joining up, Chris was determined to be a fighter pilot like Jimmy had wanted to be, rather than a 'dreary' sapper like his dad. Ironically Jimmy never achieved his

CHRIS AND JIMMY
AS SCHOOLBOYS
IN THE SUMMER
OF 1939

CHRIS GOTCH'S
FRIEND, JIMMY, IN
1943 – HE WAS
KILLED SEVERAL
MONTHS LATER

CHRIS GOTCH'S
FRIEND, JIMMY, IN
1943 – HE WAS
KILLED SEVERAL
MONTHS LATER

CHRIS GOTCH'S
WING COM-
MANDER, IAN,
PICTURED
IN 1942

ambition of becoming a fighter pilot because, by the time his turn came, what they needed was bomber pilots, and he was tragically killed when his plane flew into a hill. Chris, however, made it to the hallowed status of fighter pilot.

After three months' training in Canada, learning to fly Tiger Moths, he was posted to a squadron on a large Air Force base near Salisbury. After he'd been there about three weeks, he became aware of being scrutinized while sitting in the mess. He looked up to see the wing commander staring at him. Chris felt rather uncomfortable, not only because the man was superior to him in rank, but also because he was highly decorated, having been awarded the DSO and the DFC during the Battle of Britain. In actual fact, this splendid record had been achieved with remarkable speed since Ian, as the commander was called, was only twenty-five. When Chris left the mess and returned to his room, sitting there on the window sill was Ian. 'He just leant over and gave me a great big kiss which took me by surprise, but being a product of public school it wasn't exactly strange. He then made an assignation for me to join him in his room and so we started having sex together. He was a great character, an incredible character. He was the first bloke who ever buggered me.'

It wasn't just new forms of sex that Chris was introduced to by Ian. 'He had charm, he had personality and he had a car and he used to take me up to London and introduce me to people,' says Chris who found himself moving among the *haute monde*. One of these people was Beverley Nichols, the writer and journalist – and incidentally another Marlborough man – who had been one of the bright young things of the Twenties. Nichols had a surprisingly modern view of his own sexuality and rather shocked Cecil Beaton by saying: 'I'm not ashamed of it. I'm proud of it! Sex is everything in life . . . some people are born one way, others another. I adore my sexual experiences, they are the most thrilling moments in my life and if I were ever castrated there would be no future interest . . . to live for.'

Another, perhaps less elevated, introduction was to a rich American who was staying at Claridges. 'We all had dinner and then we all repaired to his room and apparently we all had sex in a threesome. And the next morning Ian had to go off somewhere and I had to go off somewhere separately and as I left . . . [the American] pressed something into my hand. As I walked down the street I opened my hand and there was a five-pound note . . . and that was a lot of money in those days. I was astonished and I went down the street singing, "I'm a whore, I'm a whore." I loved it,' Chris chuckles.

It wasn't all dinner at Claridges and welcome windfalls, however. Sex between men was highly taboo which, on at least one occasion, rather took the wind out of Ian's sails. By this time, Chris and Ian would meet in Ian's room to make love, which is what they were doing one evening at about

CHRIS GOTCH
(right) WITH HIS
LOVER, IAN,
DURING THE WAR

nine o'clock when there was a pounding on the door. Ian pretended to be asleep but whispered to Chris, 'Get into the cupboard.' So, stark naked, Chris clambered into the cupboard while Ian unlocked the door, pretending to be drowsy. To his astonishment, he was face to face with the group captain who wanted to discuss the following day's operations. 'So he sat down and between them they began a lengthy discussion while I was standing shivering in this cupboard, hoping to God I wouldn't sneeze because I was liable to catarrh – any sudden change in temperature and I would go off,' says Chris. Had Chris's nasal passages got the better of him, both he and Ian would have been charged and court-martialled, but taking a sexual risk was seen as no different by Chris – and no doubt hundreds of others like him – from the daily risk they were running in the war. 'It was petrifying, but . . . it was like being on an operation and under fire . . . one was frightened to death but you were optimistic about it.'

For some unfortunate gay men, that optimism was misplaced. There were more courts martial for 'indecency between males' between 1939 and 1945 than for any other category of offence. Interestingly, the number of men court-martialled for indecent conduct increased exponentially as the war progressed. In the first year of the Second World War, 1939–40, they numbered 48 but by the final year, 1944–5, they had multiplied to 324. There is no record of what arguments were advanced at these court martials but an indication of army policy is given by a War Office document made public in 1950, entitled 'The Second World War: Army Discipline', which states: 'confirmed homosexuals whose rehabilitation is unlikely should be removed from the Army by the appropriate means.' Interestingly the regulation refers to 'confirmed' homosexuals – suggesting that repeated offences were necessary and even then expulsion from the army was only considered appropriate for those confirmed homosexuals who could not be rehabilitated. This implies that at a time when all able bodies were required to fight the war, a blind eye was sometimes turned.

This was certainly the case with Bill Tawse, a medical orderly on board ship who was caught having sex with a GI and charged with indecent conduct. Bill, who had been rattled by tales that he was facing two years' hard labour, was getting very fed up and attempted suicide. 'I went and threw myself in the Mersey because we were at Liverpool at the time. I was fished up by two policemen who saw me jump . . . they were so quick. So I went into hospital and all this came out and I think in a way it went in my favour . . . the attempted suicide and being hospitalised, being visited by the sergeant major, being visited by my own colonel from Liverpool Barracks. They all put their heads together and thought, well, this lad really feels he was sorry . . . and we should be a bit more forgiving.'

To his immense relief, Bill was found not guilty at his court martial but he was not allowed to respond to the arguments that were advanced or even to listen to them. After he had entered his plea, he was asked to wait outside while a colonel and six officers deliberated and he was not called in again till a verdict was reached. 'As it was explained [to me] by the army secretary [it] was "because you were put upon by these GIs. You didn't invite them or make passes did you?" And I said "No." "Well, the officers have thought, this poor bugger . . . has been put upon by these lusty types . . . who can't have two days at sea but they want something". And that was that.'

Rude interruptions from other people were a constant fact of life during the war for gay men and women living in large same-sex institutions. Monica Still was a nurse during the war and working in a Hastings hospital where she was having an affair with Marya McLean, a fellow nurse who also ended up spending a spell in a cupboard. Because of the raids and the necessity to get people out quickly, Marya, whose room was at the top of the nurses' home, had been temporarily billeted in a basement dormitory. Not that it made any difference because she was in Monica's bed on another floor. Unfortunately the night sister discovered Marya's empty bed when doing her rounds and marched straight to Monica's bedroom and thumped on the door. "'Nurse Still! Have you seen Nurse McLean?" "Oh no, sister, she'll be sleeping downstairs," I said. "I've just been down there," the nurse said, "and she's not there." "Oh," I said. "Oh dear. One moment and I'll come and

MONICA STILL (right) AND HER LOVER, MARYA (left), IN THEIR YOUTH

MONICA
AT THE VICTORIA
HOSPITAL IN
LEWES IN 1940

help you look." And I pushed Marya into the wardrobe and went out and said to the sister, "Perhaps she's gone up to her room?"' So Monica and the night sister trotted up to the top floor, which allowed Marya to make her escape from the cupboard and sneak back to the basement dormitory. So, of course, when Monica and the night sister got down there she could plead an innocent visit to the bathroom to account for her absence. 'I don't think it washed,' says Monica drily. And the evidence that it hadn't came quite quickly.

No sooner had the hoo-ha died down, and Monica was comfortably ensconced back in her bed, then she saw the door handle turn – it was Marya creeping back into her bedroom. 'It was terribly rash, but she didn't care. I didn't care!' says Monica. Alas the night sister did care – very much – and decided to do another reconnaissance. This time she caught them and separated them. They were not to be deterred so easily, however. Before long, the door handle turned yet again and Monica and Marya were back where they belonged – in bed together. 'Even night sister didn't think that we'd try it a third time!' says Monica.

The difference between men and women was that, while men who were caught engaging in a sexual act together were committing an imprisonable offence, what women did may have been frowned upon but it wasn't actually against the law and so no action could be taken, although this didn't prevent gauleiters from putting petty restrictions in the way of women who had been found with other women. 'I was on the carpet in the matron's office the next morning and so was Marya and after that life was even more difficult for us,' says Monica. 'They put her on the male military ward. I suppose they thought that this would make her normal, and they saw to it that we were never on the same ward or had the same time off. I would be off in the morning, she'd be off in the afternoon, but we still managed it one way or another, you know. Love will find a way.'

'Well, we'll **probably** be very glad to have you, because I can see the men are going to be elsewhere.'

News Editor of the London EVENING STANDARD

Although large numbers of women served in the forces, many women who had never worked before found themselves taking over the jobs that the men had done before the war. However, it was made very clear that women were only being encouraged to do these jobs because the men were away doing something more urgent. The Minister for Labour, Ernest Bevin, said in 1943: 'Nothing that a woman can do, or can learn to do, should be allowed to absorb a man of military age.' In an era when jobs were something women did to fill in time till the right man came along, lesbians, by definition, were already in professions such as nursing or the police force or, in the case of Evelyn Irons, in journalism before the war broke out. For some of these women, war had an unexpected and very welcome side-effect. Both Evelyn and Barbara Bell, who had joined the police force just before the war began, found that with the men away, they were given responsibilities that might never have come their way otherwise. 'Because the younger men had been called up, we were left with the

BARBARA BELL
IN HER YOUTH

EVELYN IRONS
WAS A WAR
CORRESPONDENT
FOR THE *EVENING
STANDARD*

older policemen and we had to do everything without exception, everything that men did,' says Barbara. She was attached to West End Central, the busiest and probably the seediest police district in the country, and one of her tasks was to keep an eye on the prostitutes. 'We became very friendly with them – they were really wonderful girls and wonderful citizens. They weren't called up because they were already doing their duty for the country, weren't they?' Barbara recalls how the prostitute population in London included a number of gay women. 'There were one or two lesbians, actual lesbians, who were doing it. Two of them I know were doing it because they had their children at good schools – they had a child each – and they were doing it to keep these children in boarding schools.'

When war broke out, Evelyn Irons was working on the London *Evening Standard* doing the kind of thing that female reporters had been confined to until that point – soft stories about food and fashion and furniture with the odd serious piece on divorce thrown in to leaven the tedium. With the declaration of hostilities, Evelyn saw her opportunity. 'At the start of the Second World War, I didn't feel those grand feelings one is supposed to feel but I knew this was my chance to scuttle all this women's stuff and to become a proper reporter,' she recalls. So she marched over to the news editor's desk and demanded her due. 'I simply walked across the room and said to him, "I've finished with all that stuff now, I want to be a reporter," and he said, "Well, we'll probably be very glad to have you because I can see that the men are going to be elsewhere," and I became a reporter on the spot.'

Evelyn was assigned to the news desk and the first thing she had to learn to do was type. Until then she had written all her work out in longhand, partly because women weren't seen as real journalists, and if they didn't have the skills that other journalists see as a requisite, it didn't really matter. Real journalism wasn't necessarily more interesting, however – like the war itself it was long periods of boredom interspersed with extreme excitement. She might be sent to cover a blitz incident or it might be something as mundane as a change in the meat ration.

When she finished at the *Evening Standard*, Evelyn spent her evenings doing voluntary work with the Fire Service and was based at a depot in Clerkenwell in the East End of London, where the regular firemen didn't know what had hit them. A flock of glamorous females took over, sleeping in the kitchens and lining up their cosmetics on the old black iron cooking stoves. The working firemen were a bit taken aback but soon came round when they realized that the women were worth their weight in gold – or in butter which was probably just as rare and expensive during the war. 'I must say the girls did very well, there was not a funk or a coward among them,' Evelyn says with approbation.

The Clerkenwell depot was no exception. Evelyn remembers that a number of the women drivers were lesbians, as was the commandant of the volunteers who managed to wangle it so that her girlfriend and her girlfriend's son could stay in the building. 'This little boy was really marvellous,' said Evelyn. 'If there was a bad blitz on, he had a little gramophone and he used to put Beethoven's piano sonatas on the gramophone and play this while the bombs were falling all around. He was a very brave little boy.'

Evelyn was equally brave and wanted nothing more than to become a war reporter. Until quite late in the war that was regarded as men's work, so while things had changed for the better in journalism it only applied to the domestic front. When it came to the nitty gritty end of war journalism, it was still business as usual. 'Women war correspondents in England weren't like the ones in America – they weren't *personae gratae* with the Army, because Montgomery didn't like girls much . . .' It wasn't until 1944, when the Germans had abandoned Paris and were on the run and it was becoming obvious that the Allies would win, that female journalists were allowed to cross the Channel into France. Six female reporters were allowed over and Evelyn was among this pioneering group – but being at the front and getting access were two different things. The female journalist's job was to interview the wounded in hospital and write heart-warming copy about our plucky boys and occasionally they were allowed to go behind the lines and pick up what stories they could. What they weren't allowed to do was witness any fighting and, without that, war reportage is just human interest stories dressed up in khaki. Evelyn was getting very fed up with this, but then ran into an American friend from before the war who was working on the *New Yorker* to whom she complained about lack of access. She suggested Evelyn should dump the British Army with its petty restrictions and attach herself to the French. 'I said, "*The French!* Look at their attitude to women!" and she said, "My dear, you don't understand the French. The minute a woman gets into uniform, she ceases to be a woman, she just becomes an object. You just try the French Army."' So Evelyn did.

The French, as her friend had perceptively predicted, welcomed her with open arms, gave her a superb view of the fighting and were conscious of the finer things of life as well – vineologically speaking. To her delight, Evelyn found herself attached to a division of the French Army in Cognac where the brandy flowed as freely as the Seine. 'We used to go in an observation plane and watch the fighting in the morning and tend to the brandy in the afternoon.' Evelyn's news editor, who wasn't without his sense of humour, soon caught on and sent her a telegram saying: '"What the hell are you doing down there, the news is in Germany." So I had to go to the real war after that,' Evelyn chuckles.

Reality when it came had a horrific visage. The following year, in the spring of 1945, Evelyn was with a detachment of the French Army and a group of correspondents – among whom Evelyn alone represented Britain – when they came across one of Hitler's extermination camps.

'It was a spring morning and all the fruit trees were in bloom – it was simply beautiful – and then there was this horrible place where the morning's dead were just flung into an open grave. And the live people were even more horrifying because they could hardly stand. They were clinging to the wire fence and shouting at us: "Why didn't you come sooner? It's too late, we've lost all our people." We were frantic with horror. It was really a shattering experience. And inside were the ones who were too weak to come to the fence. They didn't have gas ovens, the system was to leave them there till they became so sick, they couldn't move, and the infection was rampant, of course, so they infected each other and died. And each morning they took the dead bodies and threw them into an open grave. And we saw all this. Now when people say there was no Holocaust, that it was a cooked up thing, it just makes me so mad, I could kill them. But there it was. A really terrible, terrible thing.'

In fact Evelyn didn't have to wait for long before people began to deny that millions had died simply for being who they were. Within months of the camps having been liberated by soldiers, senior Nazis began to say that the Holocaust was a figment of overheated imaginations and Allied propaganda. Frau Hess, wife of the Deputy Führer, had been put under house arrest by the French Army which gave Evelyn an opportunity to interview her. 'She didn't believe that the Holocaust had ever happened. I just held myself in as long as I could and then finally I said, "Look, the day before yesterday, I saw one of those camps," and I told her all about it. She was weeping by the time I'd finished with her and she said, "You're a very hard woman."'

For people like Frau Hess, who'd probably never seen the camps at first hand, it would have been easy enough to ignore because the horror was covered over by a tissue of refinement like gossamer overlying a dung heap.

The Nazi élite cultivated a polished façade which allowed Diana Mosley, when recalling her meetings with Hitler, to claim that he had charming manners. Evelyn soon saw at first hand how the hideousness was covered by a thin skin of civilization. She and a reporter from a French agency were to be the first female journalists to visit Hitler's private apartments in Bavaria, where he had a villa. The jeep that had brought them there could only take them as far as the main building but there was little to report on there because it had already been bombed to bits. The real story was up a mountain where Hitler's lofty sanctum – known as Eagle's Nest – was perched. The problem was that the lift that transported Hitler and his guests to Eagle's Nest was broken and, to make matters worse, the weather was bad. Evelyn and her colleague were not to be deterred. They clambered up the hill in the snow on their hands and knees. What greeted them made the journey worth it: 'When we got there we found it was an absolutely marvellous place. We found that Hitler had left quite a lot of very pleasant white wine there and magnificent china, magnificent appointments of every sort . . . the French Army had taken it in the first place and, of course, they'd made great inroads into the drink supplies and we proceeded to do the same.' Evelyn even managed to get a small souvenir of that assignment. 'His dining room was fabulous and his china was really out of this world and I helped myself to a saucer with red dragons running all round it and took it home with me, but of course it's long since broken . . . So finally, a little bit the worse for wear we slid down the snow on our bottoms.'

Incidents like these, which provided a glimpse of other lives, were welcome respite from the war. Like Evelyn, Bert Bartley discovered that there was more to war than the daily grind of bombardment and bully beef. In Bert's case, the chance to escape came through opera. Bert, who was in the Royal Signals Corps,

BERT BARTLEY
DURING HIS TIME
WITH THE ROYAL
SIGNAL CORPS, IN
ALGIERS

was stationed in Italy and managed to go to performances at the Naples opera house more frequently than most soldiers changed their socks. 'If we were off duty and wanted a liberty truck it was always put on and you paid your half a crown and got a stall seat. I went every possible time. Sometimes I'd been to an opera in the afternoon, gone to the NAAFI and had tea, and gone back and seen another one in the evening.' The music allowed Bert to fill in gaps that might have otherwise have seemed dull – for instance, finding himself in Rome at Christmas time with no prospect of home leave, he went to an opera on both Christmas Day and Boxing Day.

The high point of Bert's war career in terms of meeting other gay men was when he was posted to Algiers which was notorious. 'There was a certain bar in Algiers where the officers used to come and the Americans used to be there too and gay Americans are great fun to be with. They're much more outgoing and they've got the patter and they're telling jokes all the time. We used to have some fabulous evenings and catch the liberty truck back home.'

There was, however, more to war than sex, sopranos and Sèvres china from Hitler's collection. There was the real business of war – fighting the enemy – and gay men and lesbians distinguished themselves on that front.

> '1 got through about **nine** lives in the War.
> 1 was very lucky – nearly all my friends were killed.'
> Chris Gotch

Fifty years after the event, it is all too easy to ridicule that wartime spirit when everybody was rolling out the barrel and packing up their troubles in the old kit bag, but there was a genuine sense of camaraderie and patriotism. Although there were a number of people who refused to fight on principle – Hallam Tennyson and Frith Banbury for example – the majority of gay men and lesbians were just as enthusiastic as most of their compatriots. The difference, of course, was that gay men and lesbians were fighting for a country which didn't recognize their right to be who they were without fear. In that sense they were ahead of their time and living examples of a dictum expressed by John F Kennedy several decades later: 'Ask not what your country can do for you – ask what you can do for your country.'

'I wanted to fight for my country during the war, almost everybody did,' explains John Beardmore. 'There was a great nationalist feeling and I wanted to go right from the word go. There's a great anti-war feeling now and

BERT BARTLEY IN
ALGIERS DURING
THE WAR

rightly so and there always should be, but when it actually happens people do rush to the colours – it happened again during the Falklands War – and I was just one of them, I suppose.'

When John rushed to the colours and joined up, it was with a feeling of patriotism which conjures up visions of pageantry and rousing renditions of 'Rule Britannia'. But, as John discovered, the reality of a patriotic rush to battle is messier and a much greater threat to mortality.

The most terrifying moment for John was in early 1942 in what became known as the PQ17 incident when a convoy of thirty-six ships sailed from Iceland and got scattered because the Admiralty thought that it was under attack from a German battleship. John's ship was stuck in Archangel because the Admiralty cancelled all sailings throughout the summer – with the northern tip of the European land mass basking in almost continuous daylight, any convoys would have been sitting targets for the air forces that were under the command of the German Army in Norway. Conditions for British sailors who had been on the Russian convoys were tough. Food was scarce and rations got smaller and smaller. In the end they were reduced to eating the biscuits from the ships' lifeboats.

If John Beardmore and his fellow matelots were having trouble finding something to eat, Chris Gotch was having problems at the other end. In late 1943, Chris had been sent out to India where he was a flight lieutenant in charge of a detachment at Chitagong, positioned to fend off an invasion by the Japanese which was feared although, in the end, never took place. 'Dysentery was fairly common, of course, with the food and heaven knows what else. I spent my twenty-first birthday having the shits at this dreary place called Chitagong which we all called Shitagong.' Chris saw his way out when there were invitations to join a Mosquito squadron.

When Chris arrived at the new squadron he found that most of the pilots were Australian, as was the commanding officer who told him quite bluntly that he wanted to make it an all-Australian squadron. He could stay if he wanted but he could forget about promotion. Chris, who was mad keen, stayed anyway and found himself promoted by default when his commanding officer got taken prisoner. 'He [the commanding officer] had sat behind a desk in Delhi for most of the war and he wanted to do ops for the first time. We were moved to the Assam battle front and, on the first op, he went mad trying to shoot up sampans on the Irrawady. He went too low, hit his wing tip in the water and crash landed and was taken prisoner. He was a prisoner in Rangoon jail for the rest of the war.' As a result, Chris was promoted to squadron leader and flight commander of one of the two flights which led to one of the most frightening experiences of his war career.

Chris was leading a flight of four Mosquitoes doing long-range pene-tration and their mission was to attack an airfield in central Burma. The plan was to approach from two different angles, drop the bombs, strafe as they went over and then come home. Alas, things didn't work out quite that way because the Japanese heard them coming and flung every mis-sile they had at the attackers. 'Every gun in sight was trained on us and we were only about 100 feet up. I dropped the bombs and suddenly there was an almighty crack and air came in. I realized somehow we'd been hit and I was pushed forward by something hitting me on the shoulder and almost within the next second we were over and climbing. I said into the intercom "Are you all right?" to my navigator and there was no answer. So I turned and his face had been shot off from below the bridge of the nose, just one sort of great ghastly red wound, you know, and his eyes were goggling at me. The stench of blood was ghastly. I was flying the air-craft and there was little I could do. I took off my scarf and handed it to him but he really couldn't do anything and I couldn't do anything for him. He gave me the impression he wanted to pray – he was orthodox Jewish – so I managed to bang his seat belt thing and he sort of collapsed on his knees and actually started to pray.'

It took Chris and his wounded navigator two and a half hours to get home during which time the navigator's condition grew worse and worse. Chris radioed ahead to get ambulances ready for when they landed and the last he saw of his colleague was him being wheeled off to be examined by the medics. 'He died about an hour later through loss of blood,' Chris recalls. 'Sad because he was a twin and his twin brother had been killed on bombers almost exactly eighteen months before and I had to write to his mother and so on.'

Being shot at while in the air was not a new experience for Chris. He'd taken some flak earlier in the war in a raid over Dieppe: 'I felt an almighty pain in both legs and I just knew I had been hit in both knees – so much so that some bits of shrapnel had come through my hand on the throttle.'

He jokes that he got through nine lives during the war and considers himself lucky to be alive. Most of his friends were killed, many, like Jimmy, in flying accidents. Chris expresses some surprise that he lasted as long as he did. He was on operations almost non-stop for something like four years.

NEWSPAPER
REPORT OF THE
DISAPPEARANCE
OF IAN GLEED
DURING A
FIGHTER SWEEP
IN THE MIDDLE
EAST IN 1943

Fighter Gleed is missing

Cairo reported last night that Wing Commander Ian C. Gleed, D.S.O., D.F.C., a Battle of Britain pilot and author of the best-seller, "Arise to Conquer," is missing after a fighter sweep.

Gleed, one of the shortest leaders in the R.A.F.—he is little more than five feet tall—was leading a Spitfire wing of the Desert Air Force.

He has probably more fighting experience than any other man in Fighter Command. He fought in France, and in the sweeps across the Channel, and he was a great night intruder pilot when that technique was first developed.

His book gives a picture of a nervous, sensitive man in the late twenties, painfully aware at moments of crisis of a sinking feeling in the stomach. He wrote after a dogfight :—

GLEED, D.S.O.

"I did not feel at all hungry, only slightly sick. My hand was shaking so much that the coffee cup rattled against the saucer."

FAMOUS FIGHTER ACE MISSING

CAIRO, Friday.

Wing-Commander Ian R. Gleed, D.S.O., D.F.C., one of the most outstanding fighter-pilots of the war, and author of the best seller "Arise To Conquer," is reported missing after a fighter sweep over enemy territory.

He was in command of a fighter wing of the Desert Air Force.

'I think I marked up something like 321 which, all right, isn't that great, but when you consider that a normal tour is thirty ops it gives you an idea of how busy I was.'

The great irony about this is that while gay people were carrying out feats of astonishing endurance and bravery, the conventional wisdom was that homosexuals were cowards, couldn't fight their way out of a chiffon scarf and would let you down if you were in a tight spot. 'It's absolute rubbish!' says Chris. 'They maintained that every homosexual had no guts and would let you down if you were in a fight and that it destroyed morale and all the rest of it, and here was Ian – DFC [Distinguished Flying Cross] etc – and he can't have been the only one.'

He certainly wasn't. Plenty of gay men and lesbians were decorated for their war efforts which included not only those who had battled against the physical odds, but also those who had grappled with the enemy intellectually, like the mathematician Alan Turing. He was a cryptographer at Bletchley, a stately mansion in the Home Counties, where the intelligence service intercepted Nazi communications, and was instrumental in cracking the Enigma codes without which Britain may have lost the war. He later went on to produce the first modern computer. He was given the OBE in June 1946 for his war service and was furious when the letters OBE were added to the nameplate outside his lab. Turing did not go to the palace to be awarded his medal, but received it in the post and kept it in his toolbox.

Evelyn Irons, who was given the *Croix de Guerre*, also missed the awards ceremony because, by the time it was held, she was no longer in France. One of the few foreign journalists to be awarded such a high honour by the French government, Evelyn is rather self-effacing when it comes to owning up to her clearly distinguished record. 'When I got the citation they wrote about helping with the wounded and various things to do with the Army outside my reportorial duties and they said that I hadn't been quite a coward.'

John Beardmore received a whole clutch of medals, including the Russia Star, the Africa Star, the Atlantic Star, the Arctic Star and the Malta Star as well as being mentioned in dispatches twice, but like all the others he is modest to a fault about his record. 'These things came up on a belt and it was like serving out cigarette cards or mottos, or at least I like to think so,' he explains. 'I don't regard myself as a hero, I was just lucky. I don't really approve of awards as such because everyone should be awarded, I mean, we were all heroes.'

'We'll Meet Again'

Sung by Vera Lynn

When the forces' sweetheart sang of blue birds and white cliffs, sorrowful partings and hopeful hearts, millions sang along with lumps in their throats, proving the eternal potency of cheap music at times of high emotion. Gay men and lesbians sang just as lustily and just as loud as their straight counterparts. Ironically, the war, which had thrown legions of lovers together, was also to cause them to part – in some cases for ever. The difference, of course, was that gay people had to pretend to be gay – in the generally understood sense of the word at the time – while a man who had been separated from his girlfriend or a lass who'd waved goodbye to her man could indulge in sentimental shows of sadness to general sympathy.

For a start, it was impossible even to say goodbye properly. While railway stations were heaving with heterosexual couples engaging in lip-to-lip combat as they parted, gay men and lesbians had to restrain themselves. However some people did find a way at least to hold hands with each other without anyone seeing, but it took a lot of subterfuge.

Gerald Dougherty, for instance, fell in love with another twenty-three-year-old who was on leave from the front and living with his parents.

Gerald saw the chap – also called Gerald – every single day of his leave and would see him off at Liverpool Street station so he could catch a train back to his parents. There was nowhere for them to go where they could be intimate, but the pair found a way of at least entwining fingers. 'We used to go to theatres and concerts together and I suddenly realized there was one place we could go without anybody knowing very much about it.' This was the HMV shop in Oxford Street, which had little cubicles where people could listen to records. Although the cubicles had glass fronts down to the door handles, it was possible to lean against the door and get a modicum of privacy: 'So we sat there holding hands and talking for an hour. Of course, we couldn't do it more than once because they would get to recognize us.'

When lovers met – even though they had to be circumspect – they could at least speak the words they wanted. Once they were apart, gay men and lesbians found it difficult to express what they wanted to in their letters in case the ever-vigilant officers got a whiff of something which could land both correspondents in serious trouble.

At the beginning of the war, John Beardmore had met Steve, a private in the Royal Artillery, but Steve was sent overseas almost immediately and ended up in North Africa attached to the American forces, while John went

VERA LYNN, WHOSE MELANCHOLY WARTIME SONGS SPOKE TO GAY AND STRAIGHT ALIKE

to sea. So, for the best part of six years, their relationship was conducted via the Royal Mail which, John reckons, carried between six and eight hundred letters between the two of them.

'One had to be very discreet in writing letters because of the legal situation. It was very difficult to express one's innermost feelings and I think we rather took those for granted. You couldn't say "love and kisses", but you could say "yours affectionately" or things like that.' John wrote about the Russian convoy and the lot of the peasants which made the sailors' privations seem minor but the letters back from Steve were much more candid – censor or no censor: 'Stevenson Sergeant 23512049 c/o The US Army. Glad you have started numbering your letters, they come in batches. The Yanks are very good to me, in fact can't do enough, if you see what I mean. And I'm the only Limey sergeant attached to the US brigadier who is quite a dear and very camp to boot. He calls me Steve, even in front of Monty who clearly hates my guts and regards me as a jumped-up Durham miner's son. Which, let's face it, my dear, is what I really am. Food, fags and sex in great supply from the Yanks, they love it. Everything is fabulous, faggot or gay, it's a new language, my dear. Queer means you've got a headache. Keep writing. I look forward to your letters and hearing all about the Russians. They don't sound a very sexy lot, do they? Love, Steve.'

During all these years, John and Steve were only able to speak to each other once when John was sent down to the Mediterranean for the invasion of Algiers. When things had settled down a bit, John discovered that there was a telephone on the jetty, in an office manned by the Army, which was in communication with the front. John bribed the Army sergeant with a few bottles of Worthington which the sailors had on ship but which the soldiers couldn't acquire abroad. He spun a line about wanting to speak to his cousin at the American headquarters and was put through. By pure fluke, Steve happened to be on duty and picked up the phone. 'We exchanged a conversation and then finally he said, "I think really we'd better hang up because this is the only [telephone] line between us and the front line – we're actually holding up the war." So we quickly rang off and I had this great big British Army sergeant standing at my elbow getting more suspicious every moment, realizing I wasn't talking to my cousin at all!'

Steve and John were separated for the duration of the war but for others who parted during the war, the separation lasted much longer. One such pair were the two nurses, Monica and Marya, who met in 1943. 'She was very beautiful with high cheekbones – she looked like the young Ingrid Bergman,' says Monica of Marya. 'You know I think I loved her from the word go. We had only a year together and because we had so little time together we didn't talk a lot about our backgrounds – it was all here and now. We were very much in love. I remember we even went to a church and we made little vows and promises to each other in a sort of wedding.'

The separation came when a jealous older friend – not a lover – demanded that Monica choose between her and Marya. For some reason this caused Marya to turn on her heel and refuse to see Monica. Monica, who was due to leave, was frantic and realized that the only way to get to see Marya for one last time was to intercept her while she was on duty. 'I thought, as soon as I know night sister has done her round in that ward I'll go up the fire escape and have a word with her. So I did and Marya saw me and she just swept past while I was banging on the window saying, "Look, I must talk to you, I must talk to you." She didn't come back that way for an age so I stood there waiting and it was all dark because it was wartime, no light. And then it started to rain and I'm soaking wet and I'm out there for half an hour, then an hour and then I see her again and I bang and she still won't come. And I still waited, getting wetter and wetter and more bedraggled and desperate. Finally as the grey dawn came up I just gave up and went down and I left. I wasn't to see her again for a very long time.'

Although Monica and Marya's story is a poignant one, it has a happy ending. They were able to meet after several decades when Marya got a glimpse of Monica on television. Monica became a renowned breeder of dogs and did a commercial for Pedigree Chum in the Seventies which Marya saw. They made contact again (*see* page 203) and ended up living together until Marya's death.

For other wartime friends the parting, though just as abrupt, was much more final. Chris Gotch and Ian, the wing commander, stopped seeing each other when Ian was posted to Stanmore, where there was a military air field, and was then sent to the Middle East. About a year after they'd met, Chris heard that Ian had been reported missing in the desert. 'They later found the aircraft with the skeleton sitting in it,' Chris recalls.

Although the war had meant privation and loss, it had also given a sense of purpose, even excitement, and many people found the end of hostilities bewildering because they were expected to return to a world that they had almost forgotten existed. For many people it was important to maintain links with the life they had lived in the Second World War and, in at least one case, that proved to be fortuitous. Ray Bagley and Bert Bartley met soon after the war through mutual friends on their way to a service for ex-servicemen and have been together ever since. For others, relationships that had seemed secure during the war fell apart with peace.

John Beardmore and his friend Steve, who had exchanged hundreds of letters during the war, had always promised themselves that once the war was over they would be together, but the promised land didn't turn out to be

RAY BAGLEY IN
HIS RAF UNIFORM

quite the territory they expected. 'What sustained us throughout the war was that we thought it was going to be a great romance . . . and we would settle down after the war was over – if we got through it. On what basis I don't know because we really didn't know each other at all. In fact we didn't know each other till the end of the war – we lived together for three weeks and we realized we were incompatible. But we are still very good friends.'

The war had broken down all the old certainties and when it ended there was an anxiety to return to the old, familiar ways. The government was very concerned that women who had developed a taste for independence while the men were away should be encouraged to go back to tending hearth and home and public information campaigns were launched to achieve this. The post-nuclear age became the age of the nuclear family. The all-pervasive image in advertising and popular culture was that of Mummy, Daddy and their little darlings, and the post-war baby boom soon made this into a reality for most people. The reality for gay men and lesbians was much tougher because, when conformity became fashionable, any deviation from convention was dealt with more harshly than ever before.

BERT BARTLEY
AND RAY BAGLEY
AFTER THE WAR

PART THREE   1945-67

> 'We must **accept** the fact that total war relaxes moral standards on the home front . . .'
>
> Herbert Hoover on how things had to change
>
> after the Second World War

After the victory parade decorations had been taken down and the last of the champagne had been drunk, the hangover came. The biggest headache for the government was how to persuade people to go back to the old routine. After six years on a war footing, a state of emergency had become normal for most people. During the war, class barriers had come crashing down, women had taken over what was traditionally regarded as men's work and as a result gender distinctions had become blurred. War had also caused people to question the old certainties and the government felt it had to establish the old familiar order – or at least as near as dammit.

The task of preparing the population for what was to come began even before the war ended. In the final months of the war, in an article which argued that military victory would be hollow without a corresponding moral victory, Herbert Hoover told his fellow Americans: 'We must accept the fact that total war relaxes moral standards on the home front and this imperils the whole front of human decency.' The great and the good spoke as if with one voice on both sides of the Atlantic – forget about the war and go back to your old ways. In Britain, the Archbishop of Canterbury gave a sermon in which he called on Britons to reject 'wartime morality' and return to living Christian lives.

While it was easy to urge a return to Christian values from the pulpit, it was more difficult for people to comply. The alarm bells started ringing pretty soon when the divorce rate shot through the roof – so much so that the administrative offices couldn't deal with the demand created. Something had to be done. A committee of inquiry was set up – the Denning Committee on Procedure in Matrimonial Cases – which recommended that divorce should be made easier to obtain to help clear the waiting backlog, but it also added that the government should take on the burden of intervening where necessary in order to support marriage. The government didn't need telling. It decided to pour money into organizations like the Marriage Guidance Council which would do the job for it. Behind the scenes help was given, with the Home Office advising on new counselling techniques which drew on Army experience.

CELIA JOHNSON AND TREVOR HOWARD IN *BRIEF ENCOUNTER*, A FILM THAT WAS EMBLEMATIC OF THE BUTTONED-UP SEXUALITY OF POST-WAR BRITAIN

In a series of five broadcast talks given after the war by David Mace, secretary of the Marriage Guidance Council, he said: 'There's a job of work to be done; a vitally important job of work – the rebuilding of family life.' He went on to elucidate how this task could be accomplished – the formula was to contain all sexual urges within the confines of the marriage: 'Beneath the surge of elemental emotion which sex lets loose, nothing will suffice to hold us steady save the stabilizing emotional power of a spiritual ideal which commands our whole-hearted allegiance.' People were willing to take his word for it. In 1946 the number of marriages leapt by fifty per cent and remained twenty per cent above pre-war levels for the rest of the decade.

The other aspect of life that needed to be tackled was women's new-found independence – not least in terms of clothes. In 1943, thirty-one per cent of all British engineers were women and an unknown – but equally large – number worked as welders, riveters, crane drivers and farm workers. They had to be persuaded to go back to tending their homes and slipping into 'more appropriate' attire. Having got used to striding around in overalls and comfortable work gear, they were reluctant to squeeze into the corsets and stays that had been a staple of fashion in pre-war days. Rationing or no rationing, women had to be given a more feminine sartorial fantasy. Christian Dior came to the rescue on that front with the New Look which he said would transform European women from the Valkyries they had become back to the shrinking violets they had been. He said he hated women who 'looked like Amazons . . . I designed clothes for flower-like women, clothes with rounded shoulders, full feminine busts and willowy waists over enormous spreading skirts.'

When the family is in fashion and fashion is all about frills, flounces and femininity, homosexuality is completely beyond the pale. The metropolitan campery of people like Noël Coward, which had reigned supreme before the war was out of fashion, and instead plays, books and films portrayed the robust wholesomeness of suburban life and suburban values. Coward himself saw the signs and turned his work round full circle. Gone was the sexual ambiguity of *Design for Living* with its love triangle between two men and a woman, in its place came *Brief Encounter* for which Coward wrote the screenplay. One of the biggest cinematic hits of 1945, *Brief Encounter* had Celia Johnson as a middle-class suburban housewife who falls in love with another man. Overcome by guilt over a few furtive meetings and bit of heavy petting, she decides the best course of action is to return to her dull but safe husband. Roll credits to enthusiastic applause and soggy handkerchiefs all round. Marriage and fidelity were in, fun and sex were out.

> '1 got **married** – that was the fashion in those days. 1 got brainwashed the same as everybody else.'
>
> **Sharley McLean** on the pressure to conform in the post-war period

With this unrelenting bombardment of propaganda, some gay men and lesbians began to wonder whether it was their sexuality that was different or whether their sexual behaviour had been influenced by the fact that they had lived through an aberrational time. Certainly, the official line was that during the war it was desperate measures to match a desperate time – and it must have been tempting to believe them. John Beardmore was one of the people who thought the previous six years might just have been a phase he was going through: 'I thought because I'd been in the Navy in an entirely male society perhaps this was why I was gay or that I was not really gay at all. I'd known this Canadian nurse throughout the war and we had a very close relationship and at the end of the war we were drawn together and were briefly married. And then we realized that there was no sexual future for us – well certainly as far as I was concerned and we decided to call it a day. She met a very nice Canadian and got married and I took up my old life . . . I still see her and we have a loving friendship.'

Hallam Tennyson – who had visited female prostitutes in the Thirties in an attempt to sample the straight life – also married, but for different reasons. He had met his wife, Margot, during the course of the war and

HALLAM
TENNYSON IN
ITALY, 1945

he felt enormous admiration for her – she had escaped from the Holocaust which had consumed much of her family. She arrived in England at the age of seventeen with barely any English and had built up a life from scratch. 'I found her courage and vitality tremendously stimulating and attractive and I already knew that I enjoyed having sexual relations with women. I wanted to get married for an enormous number of reasons – partly because my brothers had been killed and I wanted to have a family because they hadn't been able to have families and

HALLAM
AND MARGOT
TENNYSON IN
1945, SHORTLY
AFTER THEIR
MARRIAGE, WITH
THEIR 'BEST MAN'

because Margot . . . made it obvious she'd fallen in love with me and I found that very attractive.'

Others simply yeilded to the prevailing attitude. When every novel you read ends with married bliss, when every film you see has the heroine walking hand-in-hand with the hero into a bright future, when every singer croons about heterosexual love, it is difficult not to be swayed. As the Fifties wore on, the ideal woman was always depicted as a coiffed paragon whose chief concerns were how to get her washing white and how to whip up a three-course dinner at a minute's notice when the husband brought his boss home. This image continued until the early Sixties and many women succumbed to it because there seemed to be no other alternative.

'I got married because in those days it was the done thing – you left school, you went to work, you got married and you had children. That was the way it was,' explains Jose Pickering. However, following the prescribed path didn't lead to happiness as all the novels and films predicted. Jose says that as a married woman she felt like a gerbil in a cage . . . 'running round and round getting nowhere fast.' She thought that the problem might be lack of children and so she planned a pregnancy, but that didn't make any difference either.

Jose was far from being alone in swallowing the propaganda. 'I got married – that was the fashion in those days. I got brainwashed the same as everybody else,' explains Sharley McLean. Like Margot, Sharley was a refugee and getting married not only meant an outward normality in sexual terms but also belonging in a real and tangible sense in that she became a British citizen. It also helped that her husband-to-be seemed unlike the conventional British man of the period, kitted out in the regulation-issue tweed jacket: 'Alan was an attractive young man and he was different from the average sort of person . . . he used to wear plum-coloured corduroys and he was a ballet dancer and a film extra and also we agreed politically. Many of my friends had got married . . . so we got married to be part of the flock.'

Only birds of a feather can be part of the same flock, however. Sharley,

SHARLEY MCLEAN

JOSE PICKERING

like many others, realized that putting on false plumage has its costs. She found that sex with her husband was 'nauseating' and came to the conclusion that a dead mother would be a better option for her children than a miserable one. Being a nurse, Sharley knew about drugs and decided that the best method would be to inject herself with a huge dose of insulin, which was available without prescription in those days. She planned it meticulously. She didn't want the family to discover her and she couldn't afford to hire a hotel room so she spied out a thick clump of rhododendron bushes in Hyde Park and decided she would sneak in just before the park closed for the night. Once she had the place to herself, she could do the deed.

Sharley chose Hyde Park because it had a particular importance for her. As a refugee from Fascist Germany she had been taken to Speakers' Corner when she first came to England and had found the idea that, in that spot, everybody had the right to say anything, immensely appealing. It became a regular haunt for her and she went throughout the Fifties, and continues to go today, with a group of gay men and lesbians to argue with the homophobes. She describes Hyde Park as her 'church' and after her suicide attempt it took on an added significance because it marked the place where her conversion to a new life began. Although that was the last thing she expected on that day forty odd years ago.

'I made sure that I had things for the children – I bought them toys and new clothing so that they would find it on the day that I wouldn't be there . . . I didn't leave a letter – I wouldn't have known what to say.' Sharley recalls. 'I took the syringe and all the capsules of insulin and I went into the toilets of Lyons Corner House and loaded the syringe and then made my way to Hyde Park . . . I hid in the rhododendron bushes and injected myself and went into a coma . . . I hadn't realized that those particular bushes were fairly close to the Hyde Park police – they had dogs in those days – and I was found.'

Sharley was immensely lucky. 'I would not have tried to commit suicide after that – I did realize the very negative effect it has on the people left behind. It was very important for me to recognize that and move on.' Sharley was also fortunate in that the police decided not to prosecute (attempted suicides were often charged in those days) but suggested that she get psychiatric treatment, which is how she ended up at the Tavistock Clinic – one of the more enlightened institutions of its kind at the time. The staff were more progressive than most of the medical establishment who, despite – or perhaps because of – the Kinsey Report, still believed that homosexuality was a 'disease' and their job as doctors was to cure it.

SHARLEY MCLEAN
IN HYDE PARK
IN 1983

'Persons with **homosexual** histories are to be found in every age group, in every social level, in every conceivable occupation – in cities, on farms, and in the most remote areas of the country.' **Alfred Kinsey**

The publication of Alfred Kinsey's two studies – *Sexual Behaviour in the Human Male* in 1948 followed by *Sexual Behaviour in the Human Female* in 1953 upturned all conventional notions of how the sexual universe was configured. His data showed that thirty-seven per cent of American men had had at least one homosexual experience to the point of orgasm since adolescence and that four per cent of males were exclusively homosexual all their lives. Of females, twenty-eight per cent reported erotic feelings towards other females and up to six per cent of unmarried women were exclusively lesbian. Kinsey's research was difficult to refute – he had interviewed 10,000 men and women and his approach to his subject was measured and dispassionate in keeping with his training as a zoologist. However, if Kinsey's data could not be disputed many felt that it was so unpalatable that he should have kept it to himself. One doctor, writing in a professional journal, said it would have been better if Kinsey had 'stuck to his rats'. In Doncaster, the local magistrates were so incensed by the publication of Kinsey's work that they decided to ban it on grounds of obscenity. The Doncaster bench was persuaded by higher author-ities not to go ahead with its decision when it became clear that it would be almost impossible to justify. The legal definition of obscenity is material that has a tendency 'to deprave and corrupt' and anybody who has attempted to wade through the hefty volumes of Kinsey's work, full of statistical tables, will know that the reader is more likely to be baffled and bewildered – bored even – by the scientific language, rather than depraved or corrupted.

The problem with Kinsey's research was not so much its content as its implications. As Kinsey put it: 'Persons with homosexual histories are to be found in every age group, in every social level in every conceivable occupa-tion, in cities, on farms and in the most remote areas of the country.' It was this aspect of the Kinsey report that was considered the most alarming. Until then the generally accepted notion was that gay men and lesbians were a tiny minority and could be spotted a mile off. The idea that gay men and lesbians were everywhere was extremely disturbing. Even more disturbing was Kinsey's development of the spectrum theory of sexuality which ranged people in seven categories from zero to six according to where they stood on the continuum from exclusive heterosexuality to exclusive homosexuality. In reality, he added, individuals not only occupied each of the seven categories but every gradation in between. This raised the even more shocking idea that homosexuals weren't a distinct group – everyone was a bit homosexual. They were everywhere.

The news matched the atmosphere of the era which was already paranoid and edgy as a result of the Red scare – the Soviet Union which had been an ally only a few years previously was now an enemy and so Reds were seen under every bed. Now homosexuals joined them down there. The link which had been present subliminally from the late Forties onwards became tangible in 1951 with the defection of two gay spies – Guy Burgess and Donald Maclean to the Soviet Union. Much was made of the fact that communism and homosexuality were bedfellows, although allegations that Burgess and Maclean were also bedfellows were met by intense indignation by Burgess. When the gay Labour MP Tom Driberg visited him in Moscow in connection with a book he was writing, Burgess felt compelled to set the record straight and exclaimed: 'The idea of going to bed with Donald! It would be like going to bed with a great white woman!'

While Burgess was most rattled by the suggestion that he'd slept with Maclean, what really rattled the Establishment was that *any* of its men had slept with other men. Burgess had never been particularly discreet, but

GUY BURGESS (left) and DONALD MACLEAN (right) WHOSE DEFECTION TO RUSSIA CAUSED PANIC IN THE ESTABLISHMENT

nobody had taken any action because the very idea that a Foreign Office man could be homosexual had seemed absurd. After Kinsey and the twin defection, everyone was suspect.

The British were also under pressure from America where the House Committee on Un-American Activities, under Senator Joe McCarthy, was weeding out suspected communists and communist sympathizers and there was a parallel witch-hunt against homosexuals. In 1950, John Peurifoy, Under-Secretary of State, was hauled before a Senate committee investigating the loyalty of federal government workers and asked how many people had resigned as security risks since 1947. Peurifoy responded that it amounted to ninety-one people 'in the shady category, most of them homosexuals'. In the run up to the congressional elections of 1950, John O'Donnell, a political pundit on the *New York Daily News*, wrote in his column: 'The primary issue . . . is the charge that the foreign policy of the US . . . [is] dominated by an all-powerful, inner circle of highly educated, socially highly placed sexual misfits in the State Department, all easy to blackmail, all susceptible to blandishments by homosexuals in foreign nations.'

From that point on, the number of gay men and lesbians sacked from Washington governmental departments rose to over sixty per month and continued at that level until the end of 1951 but of course that didn't stop the paranoia. So, when Burgess and Maclean made their highly publicized move in 1951, the attention focused on Britain which, as America's chief ally against Russia, was privy to many state secrets. The American view was that they had put their house in order, so the British should do the same.

> 'Never tell **anybody** where you work. Never take anybody to your home, and never write letters to anybody you know to be gay.'
> **Allan Horsfall**'s survival guide for gay men in the Fifties

In Britain, the number of arrests for homosexual offences suddenly shot up. In 1938 – the last full year before the Second World War – the number of men prosecuted for homosexual offences was 956. In 1952, after pressure from the Americans, this had gone up to 3,757 – an increase of over threefold. The reason wasn't that the number of gay men had increased by over 300 per cent since before the war or that they were having three times as much sex as before. It was that the authorities were three times more zeal-

ALLAN HORSFALL
IN HIS RAF
UNIFORM

ous in their perse-
cution of gay men.

'When prosecu-
tions increased dra-
matically after the
war, it was driven
home rather sharpish
that you were vul-
nerable,' explains
Allan Horsfall, who
later became an
ardent campaigner
for law reform. 'The
knowledge that you
were committing,
maybe two or three
times a week, crimi-
nal offences each of
which rendered you
liable to life impris-
onment concentrat-
ed the mind won-
derfully . . . I think
people used to cope
rather in the way

that they coped in the blitz – by convincing themselves that the bomb would-
n't fall on them unless their name was on it . . . But there was the addition-
al danger of the unexploded bomb in the cellar in the shape of one's name
in other people's address books, letters one had written sitting in somebody's
cupboard, any of which could be uncovered at any time by the police. So,
there were the bombs from above and the bombs ticking below – very anx-
iety-creating both of them.'

Then things got much worse. On 25 October 1952 Sir John Nott-Bower
was appointed the new Commissioner of Police at Scotland Yard. The
Home Secretary, Sir David Maxwell Fyfe – who had interrogated Goering
during the Nuremberg trials – told the House of Commons: 'Homosexuals
. . . are exhibitionists and proselytizers and a danger to others . . . so long as
I hold the office of Home Secretary, I shall give no countenance to the view
that they should not be prevented from being such a danger.' Nott-Bower
was left in no doubt as to what his duties were and he made it clear that he
was going to fulfil them with a ferocious zeal.

Curiously this went unreported in the British press, but was covered in Commonwealth newspapers. In October 1953, Donald Horne, the London correspondent of the *Sydney Morning Telegraph*, filed a report which made it clear that things were going to be different from the way they were 'under laxer police methods before the US-inspired plan began and before Sir John moved into the top job at Scotland Yard as a man with a mission. Sir John swung into action on a nationwide scale. He enlisted the support of local police throughout England to step up the number of arrests for homosexual offences. They [the police] knew the names of thousands of perverts – many of high social position and some world famous – but they took no action. For many years past the police had turned a blind eye to male vice. They made arrests only when definite complaints were made from innocent people or where homosexuality had encouraged other crimes . . . Now meeting Sir John's demands they are making it a priority job to increase the number of arrests.'

With the Home Secretary in the House of Commons waving a green flag for a witch-hunt, others felt able to go much further. In April 1954, a medical journal, *The Practitioner*, devoted itself to an analysis of homosexuality. Its leader article endorsed the idea proposed by one contributor who came up with the suggestion that homosexuals should be sent to remote Scottish islands like St Kilda where 'the natural and bracing climate [would] . . . strengthen their resolve'. That's assuming that the Outer Hebrides – *pace* Kinsey – were free of homosexuals.

Given a climate where gay men and lesbians were seen as universal Aunt Sallys that anyone could take a pot shot at, a climate of fear developed. Allan Horsfall describes what it was like: 'If you could have written a survival guide for gay men at that time it would have said: never, never give anybody your surname or address. Never tell anybody where you work. Never take anybody to your home and never write letters, whether affectionate or otherwise, to anybody you're sexually involved with or even to anybody you know to be gay. And I think that would have been sound advice.'

People took it. David George, who arrived in London from Newcastle in the Fifties, remembers being interrogated by worried friends who were concerned that he shouldn't inadvertently give hostages to fortune: 'A further instruction was "Do you keep a diary?" and I said, "Yes, I've always kept a diary – since I was fourteen." And they said, "Well, now you're living in London be careful what you put in your diary because if ever there was any difficulty the police would use that . . ." and that was a lesson I kept going right until the day when the law was adjusted. I still keep a diary and I'm still very discreet because you never know, do you?'

David was lucky in that he wasn't apprehended, but plenty of people were and the police methods used would not have been tolerated had the victims been anything other than gay. If one man came under suspicion for any reason, the police would raid his home, go through his possessions, particularly his papers, and contact his circle of friends.

Jim Alexander was one of the men who found his life turned topsy-turvy as a result of these tactics. A friend of his had been stopped by the police who found a letter in his pocket with Jim's address on it which provided the link. Under questioning, Jim's friend eventually admitted that they had been having a relationship. The police decided to call on Jim's home – where he lived with his mother and sister – in the dead of night. The family was woken up by a hammering on the door and Jim was carted off to the police station on the spot with just enough time to pull on a pair of trousers over his pyjamas.

If, like Allan and David, the man had been careful about letters and diaries, he would be asked to name names and offered inducements such as lack of publicity or immunity from prosecution, none of which the police could deliver. Eventually his whole circle of friends – up to twenty people in some cases – would be rounded up and interrogated in separate rooms. Invariably, the men were told that the others had confessed and, reduced to a state of terror, many gay men were convicted out of their own mouths.

It is easy to see how gay men ended up incriminating themselves under interrogation. Indeed the process of humiliation often started long before the questioning began. In Jim's case, he was strip-searched. 'I was taken to the police station where I was told to drop my trousers and bend down . . . by a group of policemen who made very derogatory remarks about what they could do with their truncheons and [they] were giggling and laughing at the fact that I had pyjamas on underneath my trousers and wanted to know if I always wore them. It was pretty frightening.'

It was going to get a lot more frightening then that. Jim was grilled by two policemen who followed the classic good-cop/bad-cop routine of interrogation. 'One was threatening to beat it out of me and another one was saying, "Go on, tell him what he wants to know and I'll make sure you're okay",' Jim explains. The experience was made worse by a cat-and-mouse strategy. The interrogators would call a halt and lock Jim up and, while the cell was sordid enough, Jim would feel relieved because it was better than being questioned, only to find the whole process starting up again in an hour.

'Every now and then they'd send me back to the police cell which was a horrific thing. It had a wooden board for you to sleep on with the toilet at the end of the wooden board . . . and they kept shutting me in and locking the door on me. And every hour or so they'd come and wake me up again and take me back to reinterrogate me. This went on from shortly after I arrived at the police station right the way through till about 6am in the morning. In the meantime [neither] my mother nor any of my family were told that I was being kept at the police station, they were just sitting there waiting for me to return home.'

The ordeal left Jim in a state of fear. 'I was so terrified that I was totally numb at first. It didn't really sink in. It felt like a strange nightmare that I was going to wake up from,' he recalls. 'I kept saying to myself, no you're asleep, you're going to wake up soon. But I never ever woke up. I was already awake.' This waking nightmare was not endured by Jim alone. In the Fifties, it was experienced by numerous gay men and was a salient feature of many criminal cases.

When they came to court none of this was brought up; judges and magistrates simply accepted the police case and acted as a rubber-stamping device. Usually, the defendants pleaded guilty partly because they wanted the ordeal over with as quickly as possible and partly because there was no point in contesting the police evidence. With the weight of the law against you, it wasn't worth pleading not guilty unless you could afford a very good barrister and were in a position to call influential character witnesses to testify on your behalf. Even then chances of success were slim.

Like most gay men, at the time, who were prosecuted in similar circumstances, Jim Alexander pleaded guilty and ended up facing two trials, first at the local courts, which then referred his case to the Central Criminal Courts at the Old Bailey. Jim pleaded guilty at both and at his initial hearing his case was not deemed worthy of a defence counsel. 'I pleaded guilty and was told, "Well then, you don't really need a defence." When I went into the crown court, I wasn't even offered a solicitor there or a barrister . . . I was told, "Well, you know, there's not much you can say that will save you."'

The Central Criminal Courts at the Old Bailey was an intimidating place. 'You can't see the people behind you, but you can feel them looking at you,' Jim recalls. 'And you've got all these judges and barristers sitting in front of you and you're made to stand to attention in the box which is surrounded by glass ... the other guy was actually sentenced to three years in Reading Jail and I was sentenced to six months or pay a fine of fifty pounds . . . I couldn't pay fifty quid, I wasn't earning that much money, and I had to go back to prison. Then, after a short while, my mother managed to raise the money and came [to] buy me out. I did actually serve about three-and-a-half months in prison whilst my mother was getting the money together.' To cap it all, Jim discovered when he came out of prison that he'd been fired from his job.

The cuttings files on the subject are thick with yellowing newspaper clippings as case after case is arraigned. The weight of the files gives an indication of how many men were brought before the courts in the Fifties and early Sixties, charged with a crime that had no victim. Each little matter-of-fact report – often no more than a few lines at the bottom of a column – was another man quashed by prejudice. Occasionally, the reporter saw fit to quote the judge's remarks which invariably added insult to injury. While the cuttings files are a good index of the numbers involved, they give no indication of the misery caused by each of these cases and the lives blighted as a result. The most poignant cases involve those where the accused didn't appear in court because he had committed suicide. In many cases the men involved hadn't committed a crime even by criteria set down by the benighted laws of the time.

> 'And I was **terrified** to go out . . . even just to the shop. I was terrified that I was going to be picked up again by another police car, that they were after me . . . '
>
> **Michael James** on the psychological impact of being falsely arrested

The effect of being framed by the police could be devastating, as Michael James was to discover some years later. He had fronted bail for the lover of a friend and, when he hadn't heard from him, Michael got anxious and went looking for him on the night before the man was due in court. He went to the Curzon Street area where the man used to hang out when he spotted someone who could be him. 'I wasn't quite sure and this guy kept looking at me, so I went over and said, "Where have you been?" He said, "I'm a police officer and I'm arresting you for importuning." . . . I pleaded not guilty obviously – I mean what nonsense – and they concocted this amazing story of how they had been following me and had seen me stop three men – none of whom were produced as witnesses.' Michael was convicted and fined but what was far worse than the sentence was the psychological effect.

'I felt dirty, I felt that they had sort of disfigured me – I really did feel as if they had torn half my face away and . . . [I had] all these gangling nerve ends,' Michael explains. 'And I was terrified to go out . . . even just to the shop. I was terrified that I was going to be picked up again by another police car, that they were after me, and of course my sex drive disappeared completely.'

> '**I** have not the **slightest** intention of sending you any of the medals mentioned which . . . were awarded to me for service in specific theatres of war and remain my property.'
>
> Author **Rupert Croft-Cooke** to the War Office when it demanded the return of his war decorations after his conviction for improper behaviour

SIR EDWARD
MARSH (left) IN
FANCY DRESS

While arrests doubled and then tripled, what the authorities were really after were the big names. They were convinced that there was a homosexual elite whose mere existence was in some mysterious way a conspiracy against the country. Both the *New York Daily News* and the *Sydney Morning Telegraph*, in their reports about British and American plans to crack down on gay men, had referred to groups who were highly educated and socially elevated – 'world famous' even. So far the trawl had netted minnows and small fry when what the Home Secretary was after were the big fish – names that people might recognize. There was an element of hypocrisy in this since at least one member of the government who sat at the Cabinet table with Sir David Maxwell Fyfe was known to be gay and some of the Prime Minister's kitchen cabinet – like Sir Edward Marsh, who had once been Winston Churchill's private secretary – were also gay. Of course, arresting them would have been embarrassing and politically counter-productive. What was needed were men who were influential but not so close to the centre of power that they cast aspersions on the Establishment.

After Maxwell Fyfe's ringing declaration in the House of Commons, people who fitted this mould began to be arrested from 1953 onwards. In January of that year, Labour MP

(From left to right) JOHN GIELGUD, EMLYN WILLIAMS AND NOËL COWARD, AT THE CHRISTENING OF WILLIAMS'S SON

William Field was found guilty of importuning after being trapped by police *agents provocateurs*, thus bringing his career to an end. The actor Sir John Gielgud was also convicted of a trivial charge, causing the press to call for his newly awarded knighthood to be withdrawn. Interestingly, on his first appearance on stage after the conviction, Gielgud was given an ovation.

Peter Robins remembers a story that was doing the rounds of gay men's circles at the time of Gielgud's conviction. 'He was playing with Dame Sybil Thorndike in *A Day by the Sea*. After he'd paid his fine and went for that evening's show, Dame Sybil was sitting in the Adelphi Theatre and she said, "Here comes John. Remember, it could happen to you, it could happen to me." The thought of Dame Sybil being arrested in a lavatory for any reason at all was impossible!'

The next case to make the headlines in a big way was that of Rupert Croft-Cooke in the winter of 1953–4. Croft-Cooke was a well-known novelist, playwright and travel-writer as well as being the book critic of *The Sketch*. After distinguished service in the Second World War, Croft-Cooke had settled in the Sussex village of Ticehurst. The locals were less than happy about the new man in their midst and hostilities intensified after Croft-Cooke described in an article their 'determined gentility' as 'pretentious and unattractive'. Then one day, his secretary invited two sailors based at the Chatham Barracks home to spend the weekend at Croft-Cooke's house. This appears not to have been an unusual occurrence – Croft-Cooke was an eccentric host who kept open house. At his trial a gypsy described how he and his family had stayed with Croft-Cooke on one occasion and the author had returned the compliment by coming to stay in their caravan.

On their way back to the barracks the two men were involved in a fracas in which they assaulted a policeman and were promptly arrested. When the police learnt where they had stayed the weekend, the men were told that, if they gave evidence against Croft-Cooke, it would help their case. The police were soon knocking on Croft-Cooke's door and he and his secretary were both arrested. Although the police officers did not have a warrant, they spent several hours turning the place upside down. The only things they took away with them were a couple of garden canes which had been used to stake house plants.

Croft-Cooke was convicted and sentenced to nine months' imprisonment on a case so weak it could have been blown away with one puff. During an interview with the legal aid officer at the Royal Naval Barracks both men had said that their statements to the police had been forced out of them and were false. The courts none the less convicted Croft-Cooke on the uncorroborated evidence of two men whose senior officers described them as 'completely wayward and thoroughly irresponsible in every way'. Croft-Cooke, on the other hand, was given glowing testimonials by his character witnesses who included Sir Compton Mackenzie and Lord Kinross.

At a loose end in prison, Croft-Cooke wrote a book, *The Verdict of You All*, which rattled the authorities even more. Although no hindrance was put in his way while inside, on emerging from prison he was visited by a plain-clothes policeman from Scotland Yard who advised him against publishing it. Croft-Cooke describes him as saying: "'You know a second conviction is very much more easily obtained than a first, especially when the first has been well-publicized. It needs only the word of one person, a policeman perhaps. If you weren't believed before, you're scarcely likely to be believed again, are you?'"

To Croft-Cooke's credit he ignored the threat but took the precaution of leaving the country. The book is an exemplary work and gives an indication of what prison was like at that time, with gay men being convicted left, right and centre.

'As the witch-hunt of homosexuals ordered, or at least countenanced by the Home Secretary raised its disgusting hue and cry, the prison began to house a new kind of victim, men of the highest probity and idealism who'd been dragged from useful lives . . . found themselves stunned and baffled in prison,' wrote Croft-Cooke. One such man, encountered by Croft-Cooke, had reported a theft to the police by another man who got his revenge by telling them about the victim's sexuality. As a result the victim of the theft

SIR COMPTON MACKENZIE (right), ACCOMPANIED BY H MONTGOMERY HYDE, UNVEILS A PLAQUE TO OSCAR WILDE IN TITE STREET, CHELSEA IN 1954

(and betrayal) was given seven years – more than Oscar Wilde was sentenced to in 1895!

A few weeks before his release from prison, Croft-Cooke received a letter from the Army Medal Office demanding the return of his war decorations which included the 1939–45 Star, the Burma Star, the Defence Medal and the War Medal. By this time Croft-Cooke had had enough. He wrote a stinging reply which included the following passage: 'The conviction as it happens . . . was totally unjust but that is irrelevant . . . am I to assume that because of a civil conviction ten years after the event, I was not in the Army or in fact in the war at all . . . I have not the slightest intention of sending you any of the medals mentioned which, shoddy and ill-designed though they are, were awarded to me for service in specific theatres of war and remain my property.'

Croft-Cooke, who was looking forward to a further exchange, was disappointed when the officer in charge capitulated. There were other, bigger fish to fry. As Croft-Cooke describes in his book, the prisons were full of gay men and the authorities realized it wasn't having any effect. 'This was happening at a time when the country was moving away from the war and out of rationing . . . and being cheered up by the Festival of Britain . . . and things were beginning to go all wrong for gay men,' recalls Allan Horsfall. 'I think even Nott-Bower realized that he couldn't attempt to put all gay men in prison, otherwise there wouldn't be room for real criminals. So it was decided that there should be a number of high profile cases and exemplary sentences.'

The month after Croft-Cooke was convicted, another case hit the headlines and, if Croft-Cooke had seemed like a large catch, the next one made him look like a sprat next to a whale. The men facing charges were a peer of the realm, the diplomatic correspondent of a national newspaper and a wealthy landowner. The fact that the offences they were charged with had all taken place in private and with consenting adults was irrelevant. What mattered was that the names were as big as you could get.

> '"Poor boys," gasped an elderly woman in the crowded gallery.'
>
> From the **Daily Sketch**'s report on the final day of the Montagu trial

It was dubbed the Montagu Case and has since become a symbol for the hypocrisy and double standards that characterized litigation against men accused of having sex with other men in that period. The chief defendant in the eyes of the press and public was the twenty-seven-year-old Edward John Barrington Douglas-Scott Montagu, the third Baron Montagu of Beaulieu with a palace in the New Forest which had been opened to the public only three years before. Lord Montagu was educated at Eton and Oxford, had served as a Grenadier Guard and was engaged to be married to a society beauty called Ann Gage. When the news reached the papers that Lord Montagu had been charged, tremors ran through every gay man in Britain – it was the culmination of a long line of causes célèbres which sent out the message that no one was safe.

LORD MONTAGU
MUCKS IN AT
BEAULIEU

'There were a number of high profile cases . . . involving well-known people. There was Lord Montagu, there was the prosecution of John Gielgud, there was the prosecution and ruination of a Labour MP called Field . . . and there was a feeling then which spread amongst gay men all over the country of fear that was palpable,' says Allan Horsfall. 'One felt that the police were ubiquitous and omniscient with their spy-holes and their secret surveillance and their *agents provocateurs* and their trawls through people's private diaries and letters. I described it once as "emotional suffocation".'

David George who was famous for his parties – which were attended not only by Lord Montagu but also by people like Shelley Winters and Ivor Novello – was due to hold one of his dos on the day the case hit the headlines. Guests phoned up in panic – everyone thought this was the start of a huge purge. Those who could afford to left the country while those who had to stay put destroyed any evidence that might undo them – love letters preserved for decades were unceremoniously burnt, diaries and keepsakes were also destroyed. The foreign correspondent of the *Observer*, Michael Davidson, got rid of two suitcases full of letters, diaries and photographs.

The reason for this bonfire of memories was that, apart from the testimony – uncorroborated one might add – of two airmen, the only evidence in the Montagu case was a series of letters that the defendants had written.

The two other men accused with Montagu were Peter Wildeblood, the diplomatic correspondent of the *Daily Mail*, and Michael Pitt-Rivers, a wealthy landowner and a cousin of Montagu's. The trio were charged with conspiring to incite two RAF men – Edward McNally and John Reynolds – to 'commit unnatural offences'. The mainstay of the prosecution case was that Montagu and Pitt-Rivers had turned up at a beach hut on the Beaulieu estate that Wildeblood had borrowed. According to the prosecuting counsel, the three men along with the two airmen – who were Wildeblood's guests – indulged in improper behaviour which the prosecution painted as a scene that would make a Roman orgy look like a suburban whist drive. Wildeblood wrote, in his account of the trial, that 'throughout the evening the hut was encircled by girl guides, apparently engaged in bird-watching . . . which does not suggest anything lascivious took place.'

Regardless of that, the all-male jury deliberated for four and a half hours and came back with a unanimous verdict of guilty. Montagu was sentenced to a year's imprisonment while Wildeblood and Pitt-Rivers were given eighteen months each. The public seats had been packed during the course of the trial to the point where one of the counsel stood up in court to castigate what he described as a form of ghoulishness, but not all the spectators were hostile. On 24 March 1954, the *Daily Sketch* mentioned in its report that, as the sentences were delivered, an elderly woman in the public gallery gasped 'poor boys!'

The public curiosity about the case was fed by the popular press which was agog. When Peter Wildeblood's house was burgled during the course of the trial, the story pushed Senator McCarthy, the Mau Mau and a pair of Siamese twins off the front page. Interestingly Palace House, Lord Montagu's ancestral pile, had also been broken into a few days earlier. In both cases no valuables were taken. The *Daily Sketch* managed to doorstep Ann Gage, who had broken off her engagement with Montagu and gone to New York to get away from press attention. She told the reporter she had written to Montagu frequently since leaving Britain and would help him in any way she could.

Some members of the public were not quite so generous. Allan Horsfall recalls going into a pub during the course of the trial and being horrified at what he heard. 'I remember sitting in the music room of a pub in Plymouth, the pianist struck up and all the people in the room . . . [began] in chorus a song to the tune of "Happy Wanderer" which concerned the Montagu case whose words I've mercifully forgotten but which were all derogatory . . . and everyone in the room seemed to know the words.'

The press reports made much of the precedent that had been set – this was the first time that a peer of the realm had been convicted in a criminal court since the right of peers to be tried by their fellow peers, in the House of Lords, was abolished in 1948. The case had made legal history, but it was also a milestone in the history of Britain's attitude towards gay men. Not only did it mark the nadir of the persecution of gay men in this country, in retrospect it was hugely influential in persuading the liberal intelligentsia that something must be done. Peter Wildeblood, who was forced out of the closet by the police, wrote a book which was widely read and so the opposing point of view from the one that held sway in court was finally heard. In the opening pages of the book, Wildeblood writes: 'I am no more proud of my condition than I would be of having a glass eye or a hare-lip. On the other hand I am no more ashamed of it than I would be of being colour-blind or writing with my left hand.' While this might not seem like a revolutionary statement – indeed it seems a mite self-oppressive to modern ears – for the times it was the nearest one gets to any form of gay pride.

Apart from the civil liberties aspect of the case there were other disturbing elements, notably about the conduct of the police. Montagu had originally been charged with improper behaviour with some Boy Scouts who used to show visitors around Beaulieu. The charge came about when Montagu called the police to inform them that an expensive camera belonging to him had been stolen by one of the boys. Instead of investigating the theft, the police counter-charged him with interfering with the boys. Montagu was hardly likely to report the theft if any impropriety had taken place. The police could not proceed with the case because the court ruled that there were irregularities in the evidence.

Almost immediately after this case ran into trouble, Montagu was charged with the next offence. The police claimed that the case involving the airmen came about as part of a general inquiry into homosexuality in the RAF but apart from Reynolds and McNally none of the other twenty-four airmen thrown up by the inquiry was ever involved in further action; nor were any of the other men that McNally had had relationships with. Among McNally's papers, the police found love letters to a man named Gerry as well as a receipt from the Regent Palace Hotel – a hotel by Piccadilly Circus whose bar was a rendezvous for many gay men – where the pair had shared a room. No charges were brought against Gerry, which suggests that this had more to do with personalities than principles. There were also some problems with Lord Montagu's passport which had been tampered with in such a way that it could affect his alibi. The passport had been in the possession of the police before the trial.

Quite apart from the inherent anomalies of the evidence, there was the larger question: both airmen were over twenty-one and neither had been coerced into anything. Although both had willingly participated in the activities they alleged against the three defendants, they were allowed to get away scot-free while Montagu, Wildeblood and Pitt-Rivers had the full weight of the law thrown at them. Most importantly, this was only a problem because the law had made it so.

Many members of the public were keenly aware of this. Wildeblood noted that the cabby who ferried him to court had said, 'Personally, and speaking man to man, I think it's a lot of bleeding nonsense. If two chaps carry on like that and don't do no harm to no one, what business is it of anyone else's?' And he was not alone. After the verdicts had been passed, Montagu, Wildeblood and Pitt-Rivers were kept waiting in the cells because a crowd of 200 had gathered outside the court. When it was finally considered safe for the trio to be transported to prison, most of the crowd had dispersed but a die-hard few remained who surged forward towards the three men. To their astonishment the reason was to pat them on the back rather than punch them in the nose. 'When the doors [of the van] were shut, they went on talking through the windows and gave the thumbs-up sign and clapped their hands,' Wildeblood wrote.

The word got out among gay men, as Peter Robins recalls: 'The rumour was that when this poor member of the aristocracy was sentenced . . . the crowd outside booed the police not the man himself. There was also a limerick.

> *An aircraftsman named McNally,*
> *Was caught with a lord in a chalet,*
> *The judge said my dears,*
> *They're patently queers,*
> *Give them two years*
> *For being too pally.*

Now the essence of the irony is the hypocrisy of the bench.'

While the intelligentsia weren't quite so ribald in challenging the law, they too were concerned about the double standard. The Church of England's Moral Welfare Council had been considering the question of homosexuality for some time and, as a result of the publicity generated by the trial, it rushed out its conclusions in a document entitled *The Problem of Homosexuality: An Interim Report*. The Church's view was surprisingly liberal. It argued that, although sex between men was a sin, so were adultery and fornication and these were not illegal. Worse – far from acting as a deterrent, the law encouraged blackmail, suicide and corruption of the police. The report called for an immediate official inquiry and change in the law.

During the course of the trial, the Tory MP Sir Robert Boothby, who in private life had affairs with members of both sexes, had repeatedly called for

LORD MONTAGU
(centre), FLANKED
BY MICHAEL
PITT-RIVERS (left),
AND PETER
WILDEBLOOD
(right), DURING
THEIR 1954 TRIAL

LORD MONTAGU (centre), FLANKED BY MICHAEL PITT-RIVERS (left), AND PETER WILDEBLOOD (right), DURING THEIR 1954 TRIAL

a royal commission – a request which Maxwell Fyfe, the Home Secretary, had repeatedly refused. Once the trial was over, the call for law reform was picked up by the Church of England and the Hardwicke Society – the senior debating club for barristers – which carried a motion saying: 'The penal laws relating to homosexual offences are outmoded and should be changed.' Within weeks, the Home Secretary had agreed to an inquiry.

> '1 had only one **failure** and that was a big American who just grinned at me and said "Brother, 1 heard this story in the Ark," and knocked me out with one punch.' Harry Raymond on his failure to extract money from gay men by blackmail

The Departmental Committee on Homosexual Offences and Prostitution, chaired by John Wolfenden – then Vice Chancellor of Reading University – was a radical departure in that, for the first time since 1533, there was an attempt to appraise the law affecting homosexuality from the point of view of liberalizing it. In other respects it was business as usual. Two entirely

separate issues, homosexuality and prostitution (or Huntley and Palmer as Wolfenden called them to spare his secretary's blushes) were lumped together as they always had been. All major enactments dealing with male homosexuality have been drawn from acts designed to control female prostitution, including Henry Labouchère's Criminal Law Amendment Act of 1885, which made sex acts between men illegal, the 1898 Vagrancy Act and the further Criminal Law Amendment Act of 1912. Wolfenden was no exception. What was odd was that the committee's remit concerning prostitution had a volition which was diametrically opposed to the motivation behind its analysis of 'the homosexual problem'. At a time when the concern was to shore up marriage and the family, it was thought that prostitutes soliciting on the street would corrupt marital ideals. The unspoken view was that prostitutes represented the antithesis of female sexuality which, at the time, had to be ordered and contained, if it was supposed to exist at all.

The Wolfenden Committee was appointed on 4 August 1954 and consisted of fifteen members, including two High Court judges, two members of Parliament, two doctors, two lawyers, two clergymen and the chairwoman of the Scottish Association of Girls' Clubs. Over the course of three years, the committee held sixty-two meetings and received submissions from over 200 organizations and individuals.

The effect this had was to bring the subject out into the open. On 10 July 1955, the *Empire News* began a two-part series, written by a former chief of Scotland Yard's vice squad, based on a dossier that had been submitted to the Wolfenden Committee. Writing under the name Fabian, the ex-police officer dealt mainly with his capture of a blackmailer while he was working as a detective inspector at Great Marlborough Street Police Station. Harry Raymond worked in harness with an ex-Guardsman whom he had met in prison. The routine was always the same. The ex-Guardsman would make contact with a gay man and bring him back to Raymond's rooms. 'After the decoy and the mug arrived, I would wait a while then bang the front door and burst in on them,' Raymond was quoted as saying. The terrified gay man would first be spun a sob story and asked for financial support and if that didn't work the money would be demanded with menaces. The pair never made less than £100 a night and netted £15,000 within seven months. There were some victims who were more lucrative than others. Fabian records how Raymond and his accomplice managed to wring £26,000 from the head of a brewery and a further £18,000 from a country property owner. These were enormous sums in those days but gay men were forced to pay them because the alternative seemed much worse. However, Raymond did have his comeuppance once, as he told Fabian: 'I had only one failure and that was a big American who just grinned at me and said, "Brother, I heard this story in the ark," and knocked me out with one punch. When I came to, he had departed.'

Articles such as these, even though they weren't sympathetic, acknowledged that there was a problem with the law as it stood. Another less sensational approach to the subject was by the sociologist Michael Schofield who, under the name Gordon Westwood, conducted the first Kinsey-type study into British male homosexuality. Although his sample consisted of only 127 individuals it laid to rest some perennial myths such as that all homosexuals are effeminate. It also found that thirteen per cent of its respondents had been blackmailed. This was probably an underestimate. Wolfenden's own findings were that between 1950 and 1953 half of all blackmail cases reported to the police involved homosexual men, and this was at a time when gay men risked being prosecuted themselves if they went to the police for help over blackmail attempts. This meant that the blackmailer's threat – public exposure and possibly prison – was instantly realized. Trapped in this manner, it is not so surprising that when Westwood asked his entire sample what their reaction would be to blackmail, over five per cent said they would commit suicide.

On 4 September 1957, the Wolfenden Committee published its report in which it recommended that homosexual behaviour in private between consenting adults – which was defined as those over twenty-one – should be decriminalized. For the first time there was a public acceptance that it wasn't the law's business 'to settle questions of morality, to interfere in the private lives of the citizens; it is only when public decency is offended that the law is entitled to step in and institute criminal proceedings.' It was the first progressive piece of proposed legislation affecting homosexuality for five centuries when the first law relating to homosexuality was entered into the statute books.

'I very much remember the Wolfenden Report when it came out which seemed to be a marvellous breakthrough,' says Hallam Tennyson. 'I remember

REPORT ON HOMOSEXUALITY

RECOMMENDATIONS AIMED AT PROTECTION OF CITIZEN

The report of the Departmental Committee on Homosexual Offences and Prostitution, published yesterday, considers the function of the criminal law in this field to be to preserve public order and decency, to protect the citizen from what is offensive and injurious, and to provide sufficient safeguards against exploitation and corruption of others, particularly those who are specially vulnerable because they are young, weak in body or mind, inexperienced, or in a state of special physical, official, or economic dependence.

"Certain forms of sexual behaviour are regarded by many as sinful, morally wrong, or objectionable for reasons of conscience, or of religious or cultural tradition; and such actions may be reprobated on these grounds. But the criminal law does not cover all such actions at the present time; for instance, adultery and fornication are not offences for which a person can be punished by the criminal law. Not indeed is prostitution as such."

The committee's first recommendation in the matter of homosexual offences is that homosexual behaviour between consenting adults in private be no longer a criminal offence. There is one dissentient.

Consent and privacy should be judged by the same criteria as apply to heterosexual acts, and adulthood should be defined as above the age of 21, it is stated. They recommend a new scale of maximum penalties, continued protection for minors, a statute bar on prosecutions for offences (except indecent assault) more than 12 months old, and various changes in the law relating to extortion, importuning, and treatment.

CONCEPT OF DISEASE DISMISSED

FULL MENTAL HEALTH

The committee find evidence for the view that there are varying degrees of homosexual propensity. This indicates, in their view, that homosexuals cannot be regarded as quite separate from the rest of mankind, as well as having implications for possible treatment.

The committee distinguish between active and latent homosexuality. The evidence suggests that continence is relatively uncommon and may break down under the influence of such factors as alcohol, stress, or disease. Often latent homosexuality can be inferred from behaviour in spheres not obviously sexual. "Among those who work with notable success in occupations

be found not only those possessing a high degree of intelligence but also the dullest oafs."

It was found difficult to assess the extent of the problem. Any figures of offences known to the police were bound to reflect police efficiency, but many of the committee thought it improbable that the increase in known offences could be explained by greater police activity, though they thought it unlikely that there had been an increase in homosexual behaviour proportionate to the "dramatic rise" in the number of offences known to the police. But even if figures obtained in a Swedish inquiry (1 per cent. wholly homosexual and 4 per cent. indiscriminate) had any relevance to Britain, the incidence among more than 18 million males must be large enough to be a serious problem. These were the lowest figures to come to the committee's notice.

MISTAKEN FEAR OF LEGALIZATION
ARGUMENTS REFUTED

It dismisses three main arguments and one subsidiary argument against legalizing adult acts in private. The committee found no evidence for the view that such conduct is the cause of the demoralization and decay of civilizations, although like other forms of debauch it may unfit men for certain forms of employment. They have seen no reason to believe that such behaviour inflicts any greater damage on family life than adultery, fornication, or lesbian behaviour, and they accept the evidence of expert witnesses that there are two recognizably different categories among adult male homosexuals - those who seek adult partners, and paedophiliacs, who seek as partners boys who have not reached puberty. Paedophiliacs, together with the comparatively few who are indiscriminate, would continue to be liable to the sanction of the criminal law as they are now.

"Our evidence indicates that the fear that the legalization of homosexual acts between adults will lead to similar acts with boys has not enough substance to justify the treatment of adult homosexual behaviour in private as a criminal offence, and suggests that it would be more likely that such a change in the law would protect boys rather than endanger them."

REALM OF PRIVATE MORALITY
"NOT LAW'S BUSINESS"

The view is also dismissed that such a change in the law would "open the floodgates" and result in unbridled licence, as

THE TIMES
REPORT ON THE
WOLFENDEN
COMMITTEE'S
RECOMMENDA-
TIONS

it as a very positive experience . . . and a great relief - of course it was ten years at least before the recommendations were accepted.'

The report sold 5,000 copies within hours of publication and went into a second edition the very next day. People like Allan Horsfall, who lived in a small Lancashire town called Nelson, couldn't get to the HMSO to buy a copy of the report but he got hold of anything else that mentioned it. 'I was aware that the report was going to be published in September 1957 because it had been trailed so heavily,' Allan recalls. 'I remember going up to town and buying all the papers I could get my hands on and taking them into the Sunbeck Café in Nelson . . . to see what the reaction of the papers was and indeed what the committee had recommended. I was . . . delighted to see what the committee had recommended, rather less pleased to see some of the editorial reception which was mixed - fairly well received by the broadsheets, less so by the tabloids.'

The report was given blanket coverage in the press, on radio and television and for some people it seemed a foregone conclusion that its recommendations would become law. Peter Robins remembers how, as a result of the coverage, homosexuality became more talked about: 'This was the beginning of the change of tide. A loosening of the censoriousness about anybody who was gay and gradually you got things like references in radio programmes. I remember one example when an entire suburban cinema collapsed when one character [in a *Carry On* film] said, "Oh but doctor, doctor I'm a haemophiliac," and the doctor leaned over and said, "Don't worry, it will all be legal in two or three years."' In fact it was to be a decade, and not before people like Allan Horsfall had put up a spirited fight.

'The road is long and red with **monstrous** martyrdoms. Nothing but the repeal of the Criminal Law Amendment Act would do any good. That is essential. It is not so much public opinion, as public officials that need educating.'

Oscar Wilde on the impediment to law reform

The problem was that the public was split on the issue but Parliament was not prepared to take the lead. The Home Secretary – Maxwell Fyfe had been succeeded by Rab Butler by this point – said that Wolfenden's recommendations were 'in advance of public opinion' – but were they? One way of assessing it is to look at the reaction of the newspapers. Seven national newspapers, with a combined readership of sixty-one per cent of the population, gave a favourable verdict on the report, only two newspapers condemned it. The newspapers which were opposed were, however, the popular tabloids. A Gallup poll carried out at the time showed that there was only a ten per cent difference between those who wanted homosexuality decriminalized and those who didn't.

Parliament debated the report and backed the proposals on prostitution but decided not to take any action on the recommendations regarding homosexuality. 'I hoped in my naivety [that the recommendation] would lead to legislation fairly quickly but I was to be proved wrong,' Allan Horsfall recalls. 'There was legislation within eighteen months on the recommendations on prostitution because that involved a tightening up of control of sexual conduct and Parliament is always more willing to tighten things up than to liberalize things.'

The House of Lords was much more objective when it discussed the report although there was the customary invocation of Sodom and Gomorrah and how homosexuality had brought about the fall of the Roman Empire. Lord Brabazon of Tara responded to this antediluvian argument by pointing out that 'the Greeks, who had no knowledge of Sodom and Gomorrah, had a curious view of homosexuality. They almost condoned it, but no divine hydrogen bomb fell upon them.' He also put his finger on the real reason why the recommendations had not been taken up by the Commons: 'This House is a singularly good place in which to debate this difficult subject because your Lordships do not have a constituency . . . looking over your shoulder to note what you say.'

His Lordship was more prescient than he could have known. One of the MPs who had urged the adoption of Wolfenden's recommendations, in the House of Commons debate, H Montgomery Hyde, was deselected in the run-up to the 1959 election by his constituency committee which said: '[We] cannot have as our member one who condones unnatural vice.'

It rapidly became clear that if any progress was to be made, the efforts should be directed at Parliament rather than the public. In that sense things hadn't changed since the previous century when Oscar Wilde – in answer to the criminologist George Ives, who had written to him expressing the view that the law should be amended – responded in the following manner. 'I have no doubt we shall win. But the road is long and red with monstrous martyrdoms. Nothing but the repeal of the Criminal Law Amendment Act would do any good. That is essential. It is not so much public opinion, as public officials that need educating.'

If any proof was needed that public officials needed educating, it came in the same year as the publication of the Wolfenden Report when the British Medical Association produced a report which said that homosexuals existed in the church, in Parliament, the civil service, and the forces. MPs were incensed and threatened to raise the matter in the Commons as a breach of privilege, notwithstanding the fact that between 1950 and 1959 three MPs – one a junior minister – were arrested and convicted of homosexual offences.

Although gay men and their supporters were demoralized by the defeat, they had not given up. The cudgels were taken up by two friends who had been at college with a gay man who had committed suicide. A E Dyson, who was at the time a lecturer at the University of Wales, and the Reverend Andrew Hallidie Smith set up the Homosexual Law Reform Society. It was decided that since arguments based on pure principle didn't appear to work with Parliament, the alternative approach would be to line up a range of personalities to make those arguments appear more palatable. Accordingly a letter appeared in *The Times* on 7 March 1958 signed by thirty-three distinguished people – including Lord Atlee, the former Prime Minister, A J Ayer, the philosopher, Bertrand Russell and Angus Wilson – arguing that the law was illiberal and unchristian.

Allan Horsfall heard of the Homosexual Law Reform Society and wrote to A E Dyson offering his support, which eventually led to him setting up the north-western branch of the society. Allan was involved in Labour Party politics and in 1958 he was a Labour councillor in his home town, Nelson. At a Labour Party conference in Scarborough, over a few beers with Labour MPs, he asked why Wolfenden's recommendations had been rejected. He discovered, to his surprise, that they were privately supportive but were terrified of constituency opinion.

ALLAN HORSFALL

That was something Allan could attempt to change. He put down a motion at his local Labour Party branch, urging progress on Wolfenden's proposals. He found that he was blocked at almost every stage, beginning with a fellow councillor on his ward committee who was a magistrate and a pillar of the local church. '[He] objected, amongst other things, to it being discussed in mixed company,' Allan recalls. 'I was very annoyed about this and went back to a subsequent meeting of the ward committee of which I was secretary and said that I wouldn't continue to serve a committee that was so evasive . . . they were free to take whatever view they wanted . . . but simply not to discuss it I thought was unforgivable.'

At the time, campaigning for homosexual law reform was an incredibly brave thing to do but Allan is anxious not to paint himself as a fearless crusader – indeed, there were many waves of panic at the beginning. His first public pronouncement on the subject came in 1958, only a few weeks after he was made councillor. When he was canvassing for election, the Labour Party apparatchiks had edited his pamphlets to exclude anything remotely controversial – he was not allowed to mention his membership of the National Association of Mental Health or his opposition to capital punishment. So when he sent his first letter about homosexuality to *Reynold's News*, a Labour Party paper owned by the Co-operative Movement, he feared he was landing himself in a huge political row.

'I dropped it rather merrily into the post-box and then felt sickness in the pit of my stomach. . . . [I feared] that this would be picked up by the local press – "New Local Councillor Backs Homosexual Law Reform" – and I would . . . be accused of being tactless and devious and I was quite distraught for a couple of days, off my food . . . and I remember taking myself off to London and arriving on Peter Wildeblood's doorstep and he was good enough to ask me in, sit me down and give me a drink and talk

THE HOUSE AT 3 ROBERT STREET, ATHERTON, LANCASHIRE, BELONGING TO THE NATIONAL COAL BOARD, WHICH WAS THE FIRST ADDRESS OF THE NORTH-WEST HOMOSEXUAL LAW REFORM COMMITTEE, WHICH LATER BECAME THE CAMPAIGN FOR HOMOSEXUAL EQUALITY

me down from this state of high anxiety by saying that things seldom turned out quite as black as one anticipated.'

Indeed Allan's foreboding was far from realized, but there were a few more weeks of worried anticipation still to be endured because the letter didn't appear the following week. Nor the following week, nor the week after that. By this time, Allan had gathered his strength and, when the editor wrote to say that he would use an extract, was able to decree that his name could only be used in full if the letter was published – unedited.

One of the main fears that Labour MPs had about supporting a change in the law – although most of them agreed, off the record, that the law was antiquated and inequitable – was that many of them were sponsored by the National Coal Board and they didn't think that backing a man's right to have sex with another man would go down very well in the Miners' Institutes. Happily Allan was able to prove them wrong when, in the early Sixties, he launched the North-West Homosexual Law Reform Committee. 'I was not only working for the Coal Board, but living in a miner's cottage in the middle of a mining village and, because we weren't able to use any other address, I used my own address and this was emblazoned across the local press in an eight-column headline and was very calmly received by the neighbours and townsfolk,' he recalls. 'I sat back and waited for the letters of protest to come into the next week's paper, but there were none and there were none the week afterwards and in the end they had to put up their own tame columnist to attack it because nobody else was willing.'

Interestingly, just as Terry Gardener had discovered in the East End, working-class communities were often more tolerant of gay men than their middle-class counterparts. This was also Fred Dyson's experience. Fred was convicted of cottaging in the Sixties when he was working as an overman at the local colliery. He went into the canteen after his shift, as usual, and the first thing he saw was the local paper lying in a prominent place. The waitress told him that they'd carried a story on his court appearance with the headline 'Miner Admits to Being a Homosexual All His Life'.

'I thought that's it I'm done. That's it I haven't got a job, I don't know what I'm gonna ruddy do, lousy bloody newspaper men.' Fred decided to make a clean breast of it and go and see his union secretary. 'I said, "Arthur," he's dead and gone now that old fella. "I don't know what I'm gonna do," I says, "it's in the paper." He says, "I know it is, Fred, I've seen it," he says. "You've not done nowt wrong," he says. "I've played with a bloke many a time. Not done nowt wrong . . . Come on now you're going in club with me" . . . so we went in club and went into tap room and all the lads just stood there from pit and one of lads came over and said, "Fred, if thou can admit to being a poof all thou life, thou are a better man than us. Have a pint."'

The next day Fred went to see his manager who told him that he was employed for his expertise and not for what he did in his spare time. However Fred didn't escape mild ribbing from his mates and ribald comments in the baths. 'At beginning it felt strange . . . 'cos I used to get a lot catcalls and . . . I used to have to bluff it off. "Fred, come up here see what we've got for you mate," you know what I mean? "Why, what you got? Twelve inches, no it's not big enough. Owt over twelve I'm interested but under twelve, I'm not bothered." But men naked, that's never bothered me. I don't like naked bodies anyway. No I like to see people in clothes . . . [otherwise] there's no excitement at all.'

One of the reasons that Fred ended up in the local paper was that he had had a bit of an altercation with the magistrate at his court appearance. 'It were a lady judge and she says to me, "Have you ever tried to go for a cure?" right. I said, "Madam, if there were a cure, they'd be lining up outside the doctor's, they would, they'd be lining up to get the cure if there were such a thing," . . . so I were fined £50 for opening me mouth . . . the other fella got £25.'

FRED DYSON
ON HOLIDAY

After the Second World War, homosexuality was widely regarded as a disease and, like all illnesses, there was supposed to be a cure for it. Accordingly, a variety of quack treatments were offered and occasionally forced on to gay men and lesbians throughout the Fifties and much of the Sixties. This continued in a few isolated cases until the early Seventies since homosexuality was not taken off the register of psychiatric diseases until 1973. In the Wolfenden Report, the committee makes a specific point of recommending that treatment should be made available to homosexuals – particularly those who were in prison. Most of the medical establishment accepted this as the obvious and matter-of-course approach to the issue. There were however a few enlightened beings around. Charles Berg, a member of the Tavistock Clinic – one of the few progressive medical institutions in existence at the time – produced a document in 1959 which responded to Wolfenden's proposals from a psychiatric point of view. In it Berg takes Wolfenden to task in a detailed and dispassionate way but he does allow himself a small dig. 'The [Wolfenden] report opens with the statement "We were appointed on 24 August 1954" and having read [it] I am inclined to remark that they do not mention whether it was AD or BC.'

Some gay men and lesbians were lucky enough to encounter medics who took Berg's point of view on the subject. Pat Arrowsmith, who was prominent in the Campaign for Nuclear Disarmament in the Sixties, was training to be a social worker at the time. She felt the stigma society attached to lesbianism sufficiently keenly to believe that she ought to have psychoanalysis before embarking on case work. 'I wrote to an analyst in London about having analysis because I was a lesbian,' she recalls. 'She wrote back a very sensible letter saying if I felt out of accord with myself through being a lesbian it might be a good idea to have analysis. The implication being that if I didn't feel out of accord with myself there wasn't any reason for having analysis and I hadn't really looked at it that way before.' Analysts like the one Pat stumbled on were very rare indeed.

The mainstream view still saw homosexuality as an aberration to be corrected. Doctors had come up with a number of different methods for 'treating' homosexuality. There were two forms of aversion therapy – the use of emetics and, if that failed, doctors went on to electro-convulsive shock treatment. Lobotomies were also performed in some cases and in April 1954 an endocrinologist in the medical journal, *The Practitioner* analysed the surgical removal of men's testes citing 'the use of castration in over 100 cases of sexual perversion and homosexuality reported by Sand and Okkels who note gratifying results in all but one case'. The study quoted was German – mercifully castration was against the law in Britain. However, chemical castration was not only permitted but extensively encouraged.

ALAN TURING, ONE OF BRITAIN'S FOREMOST MATHEMATICIANS, COMMITTED SUICIDE AFTER ENFORCED 'TREATMENT' FOR HOMOSEXUALITY

In many cases gay men who came before the courts were advised by their defence counsel that if they elected to take a 'cure' they would be treated more leniently by the judges. This is what had happened to Alan Turing, one of Britain's foremost mathematicians – he had received an OBE for cracking the Enigma codes during the Second World War, which were a crucial factor in securing victory and, in the post-war years, he built Britain's first modern computer. In March 1952 he was sent to trial for being gay – a fact discovered by the police when Turing reported a burglary to them. He was let off with probation on the condition that he agreed to hormone therapy. Female hormones were administered to him – both orally and through implants in his thigh – even though the judge was aware that in addition to lowering his libido it would cause him to grow breasts. Although research in this area was primitive, it had also shown that the ingestion of female hormones by men led to a depression of mental activity – a fact that some of the tabloid papers reported with ghoulish zeal. A year after his ordeal by oestrogen ended, Turing killed himself by eating an apple dipped in cyanide.

Many gay men were not as robust as Fred Dyson was when asked about taking a cure by the magistrate. Indeed, some gay men and lesbians volunteered themselves. At a time when homosexuality was so stigmatized and the medical establishment had the kind of authority that it hasn't enjoyed before or since, it is easy to see how gay men and lesbians talked themselves into a form of torture.

> '**What was going through my mind was not the fear of being gay; it was the fear of not coming out of this psychiatric wing alive . . . I was a very scared young man, I didn't think that I would ever be seen again.**' Peter Price on his treatment for homosexuality

One of the most common methods of 'treating' homosexuality was aversion therapy, which involved making the individual undergo a series of psychiatric sessions, at the end of which he or she was supposed to associate sexual urges towards a member of the same sex with pain and nausea. In 1963, Peter Price put himself up for it under pressure from his family. At the time, Peter was around eighteen and had been having affairs with other men for a few years, but he wasn't sure about his feelings which induced guilt in him. At the age of twelve – and again at the age of fourteen – he had gone to his family doctor for advice and as an adolescent he'd made a half-hearted suicide attempt. 'I think I was sixteen or seventeen I actually tried to take an overdose . . . [it was] a pathetic attempt of taking a bottle of children's aspirins, orange flavour, and I had a very good night's sleep that night.'

One way of coping with the problem was to be impeccably behaved in his home town on the Wirral, and live a gay life elsewhere. He'd catch the train from Liverpool down to London and effect a transformation on the way. He lived what he called a 'Jekyll and Hyde' life – the gay aspects were lived in London and completely sealed off from his home life on the Wirral where he had become engaged to a girl. Then one spilled over into the other. His mother came across a letter from which she discovered that Peter might be gay and insisted that he seek help.

Even before he went for 'help', Peter doubted the use of it. 'I knew in my heart of hearts that I would never be cured but for my mother's sake. I decided to see if there was a road that I could go down that would help me,' he explains. The first stop on that road was the family doctor who confirmed what Peter's mother had believed – that there was a 'cure' that could be attempted. The general practitioner referred Peter to a psychiatrist who in turn suggested that Peter should go to a psychiatric hospital. The hospital was a bleak spot and Peter was housed in the bleakest bit of it – a dismal row of huts on the edge of the hospital's grounds. 'It was a dreadful, dreadful place . . . they put me in a ward along with people who had had nervous breakdowns and [other] psychiatric problems, and I remember the two nights I spent in the ward with people pissing on the wall behind me, people whispering in my ear while I was trying to sleep. People screamed out at night and I was very frightened . . . and quite, quite disturbed by the whole experience.' But there was something even more disturbing still to come.

The first section of the treatment consisted of Peter telling a psychiatrist about every aspect of his sex life in the most prurient – and to Peter 'offensive' – detail. Then they put him in a small windowless room which contained nothing but a bed, a crate of Guinness – which was Peter's tipple at the time – a stack of erotic gay books and a tape-recorder on which they played back Peter's interview with the psychiatrist concerning his sex life.

'So I'm sitting in the bed, drinking Guinness, reading the books and listening to the tape that lasted an hour. Halfway through the hour they gave me an injection that made me feel sick and I said, "Please can I have a bowl?" and they said, "No, no, just be sick", so I was sick in the bed which was quite offensive to me and quite alien because I'm a very clean person. So that lasted an hour . . . straight after that they wound the tape back and they did it again. And again. And again. And for seventy-two hours I was injected, I drank, I was sick. I went to the toilet in the bed, I had no basin, no toilet facilities nothing. I just had to sit in my own vomit and excrement . . . I was in a terrible state. What was going through my mind was not the fear of being gay; it was the fear of not coming out of this psychiatric wing alive. Without sounding dramatic, I was a very scared young man, I didn't think that I would ever be seen again.'

What Peter went through was probably the most widely used technique of aversion therapy at the time, known within the profession as the 'slide and emetic' method because in many cases the patients were shown slides of partially clothed men rather than being given magazines. Peter was made to drink alcohol because the drug he was injected with was probably Antabuse, a substance which reacts with alcohol to induce nausea. The logic behind it

PETER PRICE

was to link homoerotic stimulation with unpleasant sensations and thus create a Pavlovian reaction in the person every time they were faced with such stimuli in the future. The logic was somewhat flawed since Peter could just as easily have linked the unpleasant sensation with Guinness, which he also enjoyed at the time, and gone off that instead.

After three days of this, Peter had had enough and said so. 'The psychiatrist said, "Look, you know, it's only another two days . . . and then we're gonna try the electrodes." I said, "No, you're not, I want out, I've had enough."' Peter rang a friend of his who came and picked him up. Then he went back to his friend's home where he had repeated baths and showers and then made love as a gesture of defiance. So much for the treatment's efficacy. It did have one beneficial, if entirely unintended, effect. 'That was the turning point,' says Peter. 'From that day onwards is when I started living my life.'

There was a further sting in the tail. A couple of years later he was in a gay club in Manchester and saw the psychiatrist who had treated him standing at the bar. 'So, the psychiatrist who put me through all that was gay. What went through his sordid little mind when he was experimenting on me I'll never know,' says Peter. 'I'm not a violent person but I think it took six people to get me off him that night. I wanted him dead.'

Peter was not alone in being put through this ordeal. Thousands of gay men and many lesbians suffered in exactly the same way. Some were lucky and had narrow escapes. Hallam Tennyson who had married – his wife, Margot, was aware of his sexuality before they married – felt during the early Sixties that he might benefit from consulting a psychiatrist. 'I wanted to be cured. I wouldn't use that word any more, but we used it at the time. And there were these so-called aversion therapy treatments which I put in for at one stage. I discussed it with Margot, my wife, and she was dead against it. She said she loved me as I was and she didn't want me changed. She thought it would have a very bad effect on my personality. So with her strong advice I never actually went for the cure.' It was a close run thing. Hallam Tennyson had already spent a weekend at the psychiatric unit in Bristol for assessment, but cancelled all subsequent appointments.

Luchia Fitzgerald had an equally close shave with psychiatrists and in her case the consequences would have been immeasurably more serious since the man she consulted had recommended surgery. At the time Luchia, who was of Irish origin, was seeing a probation officer, over a minor juvenile offence, who talked her into visiting a psychiatrist. Between the two of them, the psychiatrist and the probation officer, they persuaded Luchia that she had a problem and that it was her sexuality. 'They were discussing how they could put it right and he made some suggestions of a

LUCHIA
FITZGERALD

part of my brain not being developed right and that really . . . the only way for me to go forward was to have surgery . . . I was thinking to myself maybe these people are right because they're professionals, they know what they're doing . . . I thought maybe if I was heterosexual, I could go home, settle down and be like everybody else. So I thought, well, if these people can cure me, I'm going to let them.'

Fortunately, Luchia had the foresight to discuss the proposed surgery with a friend before submitting her skull to the scalpel. At the time she was a regular at Manchester's most prominent gay bar, the Union, which provided her with most of her circle of friends. 'I toddled off to the Union that night and I was chatting to one of the older butches about this psychiatrist . . . and she was absolutely horrified when I was telling her that this guy would just cut out a little part of my brain. She just put her arms around me and she said, "Luchia, please don't go back to these people because you will not end up heterosexual, you will end up like a cabbage. You won't have any feelings whatsoever. You won't be able to love anybody . . ." When I look back now and think of what I nearly had done to me . . . it makes me really want to cringe.'

However, it wasn't all chemical cures and cutting through craniums during the Fifties and early Sixties. As homosexuality became a subject that could be discussed, gay men and lesbians began to feel less isolated; as they made contact with each other they realized that, even though society considered them diseased, there was actually nothing wrong with them, a suggestion that scientists found rather difficult when it was expressed to them. Michael Schofield, writing under the name Gordon Westwood, the sociologist who conducted the first major post-Wolfenden study into homosexuality, found that sixty-five per cent of his respondents didn't see themselves as suitable cases for treatment. Westwood felt this was a thorny issue: 'These . . . contacts present a very difficult problem. They have adopted a defensive attitude to their homosexual condition and they resent the suggestion that they are suffering from any kind of disease or need any kind of treatment.'

The witch-hunts and the trials may have been frightening but if the intention was to send gay men and lesbians scurrying, it succeeded in achieving exactly the opposite objective. Being abused and reviled was better than being ignored because it acknowledged the presence of homosexuality. Indeed, the combination of Kinsey and the red scare made people so keenly aware of the presence of homosexuality, they feared it was everywhere. The ordinary member of the public had to be taught how to detect it.

In 1963, the *Sunday Pictorial* supplied the relevant details to its readers in an article under the headline 'How To Spot a Homo'. It ran: '. . . they wear silk shirts and sit up at chi-chi bars with full-bosomed ladies. Or they wear hairy sports jackets and give their wives a black eye when they get back from the working men's club. They wrestle, they play golf, ski and work up knots of muscle lifting weights. They are married, have children. They are everywhere, they can be anybody.' Gay men and lesbians had known this for decades, of course, and knew the only way to be certain was to go to the gay bars which were springing up everywhere, and the new ones were considerably less furtive than the ones that had existed before.

'I have **occasionally** drawn a cup of coffee in the Mouse Hole myself, little knowing of my peril.' E M Forster to J R Ackerley regarding the closure of a gay coffee bar following a police raid

As gay men and lesbians began to form networks, they began to give private parties that became regular fixtures on the social scene. None were more famous than the ones held by David George. During the Fifties, David's parties were as much a part of the glitterati's social calendar as dining at the Ivy and invitations were much sought after. The guests were a mixture of gay men, lesbians and movers and shakers in show business, society and the music world – the list included Shelley Winters, Lord Montagu, Ivor Novello and Burl Ives. The high celebrity count attracted the attention of gossip columnists and diary editors and even the Pathé newsreel cameras which gave David's parties a certain renown. However, the press weren't aware that David also held other, even more exclusive parties, that would have made them drop their notebooks with surprise.

E M FORSTER (left)
WITH BENJAMIN
BRITTEN

E M FORSTER (left) WITH BENJAMIN BRITTEN

'The parties were divided into sections – there used to be always two. One was "hair up" and one was "hair down" or sometimes we changed it to "earrings in" or "earrings out",' recalls David. 'At one, the men could dance together and the girls could dance together, but at the others they couldn't because it was a "normal" party. But we found that there were lots of [straight] people that . . . accepted us as we were which was a great compliment as we, of course, were forced to accept them because that was something that the Lord demanded.'

David and his friends would put on skits and cabarets at these parties to entertain the guests, but the content changed, depending on whether it was an 'earrings in' party or not. 'We had a version of *The Importance of Being Earnest* – the interview scene which we did straight and then later we did our version and the whole scene was set in a gentleman's toilet. It was hilariously funny because . . . we kept to the script – all we did was change the setting. So for instance, "You may take a seat, Mr Worthing." "Thank you Lady Bracknell, I prefer standing."'

Those who weren't lucky enough to be invited to David's parties had to make do with the pubs and the clubs, with new ones opening as fast as the existing ones closed. There were some that endured though. The Fitzroy, which Gerald Dougherty had visited on the first night of the Blitz, was still going strong in the Fifties. Two of London's oldest gay bars, the Coleherne and the Boltons, both in Earls Court, established themselves as gay venues in the Fifties. 'The Coleherne was the first gay bar I went to. That was in

1959, and it had been established at least since 1955, and the Boltons was across the road,' recalls Michael James. 'And there were loads and loads of places in the West End like the A&B, and the Pink Elephant and then there were lots of coffee bars . . . I was more into them because I was never much into drinking alcohol.'

The Fifties and early Sixties was the era of the coffee bar with the steaming Gaggia a recent import from Italy. There were quite a number of gay coffee bars in London during this period – mainly centred in the West End – which attracted an astonishing range of clientèle from rent boys to acclaimed writers like E M Forster. One of the most famous was the Mouse Hole in Swallow Street, just off Piccadilly Circus, which the writer J R Ackerley had introduced Forster to, according to Peter Parker's biography of Ackerley. When the Mouse Hole was raided in the late Fifties, Forster was most disconcerted and encouraged Ackerley to write to the papers about it. Ackerley duly sent him a draft of the proposed letter, but Forster felt it was too open and wrote back to Ackerley suggesting he rewrite it along the following lines: 'I have occasionally drawn a cup of coffee in the Mouse Hole myself little knowing of my peril, or that a policeman might be observing me and might demand my name and address because my taste in clothes differed from his.'

Outside London, gay men often met each other in the bars of large hotels. 'Most towns didn't have what would pass now as a gay bar but there

DAVID GEORGE (second from right, wearing feather boa) AT A COSTUME BALL

were little corners of [straight] places where gay men would meet and talk in code,' explains Allan Horsfall. 'It was often in the better hotels . . . or what would pass in a small town as the better hotel because there was less hassle there. This was known to me, but there were many to whom it wasn't known and people could grow up into their twenties or thirties without ever knowing that there was a little culty meeting place in the same town.'

Most of the major conurbations outside London did have a gay bar of sorts though, the most notorious of which was the Union bar in Manchester. The Union was situated in the heart of Manchester's red-light district and it took some courage for a newly emergent gay person to enter it as Luchia Fitzgerald discovered. Luchia had emigrated from Ireland to work in the Lancashire cotton mills and was so naïve that when she heard the other women in the mill talking about pansies she thought it was a conversation about horticulture. She was soon put right when one of her colleagues told her exactly what a lesbian was. 'I must have gone red from the tip of me toes right up to me forehead,' she says. 'I didn't know where to put myself. I couldn't look at her. . . . On the other hand, after I'd gone upstairs, I felt a tingling sensation because I'd suddenly been told that there was a whole nation of people out there like me.'

Not only did Luchia learn that there were other people like her, but she also found that there was a pub in Manchester where she could meet them. She caught the bus into the city and wandered around asking people till she was directed to it by a slightly suspicious policeman who demanded to know why she wanted to go there. Luchia made up an excuse about meeting a friend at the bus-stop outside it. When she got there, Luchia was too scared to go in so she stood outside for a little while and was astonished at what she saw. 'These women would come along – really big women, they looked like Desperate Dan – and they would go into the pub and really young boys. Then I started to realize that what I thought was young boys was women dressed up like men.' And, of course, the giant 'women' were really men in drag. Luchia, who was still under eighteen and therefore underage as far as drinking was concerned finally screwed up her courage to go in. 'Honest to God, I will never forget till the day I die, the smell of lipstick and Angel face powder and as soon as I got close to these blokes [I noticed] they were caked with make-up and their beards were showing through the make-up and they were built like brick shit-houses, these blokes,' Luchia recalls.

Jose Pickering also found out about the Union through word of mouth. Although she was still married, by this time she had started having an affair with another woman and the two of them decided to pay a visit. 'There was a really good atmosphere in the Union – there was a real mixture of people. There were servicemen, there were barrow boys, there were prostitutes, there were drag queens who would get up on stage and do a turn . . . and we thought this is like Wonderland.'

While places like the Union attracted lesbians, many gay bars and clubs did not make women feel very welcome and lesbians began to find meeting-places which were exclusive to them. The best known was the Gateways in Chelsea which had been going as a bohemian club since the Thirties. The club attracted both gay and straight people but it began to take on a lesbian ambience during the Second World War and by the Fifties it was exclusively lesbian. It was a members-only club but it had literally thousands of members since the joining fee was kept low – even in 1966 it was only ten shillings. The Gateways was housed in a basement room which held a maximum of 200 people, but at weekends the place would be jam-packed. The club received a wider fame when it was featured in the film *The Killing of Sister George* with small speaking parts for the club's two managers – Gina and Smithy. There were also a number of pubs in London which became known as lesbian meeting-places, such as the Raven and the Robin Hood in West London.

Pat Arrowsmith recalls visiting the Gateways and savouring the naughtiness of it. 'I always went with a group of friends and I rather relished what seemed a slightly wicked atmosphere, all a bit underground. You know my vicar's daughter . . . background rather relished all this.' The club could boast of an extraordinarily wide membership which ranged from jailbirds to junior aristocracy. Pat was an active peace campaigner which often landed her in jail for civil disobedience and she remembers a story about a lesbian warden from Holloway arriving at the Gates – as it was known among

JOSE PICKERING

its members – to find a large number of her former charges ranged up along the bar. Pat's work as a peace campaigner later earned her an entry in *Who's Who* and when asked to list her clubs, Pat put down the Gateways. 'On the strength of this the Gates made me an honorary life member, so I was very sorry when their lease expired and the Gates faded away,' she laughs.

Sharley McLean, who had come to terms with her sexuality following her suicide attempt, remembers having the Gateways recommended to her as a way of meeting other lesbians. 'I had to write first of all to get a pass and then I went along . . . and knocked and this sort of hole in the door was slid back and somebody peered and I showed my pass and I was let in,' Sharley says. 'It was quite an experience, I felt I was being mentally undressed and lesbians in those days had a uniform and I didn't fit into that category.'

Fitting into a category was essential if you wanted to be part of the lesbian scene then, and there were only two categories available – butch or femme. Margaret Cranch (known to her friends as Crunchy), who was working as a physiotherapist in London at the time, describes what this involved. 'If you were a butch it meant that you were dressed in boyish clothes and the femmes were dressed in nice skirts and blouses and hair all very highly lacquered . . . It was aping heterosexual relationships . . . and it wasn't till years later, when people actually came to terms with being gay that they were themselves . . . [they realized] it was just their sexual preference that was different – they didn't have to look as if they were a male to be . . . in love with a woman.'

> '**Luchia, you're really going to have to make your mind up because you're neither Martha nor Arthur.**' Advice from a **gay-scene regular** about the need to decide between butch and femme

Luchia Fitzgerald discovered soon after her first visit to the Union that if she wanted to become a regular there she would have to make a choice. '[When I first saw] these women with their legs crossed, smoking cigars, big pints of beer and behaving like men, I thought I can't be a lesbian, I'm not like one of them, I must be like one of these other types of women that's sat over there . . . I realized quite quickly that you had to take some sort of role. Now to be perfectly honest with you, I couldn't see myself in ankle socks and little high-heeled shoes and the ponytail, whilst at the same time I refused mentally to dress in these butch clothes . . . until one day one of the women walked up to me and said, "Luchia, you're really going to have to make your mind up because you're neither Martha nor Arthur." I thought, well, she's right because when I was fancying the girls that was dressed as men, they thought I was a bit odd 'cos they saw me as a little bit dykie. When I was fancying the femmes, I wasn't butch enough for them.'

So Lucia decided to ditch Martha and go for Arthur and bought herself the full kit – a shirt, a tie, trousers, men's shoes and a little waistcoat. Off went the old hairstyle to be replaced by a short back and sides. The new clothes demanded a new pose too, but there were some things that Luchia found she wasn't capable of doing no matter how hard she tried: 'You had to stand with one hand in your pocket and one elbow on the bar, but I couldn't do that because I'm only four foot eleven.'

Jose Pickering was also a regular at the Union but she was one of the femmes, and unlike Luchia she loved getting up in all the feminine gear. She and her friend would have their clothes made to their precise specifications and invariably they accentuated the fashions so that the curves would be curvier and cleavage would plunge vertiginously down the torso. 'She [the dressmaker] would pin on the nearly finished dress to do the neckline and we'd be saying "cut more off, cut more off" so it would be lower at the front and then the backs would be cut away with long sleeves . . . I used to have a false front in the dress, which was made of lace, to cover the cleavage and, as soon as we got out, off it came and into the handbag till you got back. You had to remember to put your front back on before you got in because you weren't meant to be showing all that.' An image of what Jose looked like can probably be conjured up by imagining her heroine, Doris Day – Jose once queued for two hours to see a Doris Day movie – in one of her trademark bell-skirted, long-sleeved dresses but displaying considerably more cleavage.

Jose was still living with her husband at this time and was financially dependent on him, which put her in a dilemma. While she stayed with him it was difficult to live her lesbian life to the full. On the other hand, if she left him, she had no way of making a living. Then, one day at the Union, she stumbled on a way of earning money. Since the pub was in the middle of Manchester's red-light district, it was a popular hangout for prostitutes and their punters. While her friend was on holiday, Jose went to the Union alone and on her first night there she was approached by a man. Jose was outraged and told him to push off, but the next night she went to the Union, he was there again. '[He] came over and said, "Look, there's nothing to worry about, it's a chance to earn some money." I don't know to this day what came over me but I took the bull by the horns and off I went with him and he was a perfect gentleman – he could see I wasn't used to this carry-on.'

What attracted Jose to the profession was that the work wasn't too demanding. 'They wanted to grovel, they wanted to worship madam and tell me how menial they were and how fortunate they were to be in my presence. And I thought, well, quite right too!' – but the most appealing thing about it was that it sent her weekly income soaring into the stratosphere. Jose was determined that she would use it to change her circumstances, rather than spend it on fripperies as she had seen other prostitutes do. 'I'd earned fifteen pounds and that was five weeks' housekeeping money to me because I got three pound a week and that was everything I got from my husband . . . I'd seen girls in the Union frittering the money and I didn't, and still don't, agree with that. I'd been kept short of money all my life, so I decided that now I was able to get some, I wouldn't abuse it.' And she didn't. The money was saved up and helped Jose move out of the marital home and into her own.

The butches who frequented the Union also had to earn a living but their choices were much more limited. The look they had adopted meant that the minute they walked into an interview for a conventional job, the employer's prejudices were stacked against them. Their appearance made them equally unsuitable for earning money in the sex industry. There was no option but to scrape by as well as they could. The women who found work as prostitutes would occasionally slip the young butch dykes their rent money. It was never enough, though, and sometimes some of the women would go shoplifting, taking along the drag queens as a decoy. While the men distracted attention by trying on frocks, the women would start pocketing the goods.

The music that this crowd listened to was heavily influenced by black culture, partly by choice and partly through accident. After the Union closed, there was nowhere for the lesbians to go to since they weren't welcome in the male gay clubs which were rather snooty. Another group that had been excluded from clubs was Manchester's Afro-Caribbean community which had set up its own nightclubs playing bluebeat music and jazz and reggae. 'They were happy to let the lesbians in – but at their own risk. They were totally illegal. You'd knock three times at the door, the door would open a little, somebody would say to you, "Oh pussy-suckers, you're all right," and you'd be in,' recalls Luchia.

In London, too, lesbians found themselves welcomed at after-hours music and drinking places, run by black people, as Claire Andrews discovered. Claire, who used to play cricket for Trinidad, emigrated to England in the early Sixties and found herself a niche in the gay scene, but when the pubs closed 'we always found ourselves in the shebeens . . . illegal drinking clubs, but they were in houses and they were usually run by black people who were sympathetic to lesbian and gay people who didn't have a place to go.'

> '" It says it's a **boy**," or "It says it's a **girl**."'
> Claire Andrews on how gay men and lesbians were taunted
> by police during raids on gay venues

The shebeens, being illegal, were subject to frequent raids, but so were gay bars and clubs which were legitimate businesses – the only difference between them and their straight counterparts being that they served a gay clientele. The club favoured by Claire Andrews, the Casino, was raided on a regular basis although no charges were ever brought because no one was breaking the law. The intention was to intimidate and harass. A raid followed a set pattern: the police would walk in and separate the men and the women, who would be lined up on separate sides of the room; names and addresses would be taken and then people would be marched down to the station.

'The police attitude towards us was to show power . . . they were there to abuse us; they had the power to take us down to [the station] . . . they'd do the same procedure again and say, "It says it's a boy," or "It says it's a girl," and they'd keep you in the cell till the morning so you don't go back to the club.' Many club proprietors had an arrangement with the police so that, in return for an inducement, they would be left alone. Allan Horsfall remembers being in a gay club outside London in the early part of the evening 'talking to the proprietor' when they were interrupted. '[A] manager came over and said, "Excuse me, sir, but your usual Monday night visitors are here," and he went away and I went to the gents and found him halfway down the corridor looking very worried, and I said, "What's to do, who is it?" and he said, "It's the police again and I don't know whether to give them spirits or cash this week."'

The raids, though frequent, were hardly ever reported in the press because the proprietors complied with the police harassment without complaining to higher authorities. The only cases that were covered were the ones that ended up in court and, judging by what the judiciary thought constituted disorderly conduct, most proprietors were wise not to contest charges. Newspaper reports of those who pleaded not guilty make instructive reading. One such was David Browne, the owner of a club called the Kandy Lounge in Gerrard Street, who appeared at Bow Street magistrates' court in September 1962. The Kandy Lounge was visited by plain-clothes policemen who observed men dancing the twist with each other. The only proof necessary that these men were homosexual was that they were wearing 'bright shirts and tight jeans'. Browne's defence counsel tried hard by pointing to a new dance craze called the Madison where members of the same sex danced together in a crowd but it was to no avail. Browne was found guilty. Two years later, in February 1964, George Monro Wilson also pleaded not guilty to charges of running a disorderly house. Plain-clothes police had visited his club – the Witches Brew – and made the arrest because 'women were dancing together and so were two effeminate men'.

Parliament's refusal to act on the Wolfenden report seemed to have given a signal to the police and the judiciary that homosexuality was not to be tolerated in any form. In fact, there is some indication that things actually got worse for gay men and lesbians in the seven-year period between 1957 when the Wolfenden report was published and 1964 when the Director of Public Prosecutions intervened and asked the police to ease off.

Not only were gay meeting-places frequently raided and their owners harassed, but the sentences handed down to men who continued to be arrested in large numbers were more severe. It is instructive to look at just a few of the cases involved to see how the law operated. The following cases illustrate how, in a blackmail case, the victim was further victimized. Men were convicted for possessing pictures of male nudes that were so innocent that many classical paintings revealed more; how a seventy-year-old man was imprisoned for having sex in private with a consenting adult; and how a homosexual pass was considered sufficient grounds for murder.

In 1961, a wealthy business man who had been having an affair with another man, Benito Giagheddu, appeared at the Old Bailey after being

CLAIRE ANDREWS

menaced by the latter. The two men had been having an affair during which the blackmail victim had supplied Giagheddu with food and lodging, a bank account with a capital sum and a weekly income in addition to that. After two years, when the relationship deteriorated, Giagheddu threatened his lover with a knife and demanded money or else there would be a 'national scandal'. The blackmail victim reported this to the police and a plain-clothes officer witnessed the handover of the money. On the direction of the judge, Giagheddu was acquitted of blackmail.

In March 1961, a Methodist preacher, former chairman of his urban council and a Justice of the Peace was arrested for sending photographs of nude men through the post. The man, married with children, had been interrogated from early evening till the early hours of the morning. The photographs in question turned out to be so innocuous, the court heard that 'if they were of classical statues in museums . . . there would not even be the question of obscenity'. A similar case in 1963 involved Lord Horder who was apprehended for sending ten prints to a Danish magazine for publication. Again, some of the photographs were described as being 'classic nude studies as used by art students' and Lord Horder said in his defence: 'I don't consider any of my work obscene. It is only in the mind of the person looking at it.' He was found guilty and fined.

The police continued to pursue chain prosecutions where if one man was apprehended so were all his gay friends and contacts. In one such case, twenty-three men appeared at Nottingham Assizes in November 1961 where Mr Justice Stable dispensed harsh judgment. In his opinion, those who argued for law reform were ignorant of the dangers. 'A number of people, perhaps not very well informed, have said this sort of thing is not contagious . . . these cases show how such moral leprosy is spread.' Severe sentences were handed out including a year's imprisonment for a man of seventy.

One of the most celebrated cases of the period was the murder of George Brinham, a former chairman of the Labour Party and a trade union executive, who was bashed to death by sixteen-year-old Laurence Somers after Brinham made a pass at him. The Old Bailey judge told the jury to ignore the murder charge. 'I cannot see how any jury, properly directed on the evidence, can fail to find there was provocation.' Somers was acquitted of manslaughter and boasted to the press afterwards that he had gained the strength to strike Brinham on the head as a result of labouring jobs where he'd used a sledge hammer and that his experience in pig-slaughtering had helped him keep his head amidst the blood and gore.

Finally, the Director of Public Prosecutions stepped in. In July 1964, a document he had issued to all chief constables was leaked which indicated that the government was getting concerned. The story was picked up by other newspapers after the London *Evening Standard* quoted sections of the document, including the instruction that, in cases involving consenting adults in private, no prosecutions should be initiated 'until a report ha been sent to the director and his opinion obtained'. So what had changed? One newspaper report made a shrewd assessment. 'In some political circles, it was pointed out that it is just two years since Sir Peter Rawlinson was appointed Attorney-General. As Mr Rawlinson QC, he defended Peter Wildeblood, author of the book on homosexuality *Against the Law* [and one of the defendants in the Montagu Trial]; as a backbencher, one of Sir Peter's later acts was a sponsor of Mr Abse's unsuccessful measure [to effect homosexual law reform].'

However, it wasn't just a change of personnel that was the cause of this intervention. To borrow Harold Macmillan's phrase of the time, there was a wind of change blasting its way through the country and opinions were rapidly being revised as the Sixties finally began to swing. The government

DANNY LA RUE
PROVIDED CAMP
FOR LARGELY
STRAIGHT
AUDIENCES

was already looking very fuddy duddy, ruled as it was by old patrician Tories, and the opposition exploited it to the full. Harold Wilson tried to position himself – rather unconvincingly it must be said – like John F Kennedy, who had been assassinated the previous year, with talk of white-hot technology. It was election year and the issue seemed to be the old against the young. The old-fashioned against the new.

> '**It was the first film in which a man said "I love you" to another man. I wrote that scene in. I said "There's no point in half-measures. We either make a film about queers or we don't."**'
>
> **Dirk Bogarde** on VICTIM

In 1958, the government had rejected the Wolfenden report's recommendations on homosexuality because they were 'in advance of public opinion', but by the mid-Sixties it was difficult to be so certain. British society was being rapidly transformed. The Lady Chatterley trials had ended on the side of liberality; satirical programmes like *That Was the Week that Was* lampooned the government and pricked pomposity and humbug wherever it could be found; and Radio Caroline was blasting unregulated programmes across Britain giving rebellion a glamour it had never had before. Being gay may have been unusual, but the unusual was in vogue. Furthermore, gay men and lesbians were at the forefront of what *Time* magazine had described as 'Swinging London'.

By 1965, Britain's most adventurous playwright, its most acclaimed avant-garde artist and its most revered modern composer – Joe Orton, Francis Bacon and Benjamin Britten – were all gay and none of them pretended to hide it much. Danny La Rue had a thriving career and straight audiences flocked to see his shows and roar approval over jokes that were as camp as a row of tents. *Round the Horne* was one of the biggest radio comedies of the time and Kenneth Williams and Hugh Paddick left people in paroxysms of giggles over their Sunday lunch. Visibility may have made gay men and lesbians into easier targets after Wolfenden, but as the years went by familiarity also decreased public fear which had been engendered by ignorance.

An interesting index of this change is provided by the way gay and lesbian themes were handled in films – the most popular art form of the time.

THE RADIO SHOW,
*ROUND THE
HORNE,*
INTRODUCED
POLARI TO A
WIDER AUDIENCE
AND THE BBC
STILL DOES A
ROARING TRADE
IN AUDIOTAPES OF
THE SHOW

In 1960, Peter Finch took the lead role in *The Trials of Oscar Wilde*, the first time that the British cinema had attempted a sympathetic biography of the man who is almost as celebrated for his sexuality as for his works. Finch played Wilde with a dry heroism which bucked up a lot of British gay men. 'It was beautifully done and made it possible for us to understand how difficult the law was in those days, even worse than we were going through . . . an important film,' says David George. The film was equally well received by the critics and Finch won a BAFTA award for his work.

However, *The Trials of Oscar Wilde* was a costume drama and the historical perspective blunted the points it was trying to make. The real breakthrough came with *Victim*, the first British film to deal with male homosexuality as a contemporary subject. The film took its cue from Wolfenden,

PETER FINCH (left)
IN *THE TRIALS OF
OSCAR WILDE*, THE
1960 FILM WHICH
WAS THE FIRST TO
GIVE THE SUBJECT
A SYMPATHETIC
AIRING

DIRK BOGARDE
(right) IN A STILL
FROM *VICTIM*

which had finally laid to rest some of the stereotypes.

Wolfenden had given wide publication to the Kinsey findings that homosexual men weren't all effeminate; that they came from all walks of life and that some of them were even married. Most of all it provided a case study of what the Wolfenden Report argued was the inevitable consequence of the law as it stood – the vulnerability of homosexual men to blackmail.

Basil Dearden directed the film as a gritty black-and-white thriller in which the hero – a barrister called Melville Farr who is a paragon of good citizenship – finds himself enmeshed in a web of blackmail. Farr is married and the reason for the blackmail is a relationship that, in the first place, was platonic, and, in any case, took place several years before the action opens – but what made the hero even more unimpeachable was the actor who played him. Dirk Bogarde was a matinée idol who had become a home counties' heart-throb for his suave roles. Bogarde records in his autobiography that the part had been turned down by actor after actor who was offered it, and every actress who was sent the script turned the role of the wife down without even reading it until Sylvia Syms said yes.

The gay men that Farr encounters, as he unravels the web that has ensnared him unanimously tell him, to stop rocking the boat. The response was always that it was better to pay up than to be found out. Ironically, many gay men in real life found it unbearable exposure to be seen in a cinema where *Victim* was playing, even as far away as Africa. When the film opened, Peter Robins was living in Lusaka – a town in Zambia filled with British civil servants – and he and some friends decided to attend a performance. 'Three or four of us said we'll go and see this film – and

that's just how many of us there were when the lights first went down . . .
the preliminary bits of the film started coming up and we heard the
rustling of mice all around us . . . and suddenly, when I dared to glance
away from the screen, I found the cinema three-quarters full,' Peter says.
'And then at the end, as you remember in the old days . . . you had "God
Save The Queen", and suddenly before the lights went up we heard the
mice rustling and there were only half a dozen of us left standing in the
cinema for "God Save the Queen". The civil servants had run back to
their closets.'

It's hardly surprising. *Victim* was considered extremely daring for the
time because it took the matter seriously. It was also frank in its depiction
of the emotional facts of gay life. Dirk Bogarde said in 1975, 'It was the first
film in which a man said "I love you" to another man. I wrote that scene
in. I said, "There's no point in half-measures. We either make a film about
queers or we don't." I believe that pictures made a lot of difference to a lot
of people's lives.'

It certainly did in the case of David George and his circle of friends:
'The film *Victim* was a really great improvement in our lives . . . it did make
the general public aware how difficult a homosexual life was and how discreet and careful we had to be . . . It was an important film, a very important film, which helped enormously.'

> '**I** used to get **whistled** at a lot, and builders
> and labourers used to say, "Hello, ducky."'
>
> **Richard Cawley** on reaction to wearing skin-tight, baby-blue, velvet
> trousers tucked into riding boots, topped off with an afro hair-do

As the sleeping generation of the Fifties gave way to the sleeping around set of the Sixties, it became increasingly clear that the climate of opinion was changing. The old distinctions between male and female that had been so rigid for generations were beginning to shift. When straight men began to look the way girls were traditionally supposed to, it gave gay men a licence they had never had before. Peter Price, who hadn't looked back since his enforced aversion therapy, would walk down the street wearing gold leather knickerbockers with metallic snakeskin stripes and green stockings, high boots and a cloak with Mickey Mouse emblazoned on it. 'I just can't believe I had the nerve to do it,' he says now. Down in London, Richard Cawley also put on a display of plumage that would put a peacock to shame. He remem-bers one particular outfit which con-sisted of a huge jacket worn with skin-tight baby-blue velvet trousers tucked into riding boots, topped by an afro hair-do. More to the point, clothes that would have got a man's teeth kicked in a decade previously now only raised ribaldry.

'I used to get whistled at a lot and builders and labourers used to say, "Hello, ducky." It sounds so funny

DIRK BOGARDE
ON THE SET OF
VICTIM

now, but people did actually say it,' Richard Cawley remembers. 'And if anybody said, "Give us a kiss," I just used to stop and say, "Yeah, all right then," and it would break the ice and they'd just have a laugh and make some comment and you'd go on your way . . . I never had any trouble.'

The only trouble there was came from the tabloids which continued to taunt or go into shocked headlines about what was going on. In April 1965, the *News of the World* went into paroxysms of horror over a drag show at an Earls Court pub called the Lord Ranelagh. Under the headline 'This Show Must Not Go On', the reporter Roger Hall describes a 'disgusting' parade which panders 'only to the lowest taste'. Unable to endure it any longer, he ends the piece: 'I'd had enough and escaped into the Earls Court night air – not perhaps rarefied at the best of times but seldom in my experience quite so unpleasant.' Alas for the reporter, nobody else shared his feelings. In a follow-up story no members of the public could be found who shared his complaint. The landlord of the pub, Kenneth Brown, when interviewed, said there had only been one complaint – '"And this will make you roar," said Mr Brown. One night a man told me that there was a woman in the gents. I was able to reassure him that it was only a man dressed as a woman."'

As the Sixties swung on, the Homosexual Law Reform Society continued its campaign and many attempts were made to get the law regarding homosexuality amended, but all failed. Between 1958, when Parliament first debated Wolfenden's recommendations, and 1967, when the law was finally changed, the issue was raised in Parliament half a dozen times before the seventh attempt was successful and went on to its second and third readings. What gave the campaigners hope was that as the years wore on, the opposition began to dwindle both in Parliament and outside it. Indeed, by 1967 when the bill was given royal assent, the film *Victim*, which had seemed so daring that people were afraid to go and see it, had been deemed innocuous enough to be shown on television. It was screened by ITV in 1966 and may well have had an effect in shaping opinion which led to law reform the following year.

The first bid for legislative change following the Wolfenden debate was in 1960, with a private members' motion brought by the Labour MP, Kenneth Robinson, who was also on the executive committee of the Homosexual Law Reform Society. Nobody seriously expected this to get anywhere, but it was an attempt to keep the issue on the boil and remind both parliamentarians and the public that it needed to be dealt with. The motion was overwhelmingly defeated with the Tories gaining a majority of 215 to 101. The small number of Tories who voted for the motion included Enoch Powell. The next attempt was in 1962 with another private members' bill –

proposed by the Labour MP Leo Abse – which decided on a slightly different tactic and merely proposed that the worst excesses of the existing law be curbed. It too was defeated.

'Many gay people felt that it was such a meek proposal that, if passed, it would prove counterproductive and should never have been brought in the first place. These were compromised measures which I personally criticized in print because if one of them was passed they would give parliamentarians the feeling that they had done something and would probably put off the possibility of full reform for another decade or possibly more,' argues Allan Horsfall. 'In a way I wasn't displeased when they failed. The only value of them was a test of parliamentary opinion. Whenever a vote was taken, one could see people moving out of opposition, perhaps into abstention, and people who had previously abstained moving to support. This gave one an appreciation that parliamentary opinion was moving though fearfully slowly. It showed those that were prepared to study it that the move was in the right direction and that we would succeed – eventually.'

Success became more of a possibility in 1964, when even the *Daily Telegraph* – the Tory Party's parish newspaper – wrote a leader saying: 'There can be no doubt that the moral corruption which follows from the attempt to punish homosexual vice between consenting adults is greater than that which would follow from the abolition of this law. It should be abolished.' The Homosexual Law Reform Society was heartened when the Labour Party returned to power that year, after thirteen years in opposition. Although many Labour MPs, who were either sponsored by the trade unions or represented traditional working-class communities, were fearful of constituency reaction, most agreed about law reform as a matter of civil liberty.

The problem was that Labour only had a majority of five, so the House of Lords, whose members had no constituents to fear, was decided upon as a good place to test out public and parliamentary opinion. If the Lords gave it the go ahead, then an identical bill could be introduced to the Commons. Accordingly, in May 1965, Lord Arran raised the issue in the upper house. During the passage of the legislation in the Lords there was a tragic incident which served, if anything, to strengthen the case of the law reformers by indicating how the police framed innocent members of the public. Lord Moynihan, a former chairman of the Liberal Party, who was due to speak in the debate, decided to find out for himself about entrapment and went to the lavatory at Piccadilly Circus tube station. He was arrested by police officers on a charge of importuning men and put on bail, pending his appearance at Bow Street magistrates' court. Two barristers were hired to defend him and it was made clear that the charge would be vigorously contested. Alas, before the case could come to court, Lord Moynihan was discovered at home in a coma and rushed to hospital where he died of a stroke which his family said had been brought on by the stress of the prosecution.

In October 1965, Lord Arran's bill was passed by the upper house with a majority of nearly two to one. The opposition had not been silenced but it spoke in a voice that was so hysterical that nobody took it seriously. For instance Viscount Montgomery, the Second World War hero who had given filthy looks to John Beardmore's lover, Steve (*see* page 84), described homosexuality as 'abominable bestiality'and suggested that the age of consent should be set at eighty. When it was pointed out to him that this would put Britain out of step with its NATO allies almost all of whom allowed homosexual practices, Montgomery thundered: 'We are British, thank God!'

Montgomery's prejudice was countered by other, more reasonable, voices. During the course of the debate, there was a poignant address to the Lords by the Marquess of Queensberry, the thirty-five-year-old great-grand-son of Oscar Wilde's persecutor, who was making his maiden speech in the House. He pleaded for toleration and added, 'I believe these laws will be changed and that when my children are grown up they will be amazed that laws of this sort could have existed in the middle of the twentieth century.'

Queensberry needn't have waited for his children to grow up before that view became prevalent. A contemporary survey, conducted by NOP, showed that by far the majority of the public was either neutral on the issue or were in favour of change. Following the success in the Lords, a Conservative MP, Humphrey Berkeley, took it up in the lower house in February 1966. The Prime Minister, Harold Wilson, abstained, but thirteen members of his cabinet voted in favour of the bill. Everything seemed to be going swimmingly when the bill passed its second reading stage in February and went to the committee stage. Then the reformers' hopes were dashed yet again. Wilson called a general election which meant that all bets were off. Lord Arran said: 'It was necessary to start again from square one but what I call square nought.'

The Labour Party won the election with a much more comfortable majority – 100 compared to only five the previous time – and it was merely a matter of time before the law was changed. In April 1966, Lord Arran reintroduced his bill in the Lords and Leo Abse introduced an identical bill in the Commons which was approved by 244 votes to 100 against. The legislation was guided through the necessary parliamentary procedure and was given royal assent on 27 July 1967 when it entered the statute books.

The hated Labouchère Amendment of 1885 had finally been expunged, but its passing seemed such a natural and obvious event that many gay men

CECIL BEATON AT
A RETROSPECTIVE
OF HIS WORK AT
THE VICTORIA
AND ALBERT
MUSEUM IN 1971

were barely aware of it. The law had become defunct through disuse and among the swinging set it was largely ignored. Richard Cawley does not remember it at all. 'I can honestly say that all through the Sixties I was totally unaware of anything to do with homosexual law reform . . . nobody was political, they were too busy partying . . . it might have been in certain newspapers but I . . . didn't read newspapers, not proper newspapers, there wasn't time.'

Even those who had campaigned for law reform felt a sense of anticlimax. The arguments had been rehearsed to the point of tedium over the previous nine years, and there was so much exasperation over the way Parliament had dragged its feet that, when it finally caved in to the obvious, no one felt like congratulating it. 'I don't think boredom quite expresses the way we felt,' says Allan Horsfall. 'Tedium perhaps . . . I don't remember cracking any bottles of champagne or going on any carnival marches.'

For many people, however, this was seen as a fundamental acknowledgment – belated though it was – of gay men's right to exist. Cecil Beaton called it 'one of the most important milestones in English law' and wrote in his diary: 'Of recent years the tolerance towards the subject has made a nonsense of many of the prejudices from which I myself suffered acutely as a young man . . . when one realizes what damage, what tragedy has been brought on by this lack of sympathy . . . this should be a time of great celebration . . . For myself I am grateful. Selfishly, I wish that this marvellous step forward could have been taken at an earlier age . . . to feel that one was not a felon and an outcast could have helped enormously.'

There was one man, however, who celebrated the change in his own inimitable way. Fred Dyson, the miner, was on a bus with a friend when he heard the news. 'I got hold of him [his friend] and I give him a great big kiss and everybody on the bus were looking but I weren't bothered, I just kissed him. I said: "You can all look, it's legal now."'

PART FOUR   1967-

> 'My generation was **not** going to be tied down by their laws and their constraints. So, whether the law changed in 1967, or whether it had to wait till 1977, we would have been like we were at that point in history.'
>
> **Peter Burton** on the impact of law reform on the hip London crowd

The distinct lack of euphoria that greeted law reform was not misplaced. Parliament had provided too little too late. When gay men sat down and analysed what had actually happened, they were bitterly disappointed. The Homosexual Law Reform Society – whose contribution was rejected when it came to drafting the Leo Abse bill – pointed out that the new law applied only to England and Wales. Even worse, in many ways it was more restrictive than what had gone before. For example, the definition of private was such that a locked hotel room was deemed to be a public place and therefore two men in such a situation could still be prosecuted. Worst of all, the people who had pushed reform through made it clear that gay men (and by implication lesbians) should be grateful for what they'd got and should now shut up.

Lord Arran's final statement in Parliament made his feelings plain. 'Homosexuals must continue to remember that, while there may be nothing bad in being a homosexual, there is certainly nothing good,' he argued. He added that legislation or not, homosexuals would continue to be objects of 'dislike, derision and, at best, self-pity'. He had misread the writing on the wall, even though it had been daubed on in five-foot psychedelic letters. The mood of the times was not one of self-pity but of self-celebration.

Peter Burton was running a club called Le Duce in 1967 which was one of the trendiest places to be seen in London. It was filled with young people who were defining what society should be like, regardless of what the law said. 'My generation was not going to be tied down by their laws and their constraints,' he explains. 'So, whether the law changed in 1967 or whether it had to wait till 1977, we would have been like we were at that point in history.' Peter's clientèle at Le Duce included David Hockney and Andy Warhol, as well as straight stars like Rod Stewart (who later employed Peter as his tour manager) and Paul Simon, who used to strum away on his guitar on the club's folk nights. Dislike and derision were not what Peter

PETER BURTON
PICTURED
OUTSIDE LE DUCE,
THE CLUB HE RAN
IN THE SIXTIES

experienced and self-pity about being gay was as alien to him as a gas mask.

The emphasis was on fun, and the first gay magazines which began to be published, soon after the law was changed, had one thing in common – they concentrated on the lighter side of life. There was *Spartacus* and *Jeremy* – of which the latter was the more frivolous. Its glossy pages were filled with pictures of good-looking men, chic clothes that could be bought in Carnaby Street, just a stroll away from the magazine's offices, and the latest movies, carrying stills from Fellini's *Satyricon* and the Hollywood adaptation of Gore Vidal's *Myra Breckinridge*. It even carried stories about the latest in underwear for men, with special offers for those of its readers who wanted to buy some. It was clearly aimed at a young, metropolitan group – the kind of crowd that Peter Burton moved in. Indeed Peter – who had written for *Spartacus* from its second issue onwards – edited *Jeremy* for a while.

The Sixties, as well as being a time of hedonism, were also noted for their head-expanding movements, with a proliferation of single-issue campaigns and the beginnings of grass-roots politics. Many people, emboldened by the change in public attitudes towards gay men and lesbians, formed self-help groups of the sort that had never existed before. The Minorities Rights Group was one such organization which had been set up as early as 1963 by Esme Langley and Diana Chapman. It was notable for being the first explicit and dedicated lesbian social and political organization. By the mid-Sixties, it had reached its high point and subsidiary groups were being set up all over the country.

That was how Barbara Bell came across it. She was living on the south coast at the time, saw an ad for a meeting in London and decided to attend. '[I went] into this seedy pub up a seedy staircase . . . dusty wooden floor and tables that looked awful, but to see all these women who were lesbian . . . was quite a revelation.' The Minorities Rights Group was in a

BARBARA BELL

confident, expansionist phase and wanted regional representatives and Barbara found herself putting her hand up to volunteer to be the representative on the south coast. 'We used to meet in our little house, we'd have parties which was wonderful. It was a cul-de-sac so we weren't disturbing anybody. We told the gay boy on the corner he could come and join us, of course he never did. We didn't really want him but we didn't want anybody to be upset.' And far from being disliked or derided, as Lord Arran had predicted, Barbara found her straight neighbours eager to help: 'The woman was in amateur dramatics and the husband commuted to London every day and they had two little girls. But . . . she saw at once that Joan and I were in a partnership and how much in love we were. So, when we had the parties, she used to say, "Come into my house and I'll make all the puddings." It was lovely having neighbours like that.'

Many gay men and lesbians had always been politically active in other single-issue campaign groups, notably the peace movement, and many of them carried on with this. One of the most prominent activists for the Campaign for Nuclear Disarmament was Pat Arrowsmith, who had been one of the original members, having been one of the prime movers in the Aldermaston March. According to Pat, the peace movement appeared to harbour no prejudices against homosexuality: 'The question of being open about my lesbianism barely arose. Wendy and I were living together and there was no particular reason for stating we were lesbians. We just took for granted that everybody knew we were and I think it's true that anybody who knew us at all did know.'

In her career as a peace campaigner, Pat has been sent to prison eleven times. During the course of it, she noticed the changes in lesbian culture inside Holloway, from a rigid division between butch and femme to a more relaxed attitude. 'On the first of my long sentences in the mid-Sixties . . . the butch-type lesbians would strap back their busts and pad themselves out with mock cocks using sanitary towels for that purpose . . . I can remember looking up to one of the galleries, thinking am I in Wandsworth or Holloway? . . . [It] wasn't always easy to tell what sex a woman was until she spoke, not even necessarily then . . . But when I was in prison for my second six month sentence a couple of years later in the late Sixties, it wasn't that stratified any more – you could see lesbian couples both of whom were dressed as women.'

This shift in emphasis was caused initially by the hippie movement, where jeans and caftans were interchangeable garments to be worn by either sex. This was reinforced by the rise of the Women's Liberation Movement, which told lesbians that they didn't need to dress like men to have power. In any case, being butch all the time was too much of an effort, as Luchia discovered. 'Dressing up in men's clothes, I can assure you, had its advantages because you could leap over a wall, you could run like the blazes . . . But in another context you didn't like it . . . you felt as if you were actually performing to people . . . At the end of the day, when everybody's gone home and there's nobody there, only you, you look in the mirror and what's looking at you is a sort of male version of yourself.'

One day, while she was in the Union bar, Luchia had her conversion from a world where a drink always meant a pint and clothes always meant a suit and tie. Two women walked in who didn't fit either the butch or the femme mould. They had long hair and they had smudges of blue make-up on their eyelids and blouses with small pieces of mirrored glass embroidered

PAT ARROWSMITH
ON HER RELEASE
FROM PRISON IN
MAY 1969

onto them and they smelled of patchouli oil. What's more, instead of seeing the Union as a refuge from a hostile world, they were criticizing it for exploiting a captive clientèle. Luchia was intrigued by their conversation, particularly by the word 'exploited', and asked if she could sit at their table. 'And I said, "Well, I was thinking about what you were saying about land-lords and, you know, what's the word – exploitation? What's exploitation?" So they told me and I said, "You're right, they are exploiting."' It turned out that what Luchia had encountered were two lesbians from the local university who were to pull her into a new milieu.

First, however, they had to effect a transformation on Luchia's dress sense. 'I started to buy myself a nice pair of slip-on sandals, I got myself a nice little pair of bell bottoms. I asked the girls to come and help me to buy one of them little blouses with glasses on and I got right into Janis Joplin.' Luchia also started attending meetings at the local university and familiar-izing herself with the vocabulary of agitprop groups which extended far beyond the word 'exploitation'.

For some lesbians, the Women's Liberation Movement, in its early days, was less welcoming. Angela Mason recalls a particularly hostile response. 'We tried to join Women's Liberation. We sent a letter to the secretary, who was this Maoist, with a postal order for seven shillings and sixpence, and she wrote me back a letter saying that lesbians shouldn't be part of the Women's Liberation Movement and returned my postal order.' Sharley McLean recalls a similarly disagreeable attitude. 'I left several groups of lib-eration-type women because on the whole they could not hack lesbianism. I think they felt threatened . . . in awareness-raising around women's issues you could always tell who were lesbians because they had a far clearer idea . . . on women's rights.'

The hippie movement was not much better when it came to gay men and lesbians. Despite its credo of free love and peace towards all, the atti-tudes of many hippie men were inevitably unreconstructed and gay men got taunted while lesbians were expected to make exceptions when it came to sex. This combination made the time ripe for gay men and lesbians to set up their own organization. The new grouping was to combine the Women's Movement's philosophy, that the personal is political, with the hippie movement's tactics of 'zapping' hostile organizations in a spirit of jovial insolence which gave the press the photo opportunities they wanted. The result was the Gay Liberation Front (GLF).

There were plenty of things that distinguished GLF from all the other campaigning organizations – not least some of its members who went everywhere dressed in radical drag – but the most obvious one was the use of the word 'gay'. Just as the use of the word 'homosexual', at the beginning of the century, had marked a shift in the way gay men and lesbians were perceived, the use of the word 'gay' signified another major change – not only in the way that gay men and lesbians were regarded by society as a whole but, more importantly, how they viewed themselves.

All the words used to describe gay men and lesbians until that point – sodomite, invert, homosexual – either had religious, scientific or legal origins, and then there were all the pejorative slang terms. What was needed was a word which was neither abusive nor clinical. Many attempts had been made to coin such a word. In the nineteenth century a German lawyer, Karl Heinrich Ulrichs, who campaigned for law reform in the German states, came up with the singularly unmellifluous 'urning'. It didn't catch on. At the beginning of this century, Edward Carpenter, the writer and thinker, came up with another neologism. He suggested 'Uranian' – taken from Plato's *Symposium*, in which the Greek philosopher had used the word to describe his theory of an idealized love between men. Although the word acquired a brief currency among Carpenter and his associates, it too fell by the wayside, but when GLF fell upon the word 'gay' it was the obvious choice, not least because it was the term that gay people had already been using to describe themselves.

The origins of the word, as applied to homosexuals, are unclear, but it had certainly been in existence since the nineteenth century. It could have been borrowed from the French, where the word *gaie* meant homosexual – interestingly the feminine form of the word was used to describe males. By the Thirties, 'gay' had become a codeword to describe homosexuality but its use was fairly restricted although it did make a mainstream appearance from time to time as an in-joke. So, for example, in 1936, a Broadway musical called *Bittersweet*, which was a satire on Oscar Wilde and Lord Alfred Douglas, had a line-up of chorus boys singing a song whose refrain was: 'We are the reason for the Nineties being gay.' Similarly, in the 1938 film *Bringing Up Baby*, the character played by Cary Grant – about whom there were many rumours at the time – loses all his clothes and has to wear a borrowed frilly négligée. Exasperated by persistent questions about why he is in that unusual ensemble, he retorts: 'Because I just went gay all of a sudden.'

Certainly by the Fifties, gay had become a common word of self-description by homosexual men and women, most particularly in America where it served the same purpose as Polari did in Britain – a way of communicating without being generally understood. So friends could talk about being gay or advertise for 'gay' roommates where only the right person would understand the real meaning. Donald Webster Cory in his 1951 survey of homosexuality in America wrote: 'Needed for years was an ordinary, everyday, matter-of-fact word that could express the concept of homosexuality without glorification or condemnation. It must have no odium of the effeminate stereotype about it. Such a word has long been in existence and, in recent years, has grown in popularity. The word is "gay".'

The fact that the word was more prevalent in America than in Britain was no impediment to the pioneering gay liberationists on this side of the Atlantic who took all their early inspiration from America. Indeed, gay rights activists in Western Europe all date the beginning of the struggle back to the Stonewall riots in New York when a group of gay men and lesbians fought a pitched battle with the police after years of harassment. To this day, Gay Pride parades across the Western world are timed to coincide with the anniversary of that event.

The Stonewall riots take their name from the bar in Greenwich Village where, on 28 June 1969, a group of gay men and lesbians fought back for the first time in modern history. Police raids were a regular occurrence at the Stonewall – so much so that there was a secret signal to warn customers. The Stonewall, which was run by the Mafia, would often get tip-offs from its contacts in the New York Police Department that a raid was imminent. When this happened or when a plain-clothes officer was suspected of having gained entry, the tinted lights on the dance floor would be switched off and the white lights switched on. These had to be deployed at frequent intervals and any members of the same sex who were dancing together would stop instantly. However this in itself was no protection. The police would still harass anybody who was wearing more than three articles of clothing that could be construed to be garments intended for the opposite sex – this apparently contravened a state law – and most people would be turned out of the bar regardless.

'We are the **Stonewall girls** – we wear our hair in curls; we wear no underwear; we show our pubic hair.'
The battle-cry of the **Stonewall drag queens** as they charged the police

On that night in 1969, the Stonewall was raided as usual, but, as each person was questioned and turned out of the bar, instead of dispersing, they hung around. As the paddy wagons arrived, the mood became angry and missiles rained down on the police who retreated into the bar. Parking

meters were uprooted and hurled into the bar, lighter fluid was squirted in
followed by burning matches. Howard Smith, a reporter from the New
York paper, *Village Voice*, who found himself inside the bar with the police,
reported: 'The sound filtering in [didn't suggest] dancing faggots any more,
it sounded like a powerful rage bent on vendetta.'

The drag queens had discovered that a stiletto could be as powerful a
weapon in the hand as it was decorative on the foot. Thus empowered, they
fought back, tooth and varnished claw. Martin Duberman, in his account
of the events, recalls how, when the police turned up the next night, they
were confronted by more angry drag queens – all dressed to kill. They had
their arms round each other's waists and proceeded to high-kick their way
towards the police lines, chanting: 'We are the Stonewall girls, we wear our
hair in curls, we wear no underwear, we show our pubic hair.' What had
happened was that gay men and lesbians suddenly discovered that they did-
n't have to put up with the harassment. Even during the course of the
Stonewall riots, this lesson was not as obvious as it seems. Duberman
describes how 'some hundred people were being chased . . . by two cops,
someone in the crowd suddenly realized the unequal odds and started
yelling: "There are only two of 'em! Catch 'em!" . . . As the crowd took up
the cry, the two officers fled.'

Symbolically, the riots began on the night of Judy Garland's funeral.
Garland had been the archetypal gay icon because she represented bravery
through adversity, but that bravery was characterized by a passive stoicism.
With the death of Judy Garland, that image of the gay man died too. The

beat poet, Allen Ginsberg, expressed it thus: 'You know those guys were so beautiful – they've lost that wounded look that all fags had ten years ago.'

What the clientèle of the Stonewall had done was express their anger; there was no planning or political agenda behind it, but interested onlookers saw how it could be used to spark off the last of the Sixties revolutions and people like Ginsberg hurried down to Greenwich Village. The decade had been marked by grass-roots agitation, starting with the civil rights movement, followed by the student revolution and the Women's Liberation Movement. Many gay men and lesbians who had been active in one or more of these other movements saw their chance. Within twenty-four hours, political slogans were appearing on the boarded-up windows of the Stonewall which read, among other things, 'Support Gay Power'. The following day another notice appeared on the Stonewall windows. It read: 'We homosexuals plead with our people to please help maintain peaceful and quiet conduct on the streets of the Village. Mattachine.'

The Mattachine Society had been going for a number of years and represented professional gay men and lesbians who wanted to lobby for equal rights by proving that they were no different from heterosexuals except in their sexual preferences. The Mattachine Society advice to its members when going out on pickets and demonstrations was that men should don white shirts, suits and ties and women should appear in skirts and dresses. Both sexes should wear glasses, if they had them, to give an added air of authority. While the Mattachine Society had done some good work in the past, its tactics were rooted in an era when respectability was what gay men and lesbians craved. What was beginning to emerge was a conflict between older, staider gay men and lesbians and their younger, angrier counterparts. Exactly the same conflict was to show itself when the Gay Liberation Front unfurled its banners in Britain.

The Stonewall riots were described by one American observer as 'the hairpin drop heard around the world', and young gay men and lesbians in Britain heard the reverberations loud and clear. In the years after law reform, police harassment was on the rise again and the gay voice was largely ineffectual. The Homosexual Law Reform Society was running out of steam. Plans to set up a series of social clubs around the country came to nothing and there seemed to be lack of direction. The North West branch of the Homosexual Law Reform Society, which had always been more adventurous, renamed itself the Committee for Homosexual Equality (CHE, later renamed the Campaign for Homosexual Equality), which, like the Mattachine Society in America, believed in doing things properly and, also like the Mattachine Society, it found itself in conflict with Britain's emergent Gay Liberation Front.

The first and most obvious difference between the Committee for Homosexual Equality and the Gay Liberation Front was one of semantics. The gay liberationists felt that to accept the word 'homosexual' as a self-definition meant also accepting all the baggage that went with it. The word 'homosexual' was clinical in a literal sense – it was a word that had emerged from and belonged in psychiatrists' clinics. More importantly, it was a word that defined a sexual category, whereas the word 'gay' defined a lifestyle. It might seem a trivial distinction but it mattered enormously, not only to gay men and lesbians but to heterosexuals too.

Soon after GLF began to make waves, British newspapers began to get upset about their use of the word 'gay'. The *People* ran a story about gay men and lesbians with the headline: 'They Call This Gay – But We Have Another Word For It – Ugh'. There was a stream of readers' letters about the hijacking of the word gay. In the early Seventies, the *Daily Telegraph*, the *Sunday Telegraph* and the *Observer* all ran letters in their correspondence columns on the issue. The general complaint was that a perfectly good English word had been misappropriated. The newly revolutionized gay men and lesbians responded by saying that plenty of other good English words – like fairy and pansy – had also been misappropriated, but nobody seemed to be complaining about them. The correspondence in the *Observer* finally came to a halt when a certain Nick Rogers wrote the following: 'It is not up to her [the previous correspondent] as a heterosexual to decide how we should describe ourselves. It is up to us to produce a description and she can like it or lump it. Why should we accept what she deems . . . to be "dignified" . . . or are we also allowed to define her identity and lay down that from now on all heterosexuals should call themselves "giraffes"?'

This jokey impertinence was typical of GLF's tactics which were transported to Britain in 1970 – by students and staff at the London School of Economics, one of the most radical campuses in Britain. During the summer of 1970, Aubrey Walter, who had just finished his sociology degree, took himself off to the States, having read about the Gay Liberation Front in *The Times*. While demonstrating in New York, he came across Bob Mellors, who was at the London School of Economics. Back in Britain, at the end of the summer, Bob Mellors and Aubrey Walter decided to hold a meeting to test out the water. Accordingly, on 13 October 1970, the first meeting of the British branch of GLF took place in a basement seminar room at the London School of Economics. That first meeting was attended by fewer than twenty people and most of whom were students or staff at the London School of Economics, but over the next few months, as the core group went round London, handing out leaflets, the attendance at meetings burgeoned.

> '*It was* **instant** *transformation. I stepped out of a three-piece suit, and into a frock. And that was it.*'
>
> **Michael James** on becoming a radical drag queen

For many gay men, like Michael James, GLF articulated what they had been feeling, but couldn't quite express. Michael, who had been living in London and frequenting the commercial gay scene, felt that 'they actually gave words to our feelings and experiences . . . it was almost as if somebody had cracked open our heads and allowed other parts of our consciousness to blossom out and start asking questions.' GLF's approach to rigid gender distinctions was radical drag. This differed from conventional drag in that it wasn't female impersonation – men with moustaches would varnish their nails and flounce around in dresses with handbags hanging from the crooks of their elbows. They knew that this would be shocking at first but that was the idea. The hope was that, after the initial indignation wore off, it would make people think about sex roles and why a piece of fabric should carry so much significance. Radical drag was something that Michael took to with alacrity. 'It was instant transformation. I stepped out of a three-piece suit and into a frock and that was it.'

GLF was just as much of an eye-opener for the lesbians who joined it. Juno Jones, who had earlier in her life joined the Carmelite nuns as a postulant,

MICHAEL JAMES

JUNO JONES
IN 1974

JUNO JONES
IN 1974

came across an article about GLF in a discarded copy of the *Daily Mirror* and decided to go along to one of the meetings which were held in a cavernous venue in Covent Garden called Middle Earth. 'I made about four or five attempts and eventually I went inside . . . and there were guys with sequins in their beards and lots of patchouli oil in the air and flowing robes . . . it was just astonishing. It really was like dipping your toe in magic,' she recalls.

Like Michael James, Juno found that GLF shifted perspectives so that her world view was now proud rather than apologetic. More importantly, she recognized that anything was possible. 'It was like somebody had taken my brain out of my head, washed out all the crap and put it back in,' she says. 'It's like trying to describe what an orgasm is. You can't describe what an orgasm is and I can't really . . . put into words what it was like for me. It was just mind-blowing. It was like the top of your head zips open and powwww!'

Most of GLF's founding members had come from other political groupings which were informed by Marxist politics, and it was one of GLF's central tenets that, by transforming the individual, society would be transformed. All mainstream *modi vivendi* came under scrutiny, from the nuclear family to private property and personal incomes. For those who were committed to GLF, the logical next step was to move into a commune with other GLF people and Michael James put his best high-heeled foot forward.

Julian Hows, who was sixteen at the time, also turned up at GLF meetings and, like Michael and Juno, felt immediately at one with what was happening. By this time, young gay men had two role models available to them – the one offered by many members of CHE which represented a distorted reflection of the heterosexual family or the GLF model. Julian was very clear which one he wanted. 'There was the whole thing in the early Seventies of homosexuals having to be respectable . . . Joe and Joe having their nice business suits and their nice 2.4 dogs and their nice little house and all the rest of it. We were there to show there was more to it than that, and if people couldn't accept whatever we were wearing and whatever we were doing then, quite frankly, it's not a sort of acceptance I wanted. That still holds true to this day. There are people wandering around saying, "If only homosexuals behaved responsibly and respectably," and, frankly, I don't want to know.'

Like Michael, Julian decided to move into a GLF commune and ended up, after a brief sojourn at a place from which they were evicted, at a former film studio in Notting Hill Gate. The building, just off Colville Terrace, became known as Colvillia. It consisted of one huge room, with a toilet and a kitchen off it. The main room, which had a gallery running along one side, is described by Julian as a 'medieval hall' and, like a medieval hall, it was used for living in, sleeping in and – most important of all – for getting dressed up in. At one end of the hall was a wall with a gap in it which was perfect as a walk-in wardrobe. All the frocks were shared, and so was all the money which was kept in a Clarice Cliff teapot. The communards would put any money they earned or received in benefit into this piece of art deco pottery and everyone would take what they needed. When things got difficult, David Hockney and his lover, who lived round the corner, would send food parcels or ask the communards to tea.

Surprisingly, among all the anarchy, there was a routine. Not having any hot water of their own, Saturday night was when they indulged themselves with a hot bath followed by an LSD trip. 'A friend of ours who lived in Kensington had this lovely bathroom and we'd go over in groups from three o'clock in the afternoon . . . the first group [back] would start preparing the dinner and there'd be big glass bowls of jellies and sweets and we'd drop our tab of acid, and put our music on and we'd trip the night away until seven o'clock the next morning when we'd stagger down to the newsagents in our high heels and distressed make-up to get the Sunday papers,' says Michael James.

It wasn't all jellies and jolly japes, there was serious work to be done. The nature of this work was to confront prejudice and pomposity wherever it existed, and during its brief reign GLF came up with some of the most imaginative demonstrations in the history of the gay liberation movement. GLF zaps exploded over London like a bomb filled with satin and sequins. What distinguished them from anything else that had gone before was their theatricality, their unashamed chutzpah and, of course, the presence of the radical drag queens.

Although there were numerous demonstrations, and in the case of the communards, every step into the outside world was a form of demonstration, the most notable being the one mounted against the Festival of Light. In May 1971, two ex-missionaries set up the Festival of Light to counter what they regarded as the moral pollution that had confronted them on their return to Britain. The organization quickly gained an enormous influence, with Cliff Richard, Mary Whitehouse, Lord Longford and Bishop Trevor Huddleston joining its board. Within a few months, the Festival of Light had become a national organization and announced plans for a huge rally in London which would compel the government to act against the 'forces of evil' as they described it. The manifestations of this evil, as cited by the Festival of Light, were Ken Russell films, sex outside marriage and the growth of open homosexuality.

This was the kind of challenge GLF was waiting for. One of the leading lights in GLF, John Chesterman, organized the event with impeccable élan. The first task was to infiltrate the organization, and one of the GLF women volunteered to work in the Festival of Light's main office, from where she filched mailing lists. These were used to send out fake mailings and misleading parking plans for coaches that were bringing Festival of Light members to their rally in Central Hall in Westminster. The most important acquisition, however, was tickets for the rally, which GLF then forged in such large numbers that there were enough to hand around to anyone who wanted to go. An early form of networking was employed and other sympathetic groups like members of the Women's Liberation Movement were brought in to join in the disruption.

Chesterman co-ordinated it so that everyone was split up into small groups and asked to come up with an inventive form of disruption. No one was aware of the complete battle plan, they only knew what the group before them was going to do. When the previous group had finished, it was the cue for the next group to do their stuff, and so on, in a chain of events that was to burst like so many water bombs over the heads of the people in the hall. In her history of GLF, Lisa Power quotes from a note handed out by Chesterman to each group. It reads: 'Enter the hall in small groups. Ones or twos. Act unobtrusively. Dress conservatively. Act cool. Make no sign of protest until it is your turn. Do not speak to each other. Sit as close to the centre of the row as possible. Let the previous demonstration finish completely before you start yours. Let everyone settle down and the speeches start again. Part of the purpose is to slow down and delay proceedings . . . Offer passive resistance only. Do not fight back. A general brawl will only confuse the media image. If there is any aggression, let them look like the villain in the press reports. Do not carry anything that could be construed as an offensive weapon . . . You may be arrested so make any arrangements . . . beforehand. Make no statements to the police until you

GAY ACTIVISTS
MARCH PAST
THE COLEHERNE
PUBLIC HOUSE IN
EARLS COURT

GAY ACTIVISTS
MARCH PAST
THE COLEHERNE
PUBLIC HOUSE IN
EARLS COURT

have legal assistance. They cannot force you to do so. Do not speak to the press or TV.'

A number of participants went one better when advised to dress conservatively – they came dressed as clerics and nuns. 'Men really sacrificed their long hair, they got their long hair cut off and had short backs and sides,' recalls Juno Jones. 'They wore suits and ties which had us on the floor laughing because we'd never seen them looking so straight.'

Michael James decided to wear a beige lace dress with pearl buttons and a voluminous lacy skirt – but under suitable disguise: 'We all met at the Embankment . . . and I had my evening dress stuffed underneath my suit, with a little bag of make-up and heels and a wig, and we got to Westminster Hall and dotted ourselves all the way around and the proceedings started.'

The first event was the release of white mice which scurried down the aisle almost as if they were clockwork toys, but the two women who released the rodents didn't escape lightly – one of them was repeatedly hit over the head with a handbag by a woman who kept shouting, 'Jesus loves you.' Then two old ladies sitting in the balcony unfurled a banner saying, 'Cliff for Queen.' Then the 'nuns' started. They consisted of a group of men and women who until then had stayed quietly in their seats, but when their cue arrived they rose as one, walked to the front and started doing the can-can.

Michael's cue was Bette Bourne – a trained actor who later started up the theatre troupe Bloolips – who was sitting on the other side of the aisle dressed like a Blimpish colonel. 'Bette has got this absolutely fabulous voice and people were being really manhandled very badly by the stewards – you know beaten and kicked, that's Christians for you – and Bette said, "This is not right," and this wonderful voice resonated throughout the hall . . . "People are being injured here, this is not right. We're supposed to be Christians. I see a steward there hitting somebody." Course they twigged that Bette was part of the demo and shoved her out.' Finally it was Michael's turn.

'By this time they'd wheeled Malcolm Muggeridge up to the microphone and he was wittering away about this, that and the other. So I gave him two or three minutes to get into his stride and then I thought now or never. I just stood up in the back in this lovely coffee-coloured frock and screamed, "Hallelujah! I've been saved," and went into the whole southern belle trip – "I've seen the light, I've seen the Lord," and of course they couldn't get to me. They had to empty the row either side and I was just standing there proclaiming the Word. Eventually they got to us and I just sort of drifted this frock over everybody as I was going down the stairs proclaiming my love for Jesus.'

Finally, it was time for the *pièce de résistance* which involved GLF people, dressed as members of Ku Klux Klan, standing up to demand 'perverts' be burnt at the stake. Afterwards, the protesters stood outside to hand out leaflets and discuss the issues with any Festival of Light members who cared to. The event was given wide coverage in the national press who found GLF enlivened what would otherwise have been very dull stories. There were dozens of other such demonstrations but the disruption of the Festival of Light rally exemplified GLF's approach to campaigning,

Branches of GLF were being set up outside London and Luchia Fitzgerald was introduced to the Manchester offshoot of it by the women she had met in the Union. Although she didn't understand all the political rhetoric, she knew she had found a way of living that would make her happy. But she had to deal with all the baffling jargon in some way. 'I went out and bought a dictionary and every night when I heard a new word at these meetings I would go home and I would open the dictionary and have a look for the word and so a whole new vocabulary was opening up to me.'

It wasn't all talk and no action. Like their London counterparts, the Manchester group were activists first and foremost. Luchia remembers going out with a pot of yellow paint one night and daubing "Lesbians Are Everywhere" on the most prominent surfaces she could find in the city. 'It went up on every bridge in and out of the city – north, south, east and west – and you should have seen it the next morning, the traffic all jammed up against one another, sitting there staring at "Lesbians Are Everywhere".'

'The lads from **GLF** were very contradictory. They were very loud in the meetings – they always wanted to chair the meetings.'

Luchia Fitzgerald on the problems within GLF

This wasn't to last long. GLF was a rainbow coalition and after a while the differences began to show. There had always been small rifts – between the women and the men – between those who espoused radical drag and those who didn't – but after a few years, those rifts widened into chasms. The gaps loomed as women felt that the men were not even interested in listening to them, let alone joining them in their fight.

'The lads from GLF were very contradictory,' Luchia explains. 'They were very loud in the meetings, they always wanted to chair the meetings. They were very butch, if you will, and we felt that they didn't have an understanding of our sexuality. They were very reluctant to share jobs and to share power and so we were fighting a battle within a battle.'

Juno Jones recalls that even though there had been divisions, the split took her aback. 'It came as quite a surprise to me when it actually happened but in retrospect I had to agree with what happened,' she explains. 'It was really the attitude of the men, just because they were gay men didn't mean that they weren't men and they basically treated us like shit. . . . The women were getting more involved in Women's Liberation by that stage and our consciousness was changing more into wanting to separate from the men because we had completely different issues. We had a different agenda by that stage like equal pay for women, wages for housework, why should women look after the children, why should women do the clearing up.'

The women involved in the London branches of GLF – still the largest and most influential in the country – were feeling much the same and now they had an alternative. The early hostility of the Women's Liberation Movement had dissipated after a group of GLF activists went up to Skegness for the Women's Liberation National Co-ordinating Conference. Initially, they were told that they were a 'bourgeois deviation', but GLF women were not

going to be put off so easily. They seized the microphone and led a grass-roots revolt which changed the tenor of the conference and put lesbianism firmly on the feminist agenda. That was in October 1971, and by the following February, women had walked out of GLF announcing that they wanted to work separately.

On 1 July 1972, when Britain's first Gay Pride parade took place, the women returned, wearing wonderful face paint, and marched under a banner reading 'Gay Women's Liberation'. The radical drag queens got decked out in fabulous frocks and the single-issue activists came as they were. The trouble was, the groups barely spoke to each other or, worse, they argued. 'The divisions were so deep that it could never have been reconciled although it did paddle along for a couple of months after that, but once the women split and the drag queens split that was it – you know, the final thing,' Michael James explains.

The demise of GLF has as much to do with a change in society as with the inherent tensions within it. GLF was an essentially Sixties organization with its emphasis on the counterculture, its suspicion of hierarchies, its opposition to capitalism and its emphasis on the individual. By the early Seventies, that approach was beginning to die off, along with the rest of the Sixties counterculture. In all, GLF had lasted for less than four years, but its influence extended far beyond its short life. During the heady days, when nobody saw beyond the next demonstration and the biggest dilemma was what you were going to wear to it, GLF members could hardly have foreseen how far-reaching their actions would be. With hindsight it has become clear.

Not only did GLF start off Britain's Gay Pride parades – which have taken place in an unbroken chain for the last twenty-four years – but it was also the catalyst for Britain's first national gay newspaper – *Gay News* was started up as a joint initiative between GLF members and CHE. Finally, GLF was also responsible for establishing a help and information line – Gay Switchboard. Indeed, when the GLF office in King's Cross closed down, it was handed on as a present to Gay Switchboard which has gone from strength to strength since then. *Gay News* soon cut itself off from its radical roots and established itself as a non-partisan, middle-of-the-road newspaper. Even though major distributors like W H Smith refused to carry the paper in the early stages, within four years it had established a circulation of 20,000 which made it the largest circulation newspaper for homosexuals in the world. In 1977 it gained even greater fame when Mary Whitehouse brought a private prosecution against the paper under blasphemy laws which had remained dormant for so long everybody thought they were defunct. Gay men and lesbians – even those that disagreed with the editorial stance that *Gay News* had adopted – rallied around staging fundraising events and

benefits to help pay the enormous costs of the court action so that the paper's future could be secured. Peter Burton, who was working for *Gay News* at this time, believes it might have even done *Gay News* some good: 'Dear Mrs Whitehouse found this [a poem published by *Gay News*] offensive and . . . took a private prosecution for blasphemous libel against *Gay News*, thereby doing the publication a great kindness, because she made us international news. Really, it was a big world-wide story,

A 1977 DEMONSTRATION AGAINST THE CONVICTION OF *GAY NEWS* FOR BLASPHEMOUS LIBEL

thereby raising our visibility, raising the readership, letting lots of lonely people, who didn't know we existed, know [that we were there]. We couldn't buy publicity like she gave *Gay News* and gays generally.'

GLF's highly visible campaigning of the early Seventies had another effect which is far more difficult to quantify – it taught gay men and lesbians not to be fearful and to ask for what they wanted. It seems that what they wanted was hedonism. What characterized gay culture throughout the rest of the Seventies was the pursuit of pleasure. The number of gay clubs, pubs and restaurants grew with such speed that it was difficult to keep pace. Gay men no longer wanted to demonstrate – they wanted to dance, and disco was the beat that they wanted to dance to.

Just as house music, which was to fuel the dance boom of the Nineties, began in small black gay clubs in Chicago, disco was born in the black gay clubs of Manhattan. The deejays in these clubs came up with a fusion of the Philly sound and traditional soul by phasing them in and out, creating a pulsating wall of sound. This was picked up by white gay clubs and soon it became the hippest sound of the moment, eventually crossing over when singers like Gloria Gaynor and Donna Summer, who had until then only been heard in gay clubs, began to have mainstream success. The group Village People camped it up with their hit 'YMCA', which they performed wearing outfits that were caricatures from gay erotica – sailor, soldier, fireman and Native American chief. The apogee of disco came when the 1977 film *Saturday Night Fever* swept all before it at the box office and the soundtrack provided hit after hit on both sides of the Atlantic.

Michael James, who went to live in Amsterdam after the demise of GLF, came back to Britain for a holiday and was astonished at the change. 'We [GLF] burst open the gates and everything else was allowed to follow through from that,' he explains. 'I came back for a fortnight's holiday and I was just amazed . . . [they] were out of the dingy venues into really good venues with good music, proper bars and the atmosphere there was wonderful and relaxed.'

Disco music and gay clubs became chic places to go to, and everybody wanted to be there as huge gay discos like Bang opened their doors. Peter Burton recalls: 'I worked on the door from the first night, doing memberships and [when new people came] Pat the doorman used to say, "Do you know what kind of club this is?" and I'd just leap from behind my desk and say, "Oh Mr Warhol, do come in, it's absolutely free for you and your 500 friends." And Rock Hudson, and Rod Stewart, and Elton and all those people used to come because it was something so unusual.'

America, which had always been the source of inspiration for British gay culture, once again provided British gay men with a new look – the clone.

BANG IN 1977 –
THEN LONDON'S
LARGEST GAY
CLUB

BANG IN 1977 –
THEN LONDON'S
LARGEST GAY
CLUB

The availability of cheap flights to New York, courtesy of Freddie Laker who was undercutting the major airlines with his own fleet of aircraft, meant that many gay men nipped over to New York to see for themselves and when they came back they were carrying a new look in their baggage. 'In the mid- to late Seventies the gay uniform was imported from the States and it was the clone look,' says Julian Hows. 'You know, the little 'tash, the white T-shirt, the Levi 501s although quite frankly that wasn't really me – at most I became a fluffy disco bunny.'

But there were plenty of other gay men who fell for the clone look hook, line and sinker. Derek Ogg, remembers that the style – which might have been at home in San Francisco was deeply unsuited for the less balmy environments of Scotland but in Edinburgh, gay men followed it to the minutest detail nonetheless. 'People were wearing hard construction helmets and cut-off jeans and work boots with rolled down socks and skimpy T-shirts in Scotland, in a climate which even in the summertime is pretty appalling . . . some people call Edinburgh the Athens of the North but I call it the Reykjavik of the South,' he jokes. 'It's a terrible place to dress like that but that was what the fashion was and that was the culture. So many of us became clones and we all had a moustache even people who looked ridiculous in moustaches had a moustache.'

The American influence was so pervasive that it dominated gay culture throughout the West. Gay men danced to American disco music and gay bars and clubs were decorated in a style which emulated their transatlantic counterparts – with American signs and posters on the walls and names like Copacabana, Fire Island or Key West.

Derek remembers how Edinburgh's most prominent gay club, Fire Island and its patrons whole-heartedly embraced this approach. 'What was going on in that disco – the music, the people, the fun and the attitude – it could have been New York City, it could have been Los Angeles or San Francisco. It could have been Paris or Amsterdam or anywhere in London. It was pure American . . . culture with a brash self-confidence and self-expression,' Derek explains. 'We felt international, we felt being gay was a passport to anywhere in the world.'

The reason for this slavish adulation was that America seemed to represent a land of hope and freedom for European gays. When the Stonewall queens hitched up their skirts and fought, they had shown their European counterparts that it was possible to resist and win. But the lesson didn't stop there. Within ten years of Stonewall, America had demonstrated that it was possible to develop a gay culture which was complete, self-contained and self-promoting. Like their American counterparts, British gay men and lesbians were forming a culture where it was no longer necessary to persuade society that it was okay to be gay – life had moved beyond that. American gay men and lesbians demonstrated that by acting together, they could garner economic and political power that hadn't been dreamt off till then. In San Francisco, for instance, gay men and lesbians were beginning to win political office and the Castro district had established itself as an enclave where gay men and lesbians could live and work in surroundings that matched their own values.

Unsurprisingly, many British gay men and lesbians wanted to go and have a look for themselves. They were helped no end by Freddie Laker with his cheap, no-frills flights to the United States.

'I don't think he [Freddy Laker] knows how many young gay guys he flew virginally across the Atlantic to America to be absolutely stunned and astonished by the scene they saw over there,' says Derek Ogg. 'They brought back from the States a lot of the music and a lot of the attitudes, a lot of politics and a lot of the social dynamics of the American gay scene. We were to learn we also brought something else back with us.' But that 'something else' didn't rear its monstrous head for a few years to come. In the meantime clubbing seemed to be emblematic of the gay way of life – certainly as far as men were concerned. While it is easy to dismiss this as pure hedonism, the reality was more complicated. Only a few years earlier, gay men and lesbians had had to make do with dingy little bars and dank basements where only relatively small numbers could gather. Dancing was a hugely symbolic activity – after all innumerable gay meeting places had been prosecuted only a few years before because they had allowed members of the same sex to dance together.

'We were able . . . to access the whole vibrant optimism and sheer confidence that went with large numbers of gay people . . . it had never happened in history and people today don't understand this,' Derek Ogg explains. 'It had never happened that you could walk into a room – 300, 500, 1,000 people all with the same sexual orientation, all loving being there, all there because they wanted to be there creating a fabulous environment.'

In addition to the imported clone look, there was an indigenous gay look in Britain which owed much to the radical drag queens of GLF. Although it was sanitized and depoliticized, in essence it was based on the same principles of gender-bending. The most prominent exponent of it was David Bowie who would strut on to stage, wearing high heels and make-up to roars of approval from the crowd. Although straight Bowie fans far outnumbered the gay ones, the very fact that he was up there, camping it up and leaning lasciviously against another man gave many young gay men the encouragement to be who they wanted, in a way that they could never have done in the past.

> '**We had to get Rod Stewart and Ronnie Wood out of the bar and into the lift, away from the red-necks who thought they were queer.**'
>
> **Peter Burton** on the problems encountered by heterosexual pop stars in the American Midwest

Pop stars – whether gay, straight or bisexual – began to flirt with gender-bending because of the element of instant rebellion and sexual frisson it provided. It started with Mick Jagger wearing a frock at the free concert in Hyde Park, but by the Seventies it became more and more overt. Peter Burton, who was Rod Stewart's tour manager, recalls that this made things rather difficult when they were in the Bible Belt. 'Rod and the band had the satin and the feather boa and sequins and the camp tat look which could be problematic particularly touring America . . . In one instance – God knows where, Phoenix, Arizona or somewhere – we were in a bar in a hotel and we had to get Rod Stewart and Ronnie Wood out of the bar and into the lift, away from the red-necks who thought that they were queer. Yet myself and the other person who were [homosexual] were perfectly all right because we weren't dressed like rock-and-roll singers. There were other people, like Marc Bolan and Mick Jagger, who were also doing it. Then there were bands, like Sweet and Mud, who were using it entirely as a commercial aid to rather mundane careers and they're not really remembered for anything – except looking like brickies in drag, I suppose.'

While Stewart, Bolan and Jagger would put on the odd androgynous garment, the leading exponent of frock rock was David Bowie. His trademark was constant transformation, and in the early Seventies he started cultivating an image which was more and more androgynous and would hint at bisexuality in interviews given at the time. One of his biographers asserts that the *Aladdin Sane* album, which pictured Bowie on the cover wearing full make-up, was originally going to be called 'Love Aladin Vein', which would have given rather a different secondary meaning to the punning title.

Young gay men got the message, even though it had been diluted. Tony Sayonas, who was a teenager in Liverpool at the time, remembers it well. 'I turned on the telly and he's on . . . singing "Star Man" – I remember me Mum and me grandmother being there, right, and like seeing this guy [Bowie] with make-up and stuff like that and suddenly he put his arm around this other guy and my heart nearly came through my chest. I thought, this is unbelievable and something snapped in me. And then when I started getting things in the paper, stuff like his bisexuality . . . I thought, my God, there's someone I can look up to . . . it filled me with hope, it really did . . . If I ever did get to meet him, which I doubt, I'd just say, "Thanks very much," you know.'

The next thing that Tony discovered was *Gay News*. 'I remember first putting my hands on this thing and reading it from cover to cover, over and over and over,' he recalls. 'This is my world . . . I'm not alone here, there's millions of us – it was a boost, it was just fantastic.'

However, the Seventies weren't all about partying, the politics was going on in the background, but was very much drowned out by the music. After GLF fizzled out in a flurry of rows and recriminations, CHE was left to battle on in its own way. Having emerged from the North-West Homosexual Law Reform Society, it spent much of its earlier years based in Manchester, but by 1977, it had acquired an office in London. There were 120 groups around the country, with a total membership of 5,000 who met on a social basis, and it had set up a counselling service called Friend. It operated as a social grouping at a local level while the central headquarters acted as a pressure group.

Its main efforts were still directed to the anomalies of the 1967 Act: the odd definition of 'private', the fact that the age of consent was higher than that for heterosexuals and that Scotland and Northern Ireland were still outside the remit of the act. In 1975, CHE, along with the Scottish Minorities Group and the Union for Sexual Freedom in Ireland, submitted a draft bill to Parliament which set out the following reforms: equalizing the age of consent for all; extending law reform to Scotland and Northern Ireland; equal freedom with heterosexuals to express affection in public (two members of the same sex holding hands in public is still technically an offence); and the removal of sanctions against gay and lesbian relationships in the armed forces. Although there was favourable coverage in the media, Parliament sidelined the initiative. Interestingly, twelve years later, Parliament has only acceded to one of these points and the other three remain as relevant now as they were then.

CHE had strong links with Scotland which had not benefited in any way from the 1967 Act. Law reform had only applied to England and Wales and not to Scotland which had a separate legal system. In 1969, a small group of people had set up the Scottish Minorities Group (SMG) but progresses was painfully slow. By the mid-Seventies there was a tacit agreement that the Scottish police would not pursue any prosecutions that would not have been pursued by their counterparts in England and Wales but that was hardly the point. The law, as it stood, outlawed all sexual acts between men of any age. It was an absurd situation. Derek Ogg, a young lawyer who had just begun his career in Edinburgh found it odd 'being told by everyone and every book I looked at that I was a criminal as long as I was in Scotland. I remember a famous Tory MP of the time saying it was ridiculous this anomaly [existed] between England and Scotland. There was a quote by him in the House of Commons saying "what are they meant to do these buggers on ... a sleeper to Scotland from London? Is the conductor supposed to blow the whistle at Carlisle?" . . . and it was as ridiculous as that . . . that over the border it was legal but here it was illegal.'

The situation was so patently inequitable that when it became clear the government wasn't going to co-operate, Scottish gay activists decided to challenge its position in the European Court. The outcome was never in doubt, it would just take a little bit longer. Accordingly three members of Scottish gay rights organisations – including Derek – put themselves forward as the individuals in whose names the action would.be brought.

The procedure was time-consuming and tedious but the case passed successfully through its preliminary phase in the European Court and the British government realized that unless a concession was made, it was facing a long and expensive battle whose outcome was obvious – defeat. It

POLICE RAID ON
A PRIVATE HOMO-
SEXUAL SAUNA,
JANUARY 1977

POLICE RAID ON A PRIVATE HOMOSEXUAL SAUNA, JANUARY 1977

decided to do the expedient thing and a tacit agreement was reached that it would not oppose law reform in Scotland. But it had to be done with a certain amount of parliamentary subterfuge. The vehicle was to be the Criminal Justice Bill of 1979 and the tactic was to propose an amendment to it late at night when it had a greater chance of getting through.

'We got Robin Cooke [a Labour MP for Scotland at the time] who was one of the vice-presidents of our organisation to [propose] . . . the amendment clause quite late at night in a sitting of the House of Commons. I think it was about eleven o'clock at night,' recalls Derek Ogg. 'It got through by a whisker and there were huge cries of foul about the way it was done . . . but it was through and we suddenly had a Bill which created equality in our law. And it was a triumph.'

Indeed Scotland nearly got itself a law which was more liberally phrased than the 1967 Act which governed sexual acts between men in England and Wales. Derek Ogg, who had drafted the clause had made an oversight. While the 1967 Act referred specifically to sexual acts between two men, the law that applied to Scotland referred only to men without specifying a number.

'I never was a very good drafter and I forgot to put in the clause. It was a genuine mistake,' explains Derek. ' . . . I remember Denis Lemon [then editor of *Gay News*] came up after we had it passed in the Commons . . . and I said . . . "By the way we're better than you in England because . . . we don't have it limited to two people" . . . and what did he do? He went down and the next edition of *Gay News* had plastered as a headline [something along the lines of] MPs PASS ORGY LAW . . . Of course the Bill hadn't passed through all its stages in Parliament, it still had to go to the House of Lords which was its final place. So the Lord Advocate of the day who was the chief law officer of Scotland called me in . . . I was a young solicitor at the time, very overawed and he sat me down with a Crown Agent sitting there and he said, in that lovely sort of Scots accent of his . . . "Now Derek, I'm sure this is completely an oversight," holding a copy of *Gay News* in front of him. "I'm sure you always intended [it] to be between two men in the Bill?" And I said "Yes, Lord Advocate, yes, Lord Advocate." He said "So you'll have no objection if we propose a friendly amendment in the House of Lords"?'

During this period in England and Wales, CHE continued its efforts. In 1976, it backed three unfair dismissal cases where individuals had been fired from their jobs because of their sexuality. It went on to organize the first gay and lesbian trade union conference in 1977, in which representatives from forty different unions took part. By this time, at CHE's instigation, the three main political parties also had gay organizations lobbying for change from within the party structure.

Given that GLF was mainly a metropolitan movement, many people who wanted to get involved in gay politics found that CHE was their only option. This was Sharley McLean's experience. 'I was never able to go along to their [GLF's] meetings but I had friends who would tell me and it was great to know that they were there and, of course, CHE came at more or less the same time and because CHE had local groups it was much easier for me to join in. That's what I did eventually and I became campaign manager.' However, CHE was largely a male-dominated organization,

DEREK OGG
AT PRIDE 1996

although it had made a small concession by campaigning for a change in the judicial approach to custody cases which mainly affected lesbians. As had happened with GLF, lesbians had deserted CHE for what they perceived as its lack of stress on the issues that concerned them. Not only was the CHE membership overwhelmingly male, the organization's main campaigning thrust was towards law reform which mainly affected gay men.

However, Sharley decided to stay because she believed the best way to effect change was to stay and fight for it: 'When I joined CHE there were quite a number of lesbians involved. Then there was a breakaway because they felt the men didn't take on board lesbian issues – I felt it was running out. I felt that those men were victims of culture as much as heterosexuals were and that they had to learn. By running away, I felt we were letting them down. I know the attitude was let them find out for themselves, but I felt it was important that somebody was there to actually put the lesbian point of view and I think it paid off, it really paid off.'

What was certainly paying off, in terms of changing opinions, was the combination of GLF's shock tactics and CHE's more reasoned approach. The former had put the gay issue in front of people's faces in a way that could not be ignored, and, when GLF fell apart, CHE could capitalize on the fact that the issue had been put on the national agenda. A measure of how far things had moved came towards the end of the Seventies when a tabloid wrote a progressive piece on gay men – the same tabloid that had vilified them not so long ago. In March 1977, the *Sunday Mirror* ran a double-page spread on the new gay visibility which was so positive it could have been published in *Gay News*. It profiled five men who represented different aspects of this new-found respectability and included a clergyman, a politician, a social worker and an actor. It also ran a piece on *Gay News* and its editor Denis Lemon. The introduction to the profiles reads: 'For some the subject is strictly taboo. From others it provokes sniggers and embarrassed jokes. But like it or not the speed with which homosexuals – or "gays" as they prefer to be known – have organized themselves is nothing short of a social revolution. Yet ten years ago homosexuality was outlawed in Britain. Today there are homosexual campaign groups, political societies, trade union groups and a gay newspaper. There are clubs, discos and phone-in organizations which will help members find anything from a gay pub to a gay plumber. And more and more people are "coming out" which in gay language means admitting in public they are homosexual . . . the gays are probably Britain's most powerful and vocal minority group.'

As the Seventies progressed, gay politics and music began to meet at some points. Punk music, whose essential ethos was to gob on everything that society cherished, embraced homosexuality because it was the ultimate form of sexual rebellion. The archetypal punk movie was *Jubilee*, directed by Derek Jarman, which featured punk icons, like Jordan, who worked at Malcolm McLaren and Vivienne Westwood's Chelsea shop selling the punk equivalent of couture. The shop was prosecuted when it produced a T-shirt which depicted two men in an intimate sexual pose. Tony Sayonas evolved from his Bowie phase of the early Seventies and espoused the punk look: 'I had the ripped jeans and everything, and I had that many pins in me arms, that go past a magnet factory and I would have gone.' Punk also threw up the first out singer who sang overtly about gay politics. Tom Robinson, who had been on the fringes of GLF in the early Seventies where he would strum 'Sing If You're Glad to Be Gay' on his guitar, had a top-twenty hit with '2–4–6–8 Motorway' and subsequently released albums which made no secret of his sexuality.

> '**Gay men these days are manlier than the straights.**'
>
> **Lucy Hughes-Hallet** in the London EVENING STANDARD

If the law seemed to have been stuck in a rut since 1967, there seemed to be inevitable progress towards greater enlightenment on the part of the public. The word 'gay', which had caused so much consternation in the early Seventies, was now becoming an accepted part of the language. Papers like the *Guardian*, the *Observer* and even the conservative *Daily Telegraph* began using the word to describe homosexuals and increasingly the word was used without quotation marks around it.

More importantly, gays began to appear in the arts and the media in a way in which they had never been portrayed before. *The Rocky Horror Show* – a spoof of American B-movies – played for years on the London stage, with Tim Curry as the 'sweet transvestite from transsexual Transylvania', camping it up to the hilt in a way that GLF gender-benders would have recognized immediately. In 1975, Hollywood picked up the rights to the play and made it into a movie. In the same year, Thames produced *The Naked Civil Servant* – after the BBC turned it down – adapted from Quentin Crisp's autobiography of the same name, to much acclaim. John Hurt, who played the leading role, won a clutch of awards for his performance and the public were besotted by it. More to the point, there was next to no hostility. A survey conducted by the Independent Broadcasting Authority revealed that, while three per cent of viewers had switched off, eighty-five per cent said

GLF'S INFLUENCE
WAS SOON SEEN
– NOT LEAST IN
*THE ROCKY
HORROR SHOW* –
AND THE FILM
OF THE SAME
TITLE WITH
ITS GENDER-
BENDING HERO
PLAYED BY TIM
CURRY

that they did not find the play shocking. The gay writer and broadcaster, Howard Schuman, wrote a gay character into his ITV series, *Rock Follies*, who was neither effeminate nor tortured and was seen to have a healthy sex life. In 1979, the ITV comedy *Agony* had Maureen Lipman as an agony aunt who was always in a complete whirl – the sane centre of her world were her two gay neighbours who weren't the usual self-loathing stereotypes. The series also took the subplot seriously and went on to deal with issues like outing and gay bereavement.

Of course, all the old stereotypes went on alongside these advances, but they weren't allowed to exist without protest. The BBC and ITV companies began to see a new kind of letter-writer in the Seventies – the gay man or lesbian who was angry about the way that homosexuals had been portrayed – and if that didn't work, the protests were carried further. In 1977, the *Daily Mirror* reported that the actor John Inman, who played a mincing shop assistant in one of the BBC's biggest rating sitcoms, *Are You Being Served?*, had been approached about his distorted portrayal and, when nothing came of that, leaflets were distributed outside a Brighton theatre where he was appearing. Inman remained oblivious. 'I'm not getting into a state,' he told the *Mirror*'s reporter.

At the beginning of the Eighties, it seemed as if there had never been a better time to be gay. The gay stereotype was changing rapidly. In the past, all dramatists and comedians had to do to denote gayness was flap a wrist. Now that image was being challenged by another one – the muscle-bound, leather-clad, moustachioed clone. In an article in the London *Evening Standard*, Lucy Hughes-Hallet asserted that 'gay men these days are manlier than the straights . . .' – a remark that would have caused apoplexy only ten years before, but it passed without comment. Gay men and lesbians got their first television series, LWT's *Gay Life* in 1980 – it was a confused and confusing programme because it never made up its mind who it was aimed at. Certainly, if it was aimed at London's gay men, at midnight on a Sunday a good proportion of them was unlikely to be sitting at home watching television. They were more likely to be dancing away in Heaven – Europe's largest night-club – with the best laser light system, which also happened to be gay.

The immense explosion in the commercialized gay scene meant that, for the first time, there were plenty of jobs that people could do where they didn't have to hide their sexuality – indeed, where being gay was a positive advantage. Julian Hows discovered this and got himself a job at Heaven. This is the same man who, when he went to sign on for the first time – wearing a green Grecian dress, hennaed hair, and long cigarette holder, finished off with boots and gold lamé clutch bag – was told that he was unemployable. 'You could not only have a gay lifestyle, but you could have a gay job as a barman, as a coat check boy, as a deejay and for some people that was absolutely fabulous. Working at Heaven, for me, was a bit of a mistake, though I met some fabulous people there, absolutely incredible people.'

TWO FLYERS FOR HEAVEN, WHICH SOON REPLACED BANG AS LONDON'S LARGEST GAY CLUB

Heaven was such a haven that it was frequented by gay men from all over Britain. Tony Sayonas remembers visiting it on a trip down to London and being bowled over: 'Heaven, for someone who's come up from Liverpool, was just amazing. To look down and see all these people . . . being themselves and not caring. [I remember] thinking this is my family. Oh yeah, you get some titheads in every family, but there's, you know, the majority of them,' he explains. 'I couldn't believe it, it buoyed you up. It

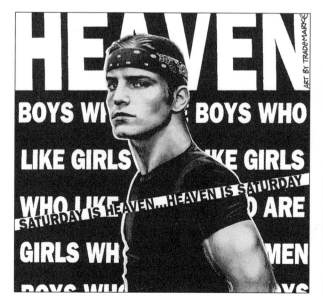

used to carry me along for days, thinking, God, I can go back to this place – it was just a buzz.'

Richard Cawley, who has been with his partner since the Sixties, also succumbed to the lure of Heaven which appealed not only to the gay man who was out looking for sexual partners, but also those who had settled into comfortable domesticity. 'I remember the early days of Heaven and it was just fabulous,' Richard recalls. 'First of all, because I was no longer one of the very very few people that wore peculiar clothes. I mean you got people wearing all those extraordinary things whether it was total drag or a leather jock-strap . . . It was all very exciting and had a kind of wonderful tacky glamour to it as well.' What nobody realized in those days of heaven was that every Eden has its serpent and for gay men it was to be AIDS.

In a subculture where four-letter words are tossed around without much thought, this one was different. The first problem was that no one knew much about it – not even the doctors, who were puzzled by the aetiology of this new disease. HIV – the virus that can lead to AIDS – had not yet been isolated and nobody had any idea how the disease was transmitted. Tony Sayonas first heard about it on one of his trips to London: 'There was three friends of mine and we went to Bang's and somebody in the company [started talking about] AIDS and I always remember that was the first time that I heard about it. I thought he was talking about these slimming things called AYDS – chocolates that you could buy from the chemist.'

The first sign that the party was over came in January 1981, when a thirty-one-year-old gay man checked in at the accident and emergency room of the UCLA Medical Centre in Los Angeles because his oesophagus was almost completely blocked by a fungal infection. A fortnight later, he developed a form of pneumonia which was only seen in transplant patients whose immune systems had been artificially depressed to prevent their bodies from rejecting the donated organs. The doctors were baffled. Their bewilderment increased over the following months as more and more physicians in America – most particularly in New York and California – began to see gay men in their clinics, displaying symptoms of diseases which in normal circumstances they should never have contracted. What they all had in common was a depressed immune system – and the fact that they were gay.

In Britain, there was concern but also a false optimism – after all, nobody on this side of the Atlantic seemed to have it. It was, in fact, only a matter of time. At the beginning of 1982, the doctors at St Thomas's Hospital were as baffled as their American counterparts when a thirty-seven-year-old man – Terrence Higgins – came in with the same rare pneumonia that the patient at UCLA had had, and the same depressed immune

JULIAN HOWS
TRAVELS IN STYLE

system. Higgins, a computer programmer, had been a regular on the circuit and was known as a warm and generous man, as Julian Hows had discovered.

Julian had gone on a Gay Pride parade where there was an altercation when one of the drag queens was taken aside because the meat cleaver she was wearing in her hat was deemed to be an offensive weapon. Julian and his friends – who had learnt about resistance in the old GLF school – decided to make a protest and sit down. 'And the police were trying to push us off and I kept saying, "Look, I'm wearing heels, I'm wearing this hat which has got spokes coming out of it and if you push me any harder, I'm going to fall over . . . I'll walk but I'll walk at my own speed." Anyway, this policeman started pushing me and I got carted off to the cells. Well, as I'm being pulled off with my lallies up in the air, still trying to do high kicks . . . I see on the back of the Heaven float this man . . . Terrence Higgins whom I knew because he was the bar manager at Heaven . . . he jumped off the float swirling a leather belt to attack the policeman who was attacking me – he was a wild and wonderful demented leather queen.'

On 4 July 1982, Terrence Higgins died. His lover was not informed of the cause of death and was told that the doctors would be writing it up in a paper and if he wanted to know more he would do so when it was published. The news that Britain's first case of AIDS had occurred did not become generally known till five months later when *Capital Gay*, the London newspaper, reported it in a story headlined 'US Disease Hits London'.

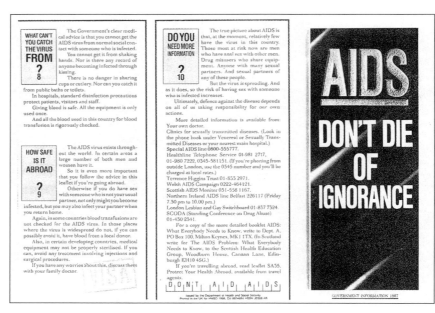

A friend of Higgins and his lover, Martyn Butler, suggested that a benefit be held at Heaven to raise cash for research into the disease which was being carried out at St Mary's Hospital in Paddington. A charity was set up to administer the money raised and it was named the Terrence Higgins Trust – which is still one of the leading AIDS charities in Britain. Its counterpart in Scotland, Scottish AIDS Monitor, was formed three months later.

By March 1983, there were six reported cases of AIDS in Britain. A few months later, in July, they had more than doubled to fourteen and the figures continued to rise. By October 1985, the number of cases had risen to 241 and, while the number of people who were infected was difficult to gauge, the most widely held assumption was that it was at least 20,000. The government had done very little – apart from giving the Terrence Higgins Trust £35,000, spread over three years, which seemed a minuscule sum to combat such a monstrous threat. However, it was becoming clear that AIDS was not going to go away; what was worse was that there was almost total public ignorance. It was vital that the government, at the very least, warn people of the risks involved. Accordingly, the health minister, Norman Fowler, announced in December of that year that £2.5 million would be spent on a public information campaign.

There were problems. The government was chary of telling people about the facts of the disease. A few advertisements appeared, but the follow-up research showed that only a small minority had seen them and, if anything, they compounded the public's confusion. A survey, conducted at

Left and right: IN
1987 A COPY OF
THIS LEAFLET WAS
POSTED THROUGH
EVERY LETTER-
BOX IN THE
COUNTRY

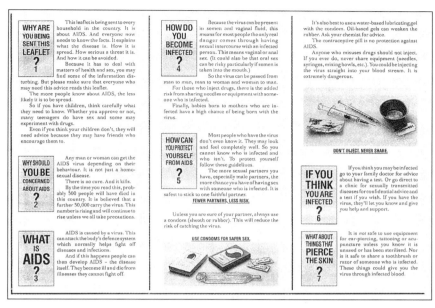

WHY ARE YOU BEING SENT THIS LEAFLET? 1

This leaflet is being sent to every household in the country. It is about AIDS. And everyone now needs to know the facts. It explains what the disease is. How it is spread. How serious a threat it is. And how it can be avoided.

Because it has to deal with matters of health and sex, you may find some of the information disturbing. But please make sure that everyone who may need this advice reads this leaflet.

The more people know about AIDS, the less likely it is to be spread.

So if you have children, think carefully what they need to know. Whether you approve or not, many teenagers do have sex and some may experiment with drugs.

Even if you think your children don't, they will need advice because they may have friends who encourage them to.

WHY SHOULD YOU BE CONCERNED ABOUT AIDS? 2

Any man or woman can get the AIDS virus depending on their behaviour. It is not just a homosexual disease.

There is no cure. And it kills.

By the time you read this, probably 500 people will have died in this country. It is believed that a further 30,000 carry the virus. This number is rising and will continue to rise unless we all take precautions.

WHAT IS AIDS? 3

AIDS is caused by a virus. This can attack the body's defence system which normally helps fight off diseases and infections.

And if this happens people can then develop AIDS – the disease itself. They become ill and die from illnesses they cannot fight off.

HOW DO YOU BECOME INFECTED? 4

Because the virus can be present in semen and vaginal fluid, this means for most people the only real danger comes through having sexual intercourse with an infected person. This means vaginal or anal sex. (It could also be that oral sex can be risky particularly if semen is taken into the mouth.)

So the virus can be passed from man to man, man to woman and woman to man.

For those who inject drugs, there is the added risk from sharing needles or equipment with someone who is infected.

Finally, babies born to mothers who are infected have a high chance of being born with the virus.

HOW CAN YOU PROTECT YOURSELF FROM AIDS? 5

Most people who have the virus don't even know it. They may look and feel completely well. So you cannot know who is infected and who isn't. To protect yourself follow these guidelines.

The more sexual partners you have, especially male partners, the more chance you have of having sex with someone who is infected. It is safest to stick to one faithful partner.

FEWER PARTNERS, LESS RISK.

Unless you are sure of your partner, always use a condom (sheath or rubber). This will reduce the risk of catching the virus.

USE CONDOMS FOR SAFER SEX.

It's also best to use a water-based lubricating gel with the condom. Oil-based gels can weaken the rubber. Ask your chemist for advice.

The contraceptive pill is no protection against AIDS.

Anyone who misuses drugs should not inject. If you ever do, never share equipment (needles, syringes, mixing bowls, etc.). You could be injecting the virus straight into your blood stream. It is extremely dangerous.

DON'T INJECT. NEVER SHARE.

IF YOU THINK YOU ARE INFECTED? 6

If you think you may be infected go to your family doctor for advice about having a test. Or go direct to a clinic for sexually transmitted diseases for confidential advice and a test if you wish. If you have the virus, they'll let you know and give you help and support.

WHAT ABOUT THINGS THAT PIERCE THE SKIN? 7

It is *not* safe to use equipment for ear-piercing, tattooing or acupuncture unless you know it is unused or has been sterilised. Nor is it safe to share a toothbrush or razor of someone who is infected. These things could give you the virus through infected blood.

Southampton General Hospital, discovered that only thirty-one per cent of people had seen the advertisements. Even worse, before the campaign five per cent of people believed there was a vaccine against the disease; after the campaign, ten per cent thought they could be immunized against it.

> '**It was total paranoia.** There was a period of about six months when it was touch and go . . . the hatred that was coming out was totally naked.'
>
> **Michael James** on press reaction to AIDS

The information campaign would obviously have to be more explicit. According to Simon Garfield's account of Britain in the time of AIDS, *The End of Innocence*, ministers needed enlightening as much as the public. The real problem the government had was that it didn't want to be accused of talking dirty to the electorate, but how else were they to get the information across? The scientists and advisors were urging the government to go ahead with a leaflet which would be pushed through every letter-box in the country. There was concern that the elderly might be literally shocked to death by it, and it was seriously suggested that the leaflets be withheld from anyone called Gladys, Albert or Daisy. Wiser counsel prevailed and the government went ahead with a blanket leafleting of Britain.

Unfortunately, in this communicatory zeal, the government forgot to pass on one vital bit of information. The phone numbers of the Terrence Higgins Trust and London Lesbian and Gay Switchboard were printed on the leaflets as places to ring for more information, but they forgot to ask these organizations' permission. Nobody even bothered to tell them. Julian Hows was one of the people who had to bear the brunt of the onslaught of telephone calls: 'I was on London Lesbian and Gay Switchboard – 0171 837 7324 – and there we were . . . the government had put out twelve million leaflets – one to every household in the country. You might have seen them – those wonderful icebergs and tombstones. And what did it do? It put our telephone number on it without telling us. Well, after about sixty volunteers burning themselves out, after the 837 exchange burning itself out several times, they gave us a new telephone system.' Tony Whitehead, of the Terrence Higgins Trust, felt that both organizations had been exploited and added, 'The very least the government could do would be an upfront thank you and a large cheque.'

The delivery of the leaflets to all British homes – which was accompanied by a press, poster and television campaign – had the intended effect : AIDS was now a household word in Britain. However, it also had another effect. It characterized gay men as being plague bearers. The tabloids had been whipping up the homophobic frenzy for the past few years and the mass information campaigns served to confirm all the lingering prejudices which had lain dormant during the Seventies. The coverage inevitably utilized plague metaphors, giving the impression that AIDS was a highly contagious disease which could be contracted through casual contact. The privacy of people with AIDS was flouted in order to get a good story and patients in the final stages of the disease were often hounded in their hospital beds. The Terrence Higgins Trust described the newspaper coverage as 'untruthful, dishonest, inaccurate, incomplete, unfair to people with AIDS and to those seen as being at highest risk of contracting it'. There was talk about compulsory testing of all gay men and even of quarantine. 'It was total paranoia,' says Michael James. 'There was a period of about six months when it was touch and go . . . the hatred that was coming out was totally naked from the *Sun* and the *Daily Mail* and all those papers. The gloves were off . . . I really believed that they were going to round up all the gays and put them into concentration camps.'

Gay men, generally, were treated like pariahs and gay men who were HIV-positive were treated like lepers. Tony Sayonas tells the tale of a friend of his who went to a dinner party where the hosts would have wrapped him in clingfilm if they had been able to: 'Ian . . . was the first HIV-positive person I met and when we were talking he just started crying. I said, "What's wrong?" and he said, "Well, I'm HIV. Do you want me to go?" And I said, "Behave yourself!" and he'd been to a dinner party the night before and they'd actually attached little pieces of cotton to the glasses and . . . on his knife and fork.'

The problem in the initial stages was that very little was known about this disease. Even its name kept changing just like the virus it described kept mutating. First it was known as the gay cancer, then it became GRID (Gay Related Immune Deficiency) and when it became clear that it didn't just affect gay men, AIDS was settled on. There was no proof that it was a virus, there was no test for it and no one knew the mechanism by which it worked. Worst of all it was impossible to tell who was affected.

'It wasn't a contact virus . . . it was a bit more hit and miss than that and you didn't know who'd got hit,' explains Derek Ogg. 'There was a kind of a feeling that you'd been in a battle in the Somme and you'd all gone over the top and all the bullets were flying and you didn't know who was hit, who the casualities were. But I sensed that there would be many, I was a kind of a prophet of doom at the time.'

Once the virus which caused AIDS was isolated, the next dilemma was being tested for it. Many insurance companies made it a condition that single men applying for life insurance should take the test. This however posed its own problems. People who had already taken the test and were found negative were still discriminated against. Insurance companies argued that taking the test implied that the individual considered him or herself to be at risk of contracting HIV and, therefore, they were a bad risk for the insurance company. For many people, however, there was no choice about taking the test – it had to be done, simply to give them peace of mind. Tony Sayonas took an HIV test after discovering that a sexual partner of his had tested positive: 'I had a relationship with somebody [whom I met] in January and at the end of June he found out he was HIV positive and I'll always remember him ringing me up and saying to me, "I'm positive," and I said, "You're positive about what?" . . . and I had to go for the test and I'm not HIV [positive], right.' Tony had a few sleepless nights and worry-filled days. He distracted himself with housework. 'In times of distress, I clean up. If anyone dies on me, I paint the house,' he says.

Others weren't as lucky as Tony. 'I found out I was positive the day before I went to Acapulco for a lesbian and gay conference, which was a stunning way to find out, wasn't it?' says Julian Hows. 'When I found out that I had HIV, I thought to myself, I'm actually not going to believe that I'm going to be dead in three years time 'cos I've been through that one already . . . I came out and the world didn't fall down, and I'm HIV positive and the world's not gonna fall down. It's more a question of what I do with my life and how I live it. I have a life-threatening illness – could be cancer, could be something else. You might as well live, let's face it, and I intend to.'

Derek Ogg was also affected by AIDS when his lover at the time, Alistair, tested positive. 'I think Alistair and I were two of the best-informed people about HIV illness and symptomology. By the time we were five years into the epidemic, Alistair and I had buried most of our friends. It was a phenomenon of the eighties that, there were a lot of gay people who didn't have any long-standing friends going back ten years. But working in the AIDS scene doesn't qualify you to be any better at handling this than anyone else. You know a lot more about it and you know a lot more about the consequences of it and arguably that's not altogether a good thing. I felt I knew what the future had in store. I was wrong because Alistair is one of the longest living asymptomatic people with HIV on planet earth.'

The bravery and courage of people faced with this immense and unexpected threat has been inspiring. Self-help organizations sprang up everywhere to provide help and support for those who needed it. Gay men and lesbians threw themselves into starting and maintaining organizations that disseminated safe-sex information, organizations that supported people who were HIV positive, that provided meals for people who were too ill to cope on their own, that visited people in hospital. A vast number of alternative therapies – such as acupuncture and massage – were examined to see if they could be of benefit to people affected by AIDS and HIV. The most rewarding – and in many cases also the most demanding – of these was the 'buddying' system. The idea, which had originated in America, involved adopting a person with HIV or AIDS as your buddy and forming a relationship with them which could include everything from doing the shopping to rushing over in the middle of the night if the person needed help.

Barbara Bell, who was now living in Brighton, volunteered to be a buddy: 'I thought, now I've got to do something about these boys because we're not suffering – look at all these women laughing their heads off and look at you boys, you need help. What can I do? I'll do anything, scrub floors, make beds, go to the launderette, make food.' Washing, cooking and cleaning was the easy bit. Being a buddy also required a high level of perseverance. 'I was very committed to the work – you had to be because sometimes you went and they may not want to see you. One fella I used to shout to through the letterbox: "Come on, Danny, let's open that door, I know you're in." They'd say, "Go away, I don't want you, go away." You hadn't to be hurt. You just said, "Oh well, I'll come round again, love, don't worry."'

OUTRAGE
DEMONSTRATION
AT THE
CENOTAPH ON
REMEMBRANCE
DAY 1995

Barbara found herself deeply affected by the work. She even found it humbling at times, when she saw the bravery with which people were dealing with their illness. She once asked one of her buddies what he wanted and he asked to have a bath so that he would be clean for the doctor's visit which was imminent. The man was covered in lesions which made the slightest touch painful but he submitted with a stoicism that Barbara found moving: 'I'm not a religious person, but I felt I was washing Jesus's feet when I was washing that body. It was all emaciated and he was suffering, and I felt so humble and I thought, well, fancy me being chosen to do this work.'

Barbara's job was to brighten things up in any way she could. To this end, she went to the Brighton Museum and cajoled them into lending pictures to cheer up the AIDS ward at the Sussex County Hospital. When it opened, it had been disused for years and, as a result, was rather bleak and depressing. Encouraged by her success with the Brighton Museum she then approached the local parks department and persuaded them to donate plants which she would take round the wards, asking patients to choose one that they liked.

Inevitably, Barbara found herself attending more funerals in this period than she had at any other period in her life: 'It was very depressing. In the beginning they were very serious affairs . . . the first funeral I went to broke my heart. I was sobbing and crying all over the place, couldn't help it. This young fella, he was only a young kid of about nineteen . . . But as time went on there was a gradual change. You don't go to weep about a life that's gone, you go to rejoice about a life that's been. It's a thanksgiving that they've been here and given such love, or pleasure or joy . . .' Working on the principle that funerals were a time to celebrate a life, not just to mourn it, Barbara and her colleagues became adept at planning them in a way that made sure that the people attending them would be aware of what sort of ceremony they were going to. For instance, in the case of Ben, who was one of her buddies, they wanted something really merry: 'So we sent out these invitations which said, "Please wear bright clothes," and we had a hundred gas-filled balloons which is quite a lot balloons . . . They were tied to the pews in the chapel and when people were coming out they were all given a balloon and then we all let go and the balloons flew into the air – bye, bye Ben, cheers Ben . . . Last year, this fellow said he wanted us all to have a firework so . . . we came out of church and we were all lighting these big sparklers for him . . . We didn't weep and gnash our teeth . . . but it doesn't mean that we are less sad or we're going to miss them any less.'

The cumulative effect of attending so many funerals can take its toll, however. Michael James says that, of all the people he knew since he arrived in London at the end of the Fifties, there are only six or eight still alive: 'So many of the people I've had close contact with, as well as people in bars whose names you don't know but who you nod and say hello to, they've all gone.' Michael's reaction to this, when he returned to London, was to throw himself into AIDS work with a zeal which eventually forced him to tone things down. He was the hospital visits co-ordinator for an organization called Body Positive. There was next to no funding and it meant that any expenses had to come out of his own pocket, even though he was on the dole.

'My little twelve pounds a week was helping to pay the bus fares from one hospital to another and occasionally buy someone who was in hospital a yoghurt or sweets . . . and also to pay telephone bills,' says Michael. 'In those days my number was published in the newsletters so I'd have people phoning me up at three o'clock in the morning and we're doing two- or three-hour phone calls – I had one lady from Southampton, about four o'clock in the morning, in tears. HIV and AIDS volunteer work was twenty-four hours a day, seven days a week.'

In order to get away from the stress of the volunteer work, Michael played hard, but going to gay places was not necessarily a break. He would look around the bar and see people he had met through work who invariably wanted advice and information or just a chat: 'Boundaries wasn't a word that was around in those days, and, even if it was, if somebody's in distress, they're in distress and you deal with it. You can't turn round and say, "Come and see me at the office tomorrow at nine o'clock." They wanted to see me there and then.'

That sort of regime has its cost. After about three and a half years, Michael was close to a nervous breakdown and he stopped being a volunteer for a year. When he returned, he couldn't face doing the hospital visits again so he worked in the Body Positive office for a further eighteen months or so. '[It was] the serial bereavement which I hadn't been able to deal with . . . it started to seep through and I just started to become very depressed . . . not knowing what was happening really, but deep down, understanding what was happening, but not wanting to recognize that I was on the edge of a nervous breakdown.' At that point Michael decided that he had to take himself out of London again and he now lives in Brighton. 'I've basically, very gently had a breakdown . . . I've got a brilliant psychotherapist . . . who's kept me together this last two years . . . it's been a struggle, but at the moment – yeah – I'm having a good time.'

The 'serial bereavement' that Michael describes has affected all gay people whose address books are filled with crossed-out names of dead friends. 'I did sit here one night, pissed, and started writing a list of friends and acquaintances who have died from AIDS and when I

PETER BURTON
AS A YOUNG
JOURNALIST

got to eighty I thought, oh let's just stop this,' says Peter Burton. 'There seems to be someone dying all the time and I still sit here thinking, well, it's a miracle that I'm here – sex, drugs and rock and roll didn't kill me.'

Peter was, however, at the receiving end of a side-effect of AIDS. The hatred stirred up by the tabloids gave a new impetus to all the homophobia that had been lying latent. When the lead is given by national newspapers and magazines, which joke that gay is an acronym for 'Got AIDS Yet?', it legitimizes hatred. Although no official figures are kept on incidents of queer-bashing, the anecdotal evidence throughout the Eighties seemed to indicate a rise in the number of gay people who were attacked.

It was Sunday night at the end of a long and bibulous weekend, when Peter went for a stroll along Brighton sea front and was rambling though a section that was a local cruising area when he heard someone say, 'That's one of them.' Alarmed by this statement Peter turned back to return the way he'd come and realized he'd walked into a trap. 'They swept through the area rather like beaters on a pheasant shoot and I happened to be the person that couldn't get away . . . I fought back, but there was only me and a lot of them.' Peter fell to the ground and was kicked in the torso as well as suffering a broken arm and numerous bruises. He dragged himself home and fell asleep at the bottom of the stairs. The following morning, he seemed lucid and cogent and rang the office to explain his absence and then went into shock: 'I couldn't eat, I couldn't smoke, I had to force myself back on to cigarettes. I had to force myself back on to alcohol and lived on jelly, which was wonderful because I lost an enormous amount of weight. I couldn't go to the loo because they had kicked me in the kidneys so I used to guess – thinking it must be time to have a pee.'

Queer-bashing has a lingering effect – long after the broken bones have mended and the bruises have faded, the battered psyche remains sore. 'I've never recovered . . . up until that point I would quite happily wander around on foot, but not since then . . . and the idea of actually going out at night is completely beyond me . . . I have a friend who lives 100 yards away with whom I usually have supper on Friday evening, and sometimes I just ring and cancel because I can't get myself out the door, particularly if there are people in the street – gangs of children I find particularly terrifying.'

The progress that had been made in the Seventies and the Eighties created a backlash that was continued by the government. After the Conservatives' third consecutive election victory in 1987, there was a move to turn attention away from making changes to the economic structure of the country, to amending what was seen as a drift away from 'family values'. At the Tories' first annual party conference after the 1987 election, Mrs Thatcher laid down the agenda for the third term and it was clear what her target was when she told delegates: 'Children who need to be taught to respect traditional moral values are being taught that they have an inalienable right to be gay.'

> '**People thought: hold on a minute.**
> I pay my taxes, I have a family, I've got a house –
> this Clause 28-thing is totally out of order.'
>
> Tony Sayonas

The AIDS backlash had led to a hardening of public attitudes towards gay men and lesbians, as evidenced by the *British Social Attitudes Survey*. In 1983, sixty-two per cent of respondents had said that they did not approve of homosexual relationships. The proportion of people who espoused this attitude increased steadily through the Eighties, rising to sixty-nine per cent in 1985 and to seventy-four per cent in 1987. It was clear to Conservative politicians that initiating legislation which targeted gay men and lesbians would not be particularly alarming for most of the public and it also served their own party political ends. Many Labour-led councils had instituted policies which sought to safeguard gay men and lesbians against discrimination. Following the lead of the Greater London Council, which had been abolished by central government the previous year, some Labour councils were also providing grants for lesbian and gay community organizations. An attack against the 'promotion' of homosexuality at a local government level served the double purpose of sounding a warning to the gay community as well as embarrassing the Labour Party at a national level, which believed that gay causes were not necessarily popular with their traditional working-class voters.

Accordingly, a mere two months after the Tory Party conference, the Local Government Bill, which was going through Parliament at the time, had a new clause attached to it which read: 'A local authority shall not a) intentionally promote homosexuality or publish material with the intention of promoting homosexuality and b) promote the teaching in any maintained school of the acceptability of homosexuality as a pretended family relationship.' This became known as the notorious Clause 28.

There was bewilderment as to exactly what was meant by it. If the government had sex education in mind, the clause was pointless since responsibility for sex education had already been taken away from councils in earlier legislation and it now lay with the governors of each individual school. The clause was so vaguely worded that, should any government be minded to, it could prosecute a local council whose schools used Oscar Wilde as a set text. Lawyers advising gay organizations said that the law was so open-ended that it could also be used to shut down gay clubs and bars or bookstores – anything that required a licence from the local council. Most gay men and lesbians, though, had no doubt what the intention behind the proposed legislation was. 'It was history going backwards,' says Michael James. 'They were trying to take away from us what we'd fought so hard for, are still fighting so hard for.'

This is not as far-fetched an analysis of what lay behind Clause 28 as it seems. The government's stated objective was that it wanted to return to the ethos of 1967. While no one was suggesting that sexual acts between men should be recriminalized, it was pointed out that the intention of the 1967 Act was not for gay men and lesbians to behave as if their relationships were as valid as heterosexual ones or as if they merited equal rights. Bernard Levin – not known for intemperate outbursts – wrote in his column in *The Times*: 'This country seems to be in a galloping frenzy of hate, where homosexuals are concerned, that will soon, if not checked, lead to something like a pogrom.' Britain which already had the strictest laws concerning homosexuality in Europe – with the exception of Bulgaria – was seeking to tighten them even further.

A MARILYN
LOOK-ALIKE AT
THE 1994 LESBIAN
AND GAY PRIDE
PARADE

THE LEGACY OF
GLF'S SLOGANS
LIVES ON AT THE
1995 LESBIAN
AND GAY PRIDE
PARADE

The move was so retrogressive, so out of step with what was happening in the rest of the civilized world that it galvanized people, who had been pondering on the brink for years, into finally taking action. One such was Sir Ian McKellen who decided to come out at the age of forty-nine. The decision was taken on the spur of the moment during the course of a radio talk show. One of the guests was the right-wing journalist Peregrine Worsthorne, who was fulminating

about gays and referring to 'them'. Unable to tolerate it any longer, McKellen finally said, '*I* am one of them.'

If the government's intention was to shut people up and make them lead quiet, furtive lives again, it backfired spectacularly. 'People thought, hold on a minute, I pay my taxes, I have a family, I've got a house, this Clause 28-thing is totally out of order,' says Tony Sayonas. 'It was making second-class citizens of us and I wasn't gonna have it. So that's why I went on my first march.' Tony wasn't to know that when he attended that anti-Clause 28 march in Manchester in 1988 that it would turn out to be the largest gay march ever held in Britain up to that point. Despite the serious issue at stake, it had a carnival atmosphere to it. 'It was a buzz, it was great,' says Tony. 'There was a line of policemen and we were going "Two, four, six, eight, is that copper really straight?" and he went, "No," and we went, "Y-e-e-e-e-e-s!"'

Michael James attended a march in London which was angrier, and for the first time in his life Michael felt that he didn't want to get involved in the mêlée. 'At one stage, going down Whitehall, a load of people broke away and it looked as if it was going to get violent. Something told me: "Don't get involved, you've been a martyr for too many years, you don't want your head kicked in. Let the younger kids do it this time."' And there were plenty of them. The AIDS crisis and Clause 28 had resulted in new protest groups, like Act Up and Outrage, which employed very much the same sort of shock tactics that GLF had employed twenty-five years earlier and, like GLF, they wanted gay men and lesbians to be known by a new name – 'queer'. Just as GLF had argued that 'homosexual' was a word that described a sex act, while 'gay' was a word that depicted a lifestyle, the new groups argued that 'queer' denotes a new approach that rejects society's labels about what is acceptable and what is not. By using a word that society has flung at gay men and lesbians as an insult, they were reclaiming it and thus taking the sting out of it.

Another organization that emerged out of the battle against Clause 28 was Stonewall, with Ian McKellen as one of its founding lobbyists. The polarity between Stonewall and organizations like Outrage and Act Up was hugely reminiscent of the relative positions of CHE and GLF. While one advocated lobbying politicians, the other recommended lobbing missiles at them. While one required its lobbyists to wear suits and talk in reasoned language, the other thought suits were anathema and talked in slogans, albeit highly entertaining ones.

Equally entertaining were the debates and disruptions that took place as the Local Government Bill proceeded through Parliament. In the upper house, Lord Rea admitted to being brought up in what the bill described as a 'pretend family'. He told the House of Lords: 'I was brought up by two women, one of them was my mother, in an actual family relationship, there was no pretence there . . . it was a good family and I maintain that there is nothing intrinsically wrong with a homosexual couple bringing up a child. I consider that I had as rich and happy a childhood as most children who are reared by heterosexual couples.' The Lords were not convinced and passed the bill by a two to one majority, at which point a group of lesbians abseiled from the public gallery on to the floor of the chamber shouting 'Lesbians are angry.' The bill was also passed by the Commons but with a much smaller majority – 254 to 201 – and on the day it happened, 19 March 1988, the lesbian protesters were out again. They infiltrated a BBC studio and chained themselves to the desks and cameras as Sue Lawley attempted to deliver the six o'clock news.

The government, according to Ian McKellen, was seriously taken aback by the reaction to Clause 28 and, depite being on the statute books, it was only enforced on a minor scale – some libraries and premises owned by

THE 1995 LESBIAN
AND GAY PRIDE
PARADE

local authorities banned the desplay of gay switchboard posters and information leaflets.

Capital Gay was in no doubt about what it represented: 'We have seen
the coming of age of the gay and lesbian movement. Well-known figures,
who have previously been quiet about their sexuality, have come out fighting, we have found support from across the political spectrum, ordinary
homosexuals have written protest letters and taken to the streets in the
biggest ever lesbian and gay demonstrations, the media coverage has been
massive (and often sympathetic) and the visibility of our community has
rarely, if ever, been greater.'

Clause 28 and the AIDS crisis had united gay men and lesbians in a
way that had not happened since the Seventies. By the Eighties, the law in
Scotland and Northern Ireland had been brought into line with the legislation in England and Wales. In 1980, law reform was extended to Scotland
after much campaigning (*see* page 177). Northern Ireland had to wait longer.
An attempt to liberalize the law, in 1977, had been scuppered by Ian Pais-
ley's Save Ulster From Sodomy campaign and it wasn't until 1982 when Jeff
Dudgeon, a gay activist, took the government to the European courts that
the government was forced to act.

During this period, many lesbians had devoted their political energies to
the peace movement, notably the Campaign For Nuclear Disarmament.
Cathy Peace, who was still a schoolgirl at the time and just discovering her

CATHY PEACE
(right)

sexuality, would go to the camp at Greenham during the school holidays. 'I went because I was really involved in CND and also because there were so many lesbians,' she explains. 'There was all the stuff in the newspapers about it being full of butch women who didn't shave and sleeping together and smelling . . . it was a bit like that on a certain level because there was no running water and it is quite hard . . . you do wear boots and lots of jumpers if it's cold and you're living out all the time.'

Apart from, and in addition to, the peace movement, lesbians were devoting their energies to women's issues. The Women's Liberation Movement had done a complete U-turn from the early days when it had rejected even the presence of lesbians, let alone their contribution. The women's movement was now largely informed by a lesbian sensibility and the concept of the 'political lesbian' – where women made a conscious choice to direct their sexuality towards other women rather than at men – had emerged. The battle with patriarchy was considered a lost cause and women developed the concept of the 'Lesbian Nation' which envisaged an alternative culture.

As the Eighties progressed, a number of women began to explore alternative forms of relating with each other. This led to a debate among lesbians, during the Eighties, over the question of sado-masochism. The accoutrements of sado-masochism – leather jackets, boots and peaked caps – had been a part of male gay culture since the Seventies; now they were beginning to make their appearance among lesbians. A number of lesbians argued that this would mean a return to the old butch/femme divides and, even worse, it was wallowing in oppressive images. Others argued that to prohibit it was to limit sexual choice. Cathy Peace moved to London to go to university and found herself living in a lesbian co-op with two SM dykes in the room next to her.

'About the first week I was there I could hear this metal clinking and I could hear this woman going [imitates the groaning noise] and I was wondering what the hell was going on next door, with these two SM dykes living together in a small space,' Cathy explains. Finally, her curiosity got the better of her. 'One day I knocked on the door and all she was doing was weights – it was so disappointing.'

While some metropolitan women were living in communes and discussing the ins and outs of sado-masochistic sex, there were plenty of other women who lived quietly in rural areas. Ann and Marika were two such people. They had met in the Sixties at an Anglican order for nuns where the attraction was immediate as far as Marika was concerned. She remembers one Christmas taking a supper tray into Ann who was ill in bed with measles and giving her a goodnight kiss. 'I kissed her in a perfectly correct,

(Below left)
ANN LEWIS ON GRADUATION DAY IN THE SIXTIES

(Below right)
MARIKA AND ANN

ANN AND MARIKA
AT PRIDE 1996

conventional fashion on the cheek, only my insides did a somersault and I fled from her room and tried to pretend it hadn't happened, but I knew then I was extremely fond of her.'

Ann left the religious community in order to have major eye surgery and did not return. Marika continued for another six years but had difficulties coming to terms with things and was given a dispensation from her vows. She left the order and got married. Years later, she returned to the order to visit a dying nun she had been particularly close to, whose last request to Marika was that she should write to Ann. Marika duly complied and all the old feelings bubbled up to the surface again. 'I'd been trying to forget Ann all that time – seventeen years. I had thought of Ann when I couldn't avoid it and I had tried very hard indeed not to think of her because I was always frightened of the consequences. And as soon as I wrote the letter to her, I knew that if she was still interested in me there was nothing else I could do about it – I'd spent too many years trying to avoid it.'

When Ann and Marika met again after the seventeen-year gap, they found that their feelings for each other were as strong as they had ever been. Marika's husband agreed that they should separate so that Ann and Marika could be together. 'I just knew that all I wanted was to be with Ann at whatever cost,' says Marika – and there was a cost. The first inkling came when a stranger came to call at their house in the depths of Somerset. 'The children came in and said, "Mummy, there's a man at the door." I did what I always do with a visitor – I said to the children, "Go and ask the man if he wants tea or coffee." And it transpired that this man was the press and a few weeks later we found ourselves splashed across one of the less reputable Sunday papers.'

The *People* carried the story on its front page with a further full page inside under the headline, 'Our Passionate Affair – By Nun in Love Tangle'. The fact that neither Ann nor Marika were nuns any longer, and hadn't been for years, didn't seem to matter. Marika was recognized by somebody who took the cutting from the *People* to Ann's boss. 'I was worried from the point of view of my father, who was a clergyman, being upset by it all and other people pointing the finger,' says Ann. There was also another problem – Ann was a primary school teacher. 'There had to be an official inquiry . . . my professional capabilities couldn't be faulted, therefore people were told that it made not the slightest bit of difference what my sexual orientation was as long as I did the job . . . As it turned out, it did us more good than harm in the end, because once we had been outed, there was nothing else anybody could do to hurt us really.'

> '‌Well, she got a **house** near Rye; and we could see the river Rother from our bedroom; and she got me instead of the French maid. But I think she was quite pleased with the deal.'
>
> **Monica Still** on being reunited with Marya after thirty years

Another couple who were united after a gap of decades were the two nurses, Monica and Marya, who had separated during the war without saying goodbye, even though Monica had spent a cold and wet night on a hospital fire escape trying to attract Marya's attention while she was on duty inside the ward. Thirty years later, they were brought together again by something as mundane as a dog-food commercial. By the Seventies, Monica was a Pharaoh Hound breeder and was asked to appear in an advertisement for Pedigree Chum, which Marya, who was living in Scotland by now, spotted. She recognized her friend even after all these years and wrote to her. 'I remember distinctly, I was . . . having my coffee at eleven o'clock and I opened this letter. I can't describe the feeling, it was great excitement and I rushed and got my best writing paper and started to write . . . and I thought, well, she hasn't mentioned whether there's a husband there or not – do I need this? Well, I thought, I'd better stop and think about this before I write.' Monica took a long time thinking about it and, before she had got round to replying, Marya managed to get hold of her phone number and rang. Fortuitously, Monica was due to visit Scotland for a dog show and the pair were finally able to meet again.

Before long Marya had moved down south and she and Monica set up house together. 'She used to say that her greatest dream was to have a house in Rye, a boat on the river Rother and a French maid,' says Monica. 'Well, she got a house near Rye and we could see the river Rother from our bedroom, and she got me instead of the French maid, but I think she was quite pleased with the deal.'

Alas, the years of happiness didn't last as long as Monica and Marya had hoped. 'We were going to live and love until we were ninety and make up for that waste of time, but sadly she got ill after we'd been together for about seven and a half years,' says Monica. 'It was cancer . . . and she had some very tough times . . . but she was very, very brave and her love for me shone through to everyone. She made no secret of the fact to all the consultants and nurses, everyone knew. I was so very proud to be loved by someone who was so proud of loving me. She was and is the love of my life. I'm on my ninth year alone now, but it's just as painful and just as bad. Don't let anyone tell you that time heals . . . I miss her so terribly and I'm just longing for the day when we meet and we're together again in some other dimension – and I know that this will happen.'

During Marya's lifetime, she and Monica got involved in restoring Radclyffe Hall's tomb in Highgate cemetery, which had gone to rack and ruin. It took them ten years to raise the money, but finally in 1994 the work was complete. Hall's coffin, which had a nasty gash in it was replaced by a larger casket made of English oak – Hall used to collect oak furniture. Artefacts within the tomb, which had been vandalized, were replaced by an oak cross and two oak candlesticks and the original gates to the tomb were put up again. A small ceremony was held on 7 October, the anniversary of Hall's death, by which time Marya was also dead, but the restoration of the tomb is as much a tribute to Monica and Marya and their team as it is to Hall herself.

The restoration of Radclyffe Hall's tomb is a symbol of how far gay men and lesbians have progressed in this century. The author of *The Well of Loneliness* was reviled in some circles within living memory and now she is hailed as the heroine that she was. Another indication of how far things have progressed is the experience of young lesbians and gay men. Grace Hughes is a young woman living in a small town in South Wales who came out to her friends at school at the age of thirteen and to her parents a year and a half later. Grace's mother's response was far from negative and the rest of the family echoed it.

THE PINK-
COLOURED TANK
REPRESENTING
GAY MEN
FIGHTING AIDS AT
THE 1995 LESBIAN
AND GAY PRIDE

THE PINK-COLOURED TANK REPRESENTING GAY MEN FIGHTING AIDS AT THE 1995 LESBIAN AND GAY PRIDE

'She was the only one out of my family – that is my parents and my two brothers – who didn't actually think I was gay. She didn't notice . . . but my Dad thought I was, my eldest brother did and my youngest brother was told by one of my teachers six months before I actually came out at home.' While Grace has come across some hostility at school, on the whole the reaction has been very positive. 'Attitudes have changed so much since the Seventies, and even since the Eighties, because it's become more accepted,' says Grace. 'People have realized that there's nothing different about them [gay people].'

Indeed, in some cases, the difference has been a positive asset rather than a liability. As the heterosexual world goes through a crisis of imagery, lesbian and gay love provides an enticing and alluring way of renewing desire. In August 1993, the New York magazine *Vanity Fair* – which has become a barometer of all that is most fashionable – had the lesbian singer kd lang sitting in a barber's chair being shaved by Cindy Crawford, at the time the highest earning supermodel in the world. The drag queen, Ru Paul, along with kd lang, have been used to advertise mainstream cosmetics to women, the reason being that their difference is appealing rather than appalling to consumers. The iconography of a gay lifestyle has become so chic that it is employed in a myriad different ways, from Madonna videos to Benetton advertisements for jumpers. In February 1994, even the British government inched towards progress, the first piece of positive legislation regarding male homosexuality for nearly thirty years being enacted when the age of consent was brought down from twenty-one to eighteen – although this still doesn't give gay men parity with heterosexuals.

At the beginning of this century, gay men and lesbians were engulfed in darkness and they have slowly moved into the light. If there is a lesson to be learned from this painfully slow progress, it is that visibility is always better than living in the dark – or as Julian Hows puts it: 'The thing that living with a life-threatening disease does is that it makes you think, why is all this nonsense going on? Why are all these people not living their lives to the full? If all these people told their bosses that they are gay, what would happen? If people turned around and explored their sexuality, what would happen? Do you want to live the rest of your life with the light off? 'Cos that's a bit what it's like. Turn the lights on! If you don't, you'll never know what anything else looks like.'

ABOUT THE CONTRIBUTORS

Jim Alexander was born on 5 December 1931. He left school at fourteen and held a number of jobs before entering the forces when he was eighteen. He saw active service in Korea after which he returned home to Middlesex to work in an engineering firm. It was during this period that he was charged and taken into custody after the police found a letter from Jim in the pocket of a man who had been arrested. When he emerged from prison, he made several failed attempts to find similar jobs before giving up and moving to London. He worked behind the bar in a 'clip joint' and lived with a couple of female colleagues before returning to Ashford to look after his mother until her death. Since then he has lived in many different parts of the country and turned his hand to a number of different jobs. 'Many of the times I have moved has been due to the prejudice I have encountered,' says Jim. He is now disabled and unable to do paid work but does voluntary service with the George House Trust and Body Positive North West.

Claire Ursula Epiphany Andrews was born on 6 January 1939 and emigrated from Trinidad in 1961 for a nursing course in England. She soon became disillusioned, however, and left to train as an electronic mechanics engineer and held various positions in industry. She entered consumer affairs after becoming a technical assistant in the Trading Standards office of Hackney council, which also led to her involvement with the trade union movement in which she has played an active part. Claire has also been closely involved with the voluntary sector and sits on a number of management committees. She is a well-known activist and ardent campaigner for the rights of minority groups. She has travelled widely and been invited to speak at an international level on a range of issues involving the black community and lesbian and gay issues. She has lobbied the European Parliament and is currently involved in building alliances across trade unions in the West Indies, Asia and Africa.

Pat Arrowsmith was born on 2 March 1930 and was educated at Cheltenham Ladies College and at Newnham College Cambridge. She has worked for Amnesty and for the National Council for Civil Liberties, as well as taking on jobs as a social worker, cinema usher and gardener. She was one of the organizers of the Direct Action Committee Against Nuclear War, the Committee of 100 and of the Campaign For Nuclear Disarmament. Pat has been jailed eleven times as a political prisoner. She has also published numerous books of fiction, verse and her autobiography and lists her recreations as swimming and watercolour painting.

Ray A Bagley was born on 14 June 1923 in Polesworth, Warwickshire. He left school at fourteen and joined the local brickworks and later became an underground electrician in a colliery. He volunteered for the RAF and gained his flight engineer brevet before being invalided out. He has worked for BOAC, the Dictaphone Company and British Telecom. Ray enjoys writing and takes his typewriter on holiday - he has had a number of poems and articles published. He has been active with his local dramatic society, with residents associations and with the Samaritans. He has lived in London for the last fifty years, forty-eight of them with his partner Bert Bartley.

Frith (Frederick Harold) Banbury was born on 4 May 1912, the son of a rear admiral. Educated at Stowe and Oxford and the Royal Academy of Dramatic Arts, he has worked as theatrical director, producer and as an actor. His first stage appearance was in 1933 at the Shaftesbury Theatre in *If I Were You*. Subsequently, he appeared in many plays and films until 1947, when he began to devote his time to production and direction. He has been involved in numerous West End productions as well as in theatrical projects in New York and Los Angeles. He enjoys playing the piano in his spare time.

Herbert (Bert) Bartley was born on 12 August 1914 in Kent. After a four-year indentured apprenticeship, he came to London aged eighteen to work as a hardware salesman. He worked in the ironmongery business for forty-two years, which included five-and-a-half years' war service in the Royal Signal Corps. Bert is an avid reader and played tennis all year round until he was seventy-one. He is fond of classical music, and opera in particular. He has lived with his partner Ray Bagley for forty-eight years.

John Beardmore was born in London in 1920 and educated at grammar school and the University of London. His early stage training at the Weber Douglas School was interrupted by war service in the Royal Navy, which he spent on the Russian convoys, the Battle of The Atlantic and the invasions of North Africa, Sicily and Normandy. After the war, he continued his theatrical career and has since appeared in over 400 stage, radio and film productions including *Colditz*, *I Claudius* and *Edward VIII*. He has also played most of the major heroic roles in Shakespeare. His hobbies are reading, writing, travel, gardening, motorcycling, swimming and, of course, Shakespeare.

Barbara Bell was born in Blackburn in 1914. She has lived in London, West Africa and in Sussex. She worked mostly as a teacher and since retirement she has worked for the last ten years as a volunteer with SACH, helping people with HIV and AIDS. She now enjoys activities like walking with Lesbian Line. She still loves and sees her old sweethearts.

Peter Burton was born on 29 April 1945 in London. He has worked in bookselling, publishing and journalism for his entire career - with periods as publicist to Rod Stewart and the Faces, assistant to novelist Robin Maugham and in such clubs as Le Duce, Bang and Bolts in Brighton. He has written, co-authored or contributed to more than thirty books, and among his titles are *Rod Stewart: A Life on the Town*, *Parallel Lives*, *Talking to . . .*, *Amongst the Aliens*, *Some Aspects of Gay Life*, *The Art of Gay Love* and the *Mammoth Book of Gay Short Stories*. He is currently literary editor for *Gay Times* and commissioning editor for Millivres Books. He has previously been closely involved with a range of gay publications including *Spartacus*, *Jeremy*, *Follow-Up*, *In Touch* and *Gay News*. His work regularly appears in the straight as well as gay press. He has lived in London and New York but now makes his home in Brighton.

Richard Cawley was born in Yorkshire and attended the local art school before gaining a place at a fashion school in Paris where he also studied at the Beaux Arts. He returned to London to study at the Royal College of Art and joined the couture house Bellville Sassoon, where he was involved in designing outfits for the Princess of Wales. He changed careers after winning the Mouton Cadet cookery competition in the *Observer*. Since then he has written seven cookbooks and writes for magazines and newspapers. He makes regular television appearances both on his own series and other programmes.

When not travelling, he divides his time between his homes in London and the South of France.

Margaret Cranch (nickname Crunchy) was born on 27 January 1939 in Plymouth. She left school at seventeen to train as a nurse and subsequently joined the WRAC and was posted at Aldershot and Cyprus. She represented the Army in hockey, athletics, swimming, badminton and tennis. On leaving the Army in 1962, she became a physiotherapist and worked in various establishments, including the Plymouth hospital where she had originally trained as a nurse. She took early retirement to care for her partner who had ovarian cancer. After her partner's death, Margaret returned to work and is currently a senior physiotherapist specializing in the needs of the elderly. She has also worked part-time in bars and clubs and sleuthing for a detective agency. Margaret has bought a home in Devon and is looking forward to returning to her roots when she retires (again) in a few years' time.

Quentin Crisp was born in 1908 in Sutton, Surrey and christened Denis. He was educated in Staffordshire and briefly attended Kings College London. In 1931, he moved from High Wycombe to London and became a fixture in Soho, with his hennaed hair and long fingernails. He became famous in 1968 with the publication of his autobiography, *The Naked Civil Servant*, which was subsequently dramatized for television. Since then he has written a number of other books and toured in a one-man show. Quentin now lives in New York.

Gerald Edward Dougherty was born on 27 September 1919 and brought up as an Anglican Catholic, which he remains. Gerald, who was born with slightly deformed feet, spent the Second World War on the home front, first as an ambulance worker and then as a light rescue worker. He studied law and qualified as a solicitor in 1943. He also worked as a pianist in bars and clubs. His final war-time occupation was in the Services Divorce Department set up to help non-commissioned men and women extricate themselves from their marriages. When this was absorbed into the Legal Aid Scheme in 1950, Gerald stayed, ending up the head of Legal Aid in the South West of England from which he retired in 1983. He would still be in Gloucestershire if he had not been overtaken by old age and disability, which caused him to return to sheltered accommodation in London. 'I always regarded myself as a Londoner living in the country and am relieved to be back in the town where I was born,' he says.

Frederick William Dyson was born on 28 January 1936 in Yorkshire, just as they were burying George V. He began work on his fifteenth birthday at Wath Main Colliery and subsequently moved to Goldthorpe Colliery where he eventually became colliery overman. Until he was made redundant in 1988, after thirty-seven years in the pits, he was a member of the First Aid Team, the Fire Fighting Team and the Mines Rescue Brigade. In his youth he was a teddy boy, complete with the hair cut and the crepe-soled shoes. The boys preferred to dance be-bop with him since he was a better mover than the girls. He subsequently became an active member of the theatrical section of the Dearne Community and Miners' Welfare Scheme and always played the villain in pantomimes.

Luchia Fitzgerald was born on 23 October 1947 in a mother-and-baby home in Cork to a fourteen-year-old mother. From the age of three, she was raised by her grandmother in Tramore, County Waterford, Eire. At fourteen she joined her mother in Lancashire but left after nine months to live rough on the streets in Manchester and London, after which she lived in a Bolton hostel run by nuns. She subsequently got a job on the buses and lived around Manchester until she became politically active in the early Seventies joining GLF and the Women's Movement. She founded the Amazon Press with two friends and helped run it until 1987. Luchia still lives in Manchester and has been unemployed since 1987. Luchia would like to dedicate her contribution to the book and the television programme to all the young lesbians and gay men who took their lives in the Sixties due to rejection by friends and family. One of whom was her best friend.

Terry Gardener was born in 1919. From an early age he was considered theatrical by his teachers – 'in other words a show-off'. Terry had an unruly mop of curls as a youngster until a naval officer during the war ordered it be cut. This was the first hair-raising experience he had in the Navy, which led to many more on duty on the Liverpool to Gibraltar convoy. The rigours of war brought on a nervous breakdown and discharge from the Navy and a return to his chosen profession in the music hall. He played his favourite role as a pantomime dame every Christmas for forty years.

David J H George was born on 25 January 1925 in South Shields, County Durham. He moved to London where he worked as a civil servant but has gained fame through his lectures on the theatre. His love of the performing arts was kindled at the age of five when he went to his first theatrical event, and he gave his first talk on the opera at the age of sixteen. In the Fifties, David gave celebrated parties at his Hampstead home which were the subject of much press attention. When David and his party were filmed by Pathé Pictorial News in costume, his mother advised: 'Please wear a little more in public, David.' He was a president of the local Rotarian Society and continues to lecture on the performing arts, having notched up well over a thousand such talks.

Christopher Gotch was born on 19 May 1923 in Kettering. After leaving Marlborough, he became an architectural student but managed to join the RAF by lying about his age. He served in Europe, Canada, India and Burma as a fighter pilot on Hurricanes, Spitfires, Typhoons and Mustangs, as well as on twin-engined planes like the Beaufighter and Mosquito. He had many close shaves during the war, including five plane crashes and being subject to an air attack while on the first war-time convoy through the Med. In over 300 operational flights, he was twice wounded. Since the war, he has worked as an architect, lecturer, journalist and author. He has written four books and has been a regular contributor to magazines, such as *Country Life* and the *Architectural Review*, as well as being a feature writer and book reviewer for the *Hampstead and Highgate Express*.

Allan Horsfall was born 20 October 1927 in the village of Laneshawbridge on the Lancashire/Yorkshire border. He spent his early years in Burnley and Nelson, apart from three years in the RAF. Since 1963, he has lived in Bolton. Allan was a Labour councillor in Nelson from 1958–61 and it was then that he introduced the subject of homosexual law reform into Labour Party thinking. Other political involvements at that time include chairing the North-East Lancashire Campaign For Nuclear Disarmament. In 1964, along with the late Colin Harvey, he founded the North-West Homosexual Law Reform Committee. After the 1967 Reform Act, the committee became the Campaign For Homosexual Equality and Allan was successively its secretary, chairman and president. Most of his working life was spent with the National Coal Board, where he worked in the estates department, but for the last few years before retirement he was employed by the Salford Education Department.

Julian Hows was born on 5 August 1958 in Brixton and has been living with HIV for seven years. He has been involved in lesbian and gay liberation ever since he was expelled from school for coming out. He has had a variety of careers, from London Underground guard to consultant to the World Health Organization. He has been a volunteer at London Lesbian and Gay Switchboard for over a decade, is a trustee of London Lighthouse and Streetwise Youth (working with male sex workers) and a director of Gay Men Fighting AIDS. Internationally he has worked with, among others, gay organizations in Slovenia, Poland, Hungary and Mexico to fight for equality and in health promotion in response to the AIDS epidemic. He is always accessible via e-mail as julian@misscane.demon.co.uk. He is single, has an extensive wardrobe of frocks which are displayed often and is always open to offers!

Grace Hughes was born on 15 April 1980 and has lived in Llantwit Major all her life. She lives with her parents and two older brothers, none of whom has any problem with her sexuality; her girlfriends are as welcome as her brothers' girlfriends are. At the moment, however, she is single. Grace is also out at the school she attends in Llantwit and says she doesn't 'get much hassle'. When Grace leaves school, she hopes to act. Another thing she would like to do would be to foster gay teenagers who have been forced out of their homes due to their sexuality. She enjoys listening to music, reading, writing poetry and spoiling her cats.

Evelyn Irons was born on 17 June 1900 and educated at St Bride's School, Helensborough and at Somerville College, Oxford, of which she is an honorary fellow. Her career as a journalist began with the *Daily Mail* and she subsequently wrote for the *Evening Standard*. During the war, she was posted with the French Army and received the *Croix de Guerre* for her war service. She was a friend of both Radclyffe Hall and of Vita Sackville-West.

Michael James was born on 2 June 1941 in Newry, Northern Ireland but moved to Plymouth at an early age where he lived until 1959. He was educated by a series of 'sadistic' nuns and Christian brothers. He moved to London and got a job at Debenham and Freebody's. When Michael hit GLF in 1971, he changed from 'a straight drag queen to a freaked-out acid queen overnight'. He then moved to Amsterdam and got unwillingly caught up in an international drug smuggling episode and spent five and a half years in jail. When he emerged, the gay community had been hit by AIDS, and Michael got involved in a number of AIDS organizations, including London Body Positive. Too many deaths took their toll and Michael retreated to Brighton to have a nervous breakdown where he still lives with a 'wonderful dog called Rusty who keeps me sane'.

Ann Lewis was born on 3 January 1945 in Devon, the elder daughter of a village policeman who later became an Anglican priest. She has led a full and varied working life as a library assistant, an NCO in the WRAF, a housemother in residential child care, a novice in an Anglican religious community (where she met Marika), and three years at a teachers' training college in Winchester before spending twenty years at a primary school in Cornwall. Ann gained a BPhilEd degree in Special Education Needs from Exeter University in 1991 and a diploma in Educational Therapy in 1994. She took early retirement from teaching in August 1995 and is now self-employed as a contract shepherd. Her interests include history – especially rural/agricultural history – reading, writing, the countryside, sheep-dog trials and anything to do with sheep. Ann recognized and accepted her sexuality in 1987 and has lived very happily with Marika in Cornwall since 1988.

Juno Jones was born in July 1949 in Stoke-on-Trent where she lived until she was sixteen when she moved down to London. She worked in an office until her involvement with GLF in 1971, which launched her into lesbian and gay politics, not only in Britain but also in New York and Australia. She has worked as a broadcaster and journalist and has begun her own collective of archives for future generations to use as a resource. Juno is crazy for opera, particularly the work of Marilyn Horne and Kathleen Ferrier and hopes to make a TV programme on the life of the latter. She lives alone in Covent Garden, lifts weights to keep fit and likes her own company a lot. Juno feels disenfranchised from the current lesbian and gay community because of its consumerism. She was keen to participate in *It's Not Unusual* 'so our stories can be told and we are not forgotten – it was very hard then and will continue to be very hard for lesbians and gay men unless they wake up and get real very soon.'

Sharley McLean cannot remember her birth but has no doubt she was present for lunch on 26 May 1923. Fondness for food has featured greatly in her life. An idyllic childhood was cut short by the rise of fascism and she came to Britain as a refugee with feelings of displacement, confusion and homesickness. She trained as a nurse and got married on 11 April 1945 – a date she refers to as 'double fools' day'. Highlights were a daughter and a son. Eventually she began a 'fantastic' long-term Sapphic relationship.

Derek Ogg was born in 1954 and is a advocate at the Scottish bar, specializing in criminal defence work. He has been a gay rights activist since his election as Student President at Edinburgh University in 1973. He was a member of the Scottish Minorities Group which became the Scottish Homosexual Rights Group and is currently called Outright-Scotland. He was founder and chair of Scottish AIDS Monitor until 1993 and is founder and trustee of Waverley Care Trust, Scotland's only AIDS Hospice. He broadcasts regularly for BBC Radio on legal and gay issues, as well as being a regular reviewer on BBC Scotland's arts programme, *The Usual Suspects*. He drafted the section of the Criminal Justice Scotland Act which equalized the age of consent in Scotland with England. He currently lives in Edinburgh with his lover.

Cathy Peace was born on 14 January 1969 in Bristol and was brought up in Hull. She developed a passion for performing and other women at a tender age. Early role models included Bet Lynch, whom she played behind a sideboard which doubled as the Rovers' bar. Cathy came out at fourteen and has never been in since. She did an English/Drama degree at Goldsmith's College, followed by postgraduate work. She works as a clown, actress and drag queen, and, in addition to solo performances, she has formed two touring companies. Cathy lives in London and has a passion for drag, big frocks, high heels, glitter and glamour. Her singing idols are Shirley Bassey closely followed by Janis Joplin.

Jose Pickering was born in the late Thirties and got married in the Fifties. She first visited the Union Bar in Manchester in 1956 and subsequently left her husband. She continues to live in the Manchester area.

Peter Price grew up on the Wirral, where he still lives. In his youth, Peter was subjected to aversion therapy in an attempt to 'cure' him. A former winner of New Faces, Peter presents programmes on Radio City 1548AM, including a dateline service which has resulted in eight marriages and a baby. During the course of his career, he has compèred many shows and interviewed numerous celebrities. He has a versatile voice and has released a record of his songs. The writer Alan Bleasdale created a cameo role for Peter in his film *No Surrender*. Peter is a self-confessed soap addict and claims that what he doesn't know about soaps isn't worth knowing.

Peter Robins, born in Twickenham in 1927, is a novelist, dramatist, journalist and broadcaster. After training as a teacher at King Alfred's College, Winchester, he taught in England and in Central Africa. Having left teaching for journalism, he covered the 1960 Congo Katanga War for the BBC, as well as Canadian radio and NBC, New York. Soon after, he joined the BBC's current affairs department, where he remained until 1986 with a short commercial break at London Broadcasting. During these years he also found time to write radio and stage plays, and many of his short stories have been broadcast, published and translated. All six of his novels are in print. He lives in Wandsworth.

Marika Savage was born on 30 December 1945 in London. The eldest of three daughters of an art dealer and writer, she joined an Anglican religious community at the age of twenty-one and left on health grounds after six years. Marika married at thirty and had two children and a lesbian affair. Having made contact again with Ann, with whom she had fallen in love almost twenty years previously, her marriage was dissolved after twelve years. Marika finally acknowledged her sexuality and settled down with Ann eight years ago. Marika's hobbies include reading and tap-dancing and she is an active member of her local church. She is now a full-time carer for Ann's elderly mother, who lives with them, and a 'happy housewife' in Cornwall.

Anthony Sayonas was born on 5 March 1957. He left school at sixteen and became a shoe salesman at John Lewis, followed by jobs at Harry Gee, Top Shop and Probe Records. Other jobs he has held include trainee tutor at NACRO. Tony has lived in Liverpool, London and Leeds and is involved in voluntary and community projects, including Healthwise, Friend Merseyside, Lark Lane Housing Co-op Committee, Homewatch, Merseyside Information Project and the Fazakerly Welfare Rights Centre. Tony enjoys going dancing, particularly the Manchester club scene. He doesn't drink or smoke and exercises daily.

Monica Still was born on 17 May 1923. Educated at Lewes County School for Girls, she trained as a nurse and met Marya Denny McLean at the Royal East Sussex Hospital, Hastings in 1943. After becoming a state registered nurse, Monica worked in several hospitals before joining two doctors in general practice in Bedford in 1947. She served on Bedford Borough Council for thirteen years. As a hobby Monica became involved in the breeding of pharaoh hounds and met up again with Marya thanks to her appearance in a dog-food commercial in 1980. They lived together in Kent until Marya's death in 1988. Monica returned to Bedford in 1995.

William Barron Tawse was born on 5 January 1912 in London and educated in Scotland. He worked for an agricultural supplies company before losing his job in the Great Depression. During the Second World War, he was a medical orderly, mainly on troop ships, during the course of which he faced a court martial for having sex with another man. After the war, he worked in the airline industry in various jobs and locations before retiring in 1972 which has allowed him to pursue his interests. Jim is a keen writer of journals, plays, short stories and poetry some of which has been published. Jim, who comes from a highly musical family, enjoys the work of Mozart, Debussy and the Russian composers and plays the piano himself. He is keen on French culture and language and can also converse in German. His other interests include climbing the Scottish hills, sketching and conversation. He says that 'like William Hazlitt' he has enjoyed a very happy life.

Hallam Tennyson, the youngest greatgrandson of the Victorian poet laureate, was born on 10 December 1920. He was educated at Eton and Oxford and was a conscientious objector during the war. In 1945 he married Margot Wallach, a German Jewish refugee and they have a son and daughter. He worked for the government of liberated Italy rebuilding destroyed villages. After the war, he and Margot worked in Bengal with the Quakers on a rural development scheme. Later he joined BBC Radio where he was assistant head of drama for seventeen years. Hallam has written seven books and innumerable plays and adaptations for radio and television. He has six grandchildren, a splendid relationship with his ex-wife, to whom he was married for twenty-six years, and a lover thirteen years younger than himself, with whom he has been involved since he received a fan letter from him in 1984 after the publication of his autobiography.

BIBLIOGRAPHY

BAKER, MICHAEL, *Our Three Selves: The Life of Radclyffe Hall*, Hamish Hamilton, 1985

BERG, CHARLES, *Fear, Punishment, Anxiety and the Wolfenden Report*, George Allen & Unwin, 1959

BERRY, PAUL, and MARK BOSTRIDGE, *Vera Brittain: A Life*, Chatto & Windus, 1995

BERUBE, ALLAN, 'Marching to a Different Drummer: Lesbian and Gay GIs in World War II' in Martin Bauml Duberman, Martha Vicinus and George Chauncey Jr (eds.), *Hidden from History: Reclaiming the Gay and Lesbian Past*, New American Library, 1989

CHESSER, EUSTACE, *Live and Let Live: The Moral of the Wolfenden Report*, Taylor Garnett & Evans, 1958

CONNON, BRYAN, *Beverley Nichols: A Life*, Constable, 1991

CORY, DONALD WEBSTER, *The Homosexual in America*, Greenberg, 1951

COSTELLO, JOHN, *Love, Sex and War: Changing Values 1939–45*, Collins, 1985

CROFT-COOKE, RUPERT, *The Verdict of You All*, Secker & Warburg, 1955

DAVIES, RUSSELL (ed.), *The Kenneth Williams Diaries*, HarperCollins, 1993

DUBERMAN, MARTIN, *Stonewall*, Plume, 1994

DE JONGH, NICHOLAS, *Not in Front of the Audience: Homosexuality on Stage*, Routledge, 1992

ELLMAN, RICHARD, *Oscar Wilde*, Hamish Hamilton, 1987

FADERMAN, LILLIAN, *Surpassing the Love of Men*, The Women's Press, 1985

GLENDINNING, VICTORIA, *Vita: The Life of Vita Sackville-West*, Weidenfeld & Nicolson, 1983

HALL, RADCLYFFE, *The Well of Loneliness*, Virago Press, 1982

HAMER, EMILY, *Britannia's Glory: A History of Twentieth Century Lesbians*, Cassell, 1996

HASTE, CATE, *Rules of Desire*, Chatto & Windus, 1992

HODGES, ANDREW, *Alan Turing: The Enigma of Intelligence*, Burnett Books, 1983

HOWES, KEITH, *Broadcasting It*, Cassell, 1993

KATZ, JONATHAN NED, *Gay/Lesbian Almanac*, Harper & Row, New York, 1983

LESLEY, COLE, *The Life of Noël Coward*, Jonathan Cape, 1976

MILLER, NEIL, *Out of the Past: Gay and Lesbian History from 1869 to the Present*, Vintage, 1995

MONTGOMERY HYDE, H, *The Other Love*, William Heinemann, 1970

MONTGOMERY HYDE, H, *The Trials of Oscar Wilde*, Dover Books, 1962

NICHOLS, BEVERLEY, *The Sweet and Twenties*, Weidenfeld & Nicolson, 1958

NICOLSON, NIGEL, *Portrait of a Marriage*, Weidenfeld & Nicolson, 1973

PARKER, PETER, *Ackerley: A Life of J R Ackerley*, Constable, 1989

PORTER, KEVIN, and JEFFREY WEEKS (eds.), *Between the Acts*, Routledge, 1991

POWER, LISA, *No Bath but Plenty of Bubbles: An Oral History of the Gay Liberation Front*, Cassell, 1995

RUSSO, VITO, *The Celluloid Closet*, Harper & Row, 1987

SOUHAMI, DIANA, *Greta and Cecil*, Jonathan Cape, 1988

SPENCER, COLIN, *Homosexuality: A History*, Fourth Estate, 1995

SPOTO, DONALD, *Dietrich*, Bantam Press, 1992

STILLMAN FRANKS, CLAUDIA, *Beyond the Well of Loneliness: The Fiction of Radclyffe Hall*, Avebury, 1982

TAMES, RICHARD, *World War Two: Life in Wartime Britain*, B T Batsford, 1993

THORNTON, MICHAEL, *Royal Feud*, Michael Joseph, 1985

TRAUTMAN BANKS, JOANNE (ed.), *Congenial Spirits: The Letters of Virginia Woolf*, The Hogarth Press, 1989

VICKERS, HUGO, *Cecil Beaton, The Authorised Biography*, Weidenfeld & Nicolson, 1993

WEEKS, JEFFREY, 'Inverts, Perverts and Mary-Annes: Male Prostitution and the Regulation of Homosexuality in the Nineteenth and Early Twentieth Centuries' in *The Gay Past*, Harrington Park Press, 1985

WEEKS, JEFFREY, *Coming Out*, Quartet Books, 1990

WESTWOOD, GORDON, *A Minority: A Report on the Life of the Male Homosexual in Great Britain*, Longman, 1960

WHEEN, FRANCIS, *Tom Driberg: His Life and Indiscretions*, Chatto & Windus, 1990

WILDEBLOOD, PETER, *Against the Law*, Weidenfeld & Nicolson, 1955

INDEX